HOW THE GIRL GUIDES
WON THE WAR

HOW THE GIRL GUIDES WON THE WAR

JANIE HAMPTON

LARGE PRINT
Oxford

First published in Great Britain 2010
by
HarperPress
An imprint of HarperCollins Publishers

Published in Large Print 2011 by ISIS Publishing Ltd.,
7 Centremead, Osney Mead, Oxford OX2 0ES
by arrangement with
HarperCollins Publishers

British Library Cataloguing in Publication Data
Hampton, Janie.
  How the Girl Guides won the war.
  1. Girl Guides Association - - History - -
  20th century.
  2. Girl Guides - - Great Britain - - History - -
  20th century.
  3. World War, 1939–1945 - - Great Britain.
  4. World War, 1939–1945 - - Children - -
  Great Britain.
  5. Large type books.
  I. Title
  369.4'63'0941'09044–dc22

ISBN 978–0–7531–5281–2 (hb)
ISBN 978–0–7531–5282–9 (pb)

Printed and bound in Great Britain by
T. J. International Ltd., Padstow, Cornwall

To my mother, who throughout her long life
as both a Guide and a Brown Owl, has
demonstrated that keeping to the rules
is not nearly as important as
Robert Baden-Powell's maxim:

*"I wouldn't give tuppence for you if you are
not jolly and laughing."*

Contents

Introduction

In my mother's attic is a green school exercise book. "Name: *Janie Anderson*. Subject: *Writing*. School: *St Mary's*. 21.10.1960". I turned to the first page. "*Brownies*" was the title. Underneath I'd written:

On the 3rd of November I am going to be enrolled. Brown Owl gave me a paper cat to put a knot on the cat's string tail when I do a good deed. I have at least sixty knots. I am a Sprite. I know the Brownie promise, law, motto and rymne, and I can plait. I am excited about wearing my Brownie tunick. I do not know wether a Commishner comes to be enrolled or just Brown Owl.

At just eight years old, I already had a sense of the structure of the Brownie movement, and knew that a Commissioner was more important than "just Brown Owl". Fifty years later, I can still remember my promise — "I promise to do my best, to do my duty to God and the Queen, to help other people every day, especially those at home" — and the Brownie song — "We're the Brownies, here's our aim: Lend a hand and play the game."

But by the time I was a teenager later in the sixties, the Beatles had arrived and I reckoned that Guides were deeply uncool. Who would choose to wear a uniform, unless it was a Sergeant Pepper fancy dress one? Why would a teenager want to attend meetings punctually, and salute a fat old Captain? I did go to Guides for a year, but at camp in Sussex, Captain got her come-uppance when a ram trotted up behind her and tossed her in the air. She spent the rest of the week lying in her bell tent, moaning. After that, how could I possibly take her seriously?

When I began writing this book, my perspective was that of a flower-child of the 1960s, who shunned uniforms and rules. I intended to write a satire on Guides and Brownies, making fun of Ging-gang-goolies and dyb-dyb-dob, standing for "do your best, do our best". But the more stories I read, and the more former Brownies and Guides I met, the more I came to realise what an important part of twentieth-century history the Guide movement was. Much to my amazement, I saw that Guides had played a crucial part in feminist history and the women's equality movement. Their achievements, though, have been largely overlooked, their influence for the most part unrecorded.

The feminists of the 1960s and '70s simply could not see past the blue, pocketed shirts and navy serge skirts of the Guide uniform to the impact these girls had on the lives of Britain's women. As well as the importance of the work they did, I learned that Guide meetings were an affordable form of further education for girls who had left school at fourteen. I came to realise that the movement's founder, Lieutenant-General Lord Baden-Powell, was not the old fuddy-duddy I had assumed, but a forward-thinking man who wanted to make a positive difference to the lives of both boys and girls, of every class, in every nation. I also learned that the Guides were never a paramilitary organisation for the Church of England middle-class. There have been companies in factories, hospitals, female Borstals, synagogues and Catholic orphanages. The uniform was designed not to force girls to conform, but to give them a sense of belonging, especially if they had few or no smart clothes.

Mention Girl Guides to many women, and the reaction will be strong. They will tell you either that they loved them or hated them; they were either proud to wear their uniform or refused to join. Once enrolled, they either adored tying knots or couldn't see the point; revelled in campfire singing or loathed damp canvas tents. They either fell in love with their Captains, or thought they were fascists and sadists. Whatever their feelings, most former Girl Guides retain strong memories of their experiences.

A survey by Girlguiding UK in 2007 found that two-thirds of Britain's most prominent women have been Guides, and three-quarters of them say they benefited from the experience. Yet few people realise the impact that the foundation of the Guide movement in 1910 had on women's equality, and on society in general. From the very start, when Robert Baden-Powell asked his sister Agnes to form the Girl Guides, the organisation was separate from the Boy Scouts, and not subservient to them. Baden-Powell died in 1941, but how much has his vision affected the social and political history of feminism in the twentieth century?

Nearly twenty years before all British women got the vote, Girl Guides were earning badges for proficiency as Electricians, Cyclists, Surveyors and Telegraphists.

In both world wars, Brownies and Guides took over the jobs of adults. When historians came to write up these wars, they spoke only to adults, who had either not been around or, if they had, were too busy to notice, and thus failed to mention the role of these girls and young women.

The impact of the Guides in World War II is particularly clear. Their activities were not confined to Britain, but also included the Commonwealth, Nazi-occupied Europe and Japanese-occupied Asia. It was World War II that brought the philosophy of the Guides to the fore, and released their skills and training to the benefit of everyone around them.

This book explores how being a Brownie or a Guide was essential training for war work. How did a Guide gaining a badge in Morse code aid fighter pilots? How did collecting 15,000 wooden cotton reels help RAF prisoners of war? And how does Guiding in those times influence the lives of women in the twenty-first century? Within days of the declaration of war with Germany in September 1939, young women were being called up to the Women's Auxiliary Air Force (WAAF), Women's Royal Navy (Wrens), and the Female Aid Nursing Yeomanry (FANYs). The military services soon realised that Guides with badges sewn on their sleeves had skills that were not only life-enhancing, but also life-saving.

Guides from all walks of life threw themselves into war work. Even Princess Elizabeth, a Guide, and Princess Margaret, a Brownie, learned how to cook on a campfire and promised, like thousands of other Guides, "to help other people every day, specially those at home". When the Blitz began, Guides kept up morale in bomb shelters with "Blackout Blues" sing-songs. They built emergency ovens from the bricks of bombed houses. They grew food on company allotments, and knitted for England. They became the embodiment of the Home Front spirit, digging shelters and providing first-aid. All over Britain, Guides held bazaars and pushed wooden two-wheeled trek carts around the streets, collecting jam jars and newspapers for recycling. In one week in 1940 they raised £50,000 to buy ambulances and a lifeboat which saved lives at Dunkirk.

Guides painted kerbs with white paint to help people find their way around in the blackout. They collected sphagnum moss to dress wounds. They helped evacuated children leave the cities, and helped to care for them when they arrived in the country. War Service Badges were awarded to Guides after ninety-six hours of work, washing up in children's homes, caring for the elderly, feeding bombed families and Air-Raid Wardens.

Their contribution was noted at the highest levels. At the Lord Mayor's Show in London in 1942, Winston Churchill took off his hat in salute as the Guides marched past. Movietone newsreels featured Guides putting out incendiary bombs, marching with gas masks and sending messages by semaphore. Older

Guides were shown helping on a farm and rowing on a river (they may have been looking out for German parachutists disguised as nuns, a common fear at the time).

Exploring archives, I stumbled across extraordinary stories. A Brownie log book from 1944 surprised me halfway through with a song the pack sang on Christmas Day:

We might have been shipped to Timbuctoo
We might have been shipped Kalamazoo
It's not repatriation nor is it yet starvation
It's simply Concentration in Chefoo!

I discovered that from 1942 to 1945 the 1st Chefoo Brownie Pack was based in a Japanese concentration camp. After the bombing of Pearl Harbor in December 1941, an entire boarding school of British children was interned in eastern China along with Trappist monks, White Russian prostitutes, businessmen and Cuban jazz players. The morale of the girls and their teachers was greatly improved by their continuing as Brownies and Guides. Their sports were organised by Eric Liddell, the 1924 Olympic gold-medal winner and hero of the film *Chariots of Fire*. I tracked down their Brown Owl, aged ninety-three and living in Seattle, and several of the girls, who told me how being Brownies had given them stability and normality during those four long years when they were separated from their parents. They led me to other Brownies who had been captured by pirates in the South China Seas in 1935, while on their way to school by ship.

Letters to local newspapers produced wonderful stories, photographs and more log books. The 1st Wantage Brownies went on a camp at the end of August 1939, and although their Brown Owl must have known that war was imminent, you would never guess it from the pictures of them swimming and standing on their heads, or from the brief note that they had had to return home a day early, on Saturday, 2 September.

A scrapbook in the Imperial War Museum revealed that during the war three spinsters from Kent ran a hostel near Perth which was filled with sixty children evacuated from Glasgow. They set up a Brownie pack, a Cub pack and a Guide company which were so well run that Guiders were sent from all over Scotland to train there. When I wrote to the house, the current owner phoned me back: "I had no idea of the importance of guiding here. Lady Baden-Powell was my grandmother-in-law. I knew her well." I found one of the Brownies who had lived at the hostel, in Weymouth. Brought up in a tenement in Glasgow, she went on to become Mayor of Weymouth, and put it all down to being a Brownie.

One afternoon I told my husband about a story published in 1947 about a Dutch family who rowed across the English Channel in May 1940. The thirteen-year-old daughter was a Guide, and had used her skills to keep them afloat. "Wouldn't it be great if you could find her now?" said my husband. "Well, she was called Josephine Klein," I replied. He dashed out of the room and returned with a pile of books. "These are by Josephine Klein. She's a leading London psychotherapist. I've seen her give a talk, and she's the right age." I found her in Waterloo, and she invited me to visit. We spent a morning with her lying on her therapist's couch, telling me the whole story, and how Guiding had provided her with instant friendship in a country where she knew nobody.

Guides were among the first civilians to enter Belsen concentration camp, and in the aftermath of World War II their outstanding service continued. Financed by Guides and Brownies from all over the Commonwealth, teams of former Guides and Guiders worked with refugees in Holland, Germany, Greece and Malaya.

When you go camping with only a rucksack, you cannot take all the things you want: you have to choose the most important, and leave the rest behind. I have almost certainly left things out of this book that some people will feel should have been included. Brownies and Guides did so much in World War II that it is impossible to cover even a small amount of it. I hope, however, to give some understanding of the extraordinary and important part that Guides and Brownies played during that time of crisis.

Their stories form an unofficial history, told by the girls themselves, first-hand as well as through letters, diaries and log books. Celebrities and ordinary women describe the fun and frustration, the characters they met, the places they went, the art of tying a reef knot behind your head during a blackout and the thrill of a midnight feast in an Anderson shelter during the Blitz.

I realise now that it was through Brownies that I learned about values, caring for other people, and trying to do a Good Deed every day. This book gives a taste of one of the most extraordinary movements of the twentieth century, and how it influenced people all over the world.

Janie Hampton
Oxford

Prologue

Pax Ting

On a hot evening in mid-August 1939, silver trumpets sounded from the battlements of an old castle in a forest in Hungary to mark the end of an extraordinary meeting. The blue and gold Guides' World Trefoil flag which had flown from the main tower for just over two weeks was hauled down for the last time. The first world gathering of 5,800 Girl Guides from thirty-two countries, as far apart as India, Holland and Estonia, had set up camp on the royal hunting estate of Gödöllő. In typical international style, Lord Baden-Powell had put together Latin and Norse words to name the occasion "Pax Ting", or Peace Parliament.

Gödöllő was twenty-two miles from Budapest, and was described by the Guides of Hungary as "in a very healthy wooded part, surrounded by vineyards on the plain of the river Rakos. Its principal curiosity is the famous royal castle, now residence of the Regent of Hungary, a one-floor building built in French rococo style, with more than a hundred chambers. 3/5 of which estate being wood and excellent hunting ground, and the station for potato researches."

The World Association of Girl Guides and Girl Scouts (WAGGGS), founded in 1928, was already the largest organisation of its kind anywhere on earth, with a mission "to enable girls and young women to develop their fullest potential as responsible citizens of the world". When WAGGGS decided to gather in Hungary, the association had ignored the signs of impending war.

There were 246,202 Guides in Great Britain, but only two hundred were invited to go on this epic trip. The lucky few who were chosen had to be physically fit for the long journey by train and the dry heat of Hungary in August, as well as keen campers and efficient Guides who would both give a good impression of British Guiding and have the wits to bring back useful observations of the gathering.

Leading the British contingent was twenty-four-year-old Alison Duke, who had recently graduated from Cambridge with a first-class degree in Classics. She was known as "Chick" and had joined the 1st Cambridge Guide Company as a girl; now she was the company's Captain. With the Nazis already in control of Germany, Austria and Czechoslovakia, Alison's fluent German had helped to secure her selection as leader, and it was her task to escort the British Guides across Europe. As their train passed through Germany, at each station they were greeted by members of the Girls' Hitler Youth Movement, the *Bund Deutscher Mädel* (BDM). A group of BDM girls were at Aachen station at 3a.m. to present the British Guides with fruit and flowers. Their leader travelled to Cologne with the party to ensure that more BDM girls further down the track provided breakfast. "Nothing could have been more friendly or helpful," said the Guides later.

For two whole years, the 7,500 Guides of Hungary had been preparing for Pax Ting. They had learned new languages and garnered badges such as Health, Fire, Gymnast and Police; older Guides and Rangers (aged sixteen to twenty-one) had learned about the local history so they could lead expeditions to places of interest. "No time and no trouble had been spared to ensure the great gathering being well organised and the guests well cared for," said the official programme. However, in the summer of 1939 most adults in Europe knew that war might break out at any moment. It took much courage on the part of Guide leaders to allow the camp to go ahead. If war had begun while 5,000 girls were hundreds of miles away from their homes, what would have happened to them all? The Polish contingent understood better than anyone the threat of war, and at the last moment they altered their plans. The night before they left for Hungary, the younger Guides were replaced with First Class Rangers experienced in mountain expeditions. They were issued with special maps which they sewed into their uniforms, so that even if they lost their haversacks they could find their way home. If, as was thought likely, the German army invaded Poland during Pax Ting, these Guides were to return home on foot over the Carpathian mountains that separated Hungary and Poland, in small groups or alone. "Be prepared" had always been the Guides' motto; now these girls might have to put it to the ultimate test. Only weeks later, many of them would travel in the opposite direction, out of Poland, on even more dangerous adventures.

At Pax Ting, Guides from each country pitched their ridge tents in circles or rows in the pine woods, each encampment marked with a gateway featuring their national emblem or a peace symbol. The British camp's gate was flanked by a lion and a unicorn made from painted cardboard; the Danes had constructed a pair of giant doves. The Hungarian Guides had never camped under canvas before, and their tents were quite a spectacle: "They varied enormously, from holding 16 children to two," wrote Christie Miller, a Guide from Oxfordshire. "They nearly all had their beds raised off the ground, and were covered in the most beautifully embroidered counterpanes. The tent pole was decorated with coloured ornaments. All tents were trenched but judging by the effects of the first thunderstorm, not very effectively."

The Finnish Guides brought tepees, like those still used by the Suomi people in Lapland, and invited everyone to autograph them. These tepees fascinated the British Guides: they had their ground-sheets sewn to the tops, and were held up by bent bamboo poles threaded into the canvas — a foretaste of twenty-first-century tents.

The Guides from Poland were the "real heavyweight campers", wrote Christie Miller. "All the beds were made of wooden planks raised off the ground on logs. They made shelves for shoes, rucksacks etc. Each Guide carved an emblem at the doorway of her tent. In

4

their grey uniforms they were one of the smartest contingents. In the evening they all wore long cloaks."

At all camps, including Pax Ting, the Guides wore their camp uniform. For the British this was a blue cotton tunic with a leather belt, a triangular cotton scarf and a floppy cotton hat. At a time when most girls had few clothes, wearing a uniform gave them both a smart outfit and a sense of belonging. The early uniform reflected the relaxed post-Edwardian approach to women's wear: an A-line skirt above the ankle and a practical, comfortable shirt — often a cricket shirt borrowed from a brother and dyed blue.

Lord Baden-Powell had also designed the Guides' equipment to be practical: the long wooden staffs they carried were marked in feet and inches so they could measure objects and the depth of streams. They could be used for rescuing struggling swimmers, scything a path through nettles or brambles, or vaulting streams. Two staffs with a coat fastened around them could form a stretcher, and several strung together made a tent frame. The scarf was used as a handkerchief, bandage, sling, pressure pad to prevent bleeding, or to tie on a splint. The whistle could be used to send Morse messages or to summon help. The hats not only kept off the sun and rain, but could also be used for carrying water or fruit, or fanning a reluctant fire.

Once the Pax Ting camp was set up, all the Guides were led by a Hungarian army band on a parade through the local town. They then spent the fortnight occupied by the usual camping activities such as constructing drying-up stands with sticks and fancy

5

knots, collecting firewood, cooking dampers (a kind of doughy bread made from flour and water) and singing around the campfire before going to bed. The Hungarian Guides had laid on a programme which included "Move in open air; an excursion by steamer to Esztergom; and Funny Evening in the English Garden (not obligatory)".

The theme of Pax Ting, suggested before the camp started by the British Guides, was "How can Guides help towards world peace?", and it was decided that English should be adopted as their "agreed international language". The host was Prince Horthy Miklos, Regent of Hungary, who rode to the camp on his horse. The aristocracy of Hungary were out in force: the Patroness of the Hungarian Girl Guides was the Archduchess Anna, daughter-in-law of the last Austro-Hungarian Emperor. Antonia Lindenmyer, President of the Hungarian Girl Guides and Chief of Pax Ting, was accompanied by the formidable Zimmermann Rozsi, Chief Secretary of the Hungarian Guides. Count Paul Telki, Prime Minister of Hungary and Chief Scout of Hungary, also came to sing round the campfire. Her Royal Highness Princess Sybilla of Sweden, great-granddaughter of Queen Victoria, was there too, eating roast cobs and slices of watermelon. Princess Ileana, daughter of the King of Romania, whose full title was "Her Imperial and Royal Highness, The Illustrious Ileana, Archduchess of Austria, Princess Imperial of Austria", had been Chief of the Romanian Guides. After marrying the Archduke of Austria she became President of the Austrian Girl Guides, which had recently been banned by the Nazis, but she had come anyway. Lord Baden-Powell, now aged eighty-two, sent greetings from his home in Kenya. The Royal Hungarian Post designed "a fine collection of stempis" to commemorate the occasion.

At the end of the camp, every Guide received a certificate signed by Lindenmyer, saying, "We believe that the Spirit of Guiding so splendidly manifested during the Pax Ting will bear its fruits for the common good of the world in time to come."

A growl of thunder sounded menacingly as the trumpets called out on the last evening. As the Guides all said goodbye to each other on the following wet, stormy morning at the end of August, they must have wondered how long it would be before they would meet again. What might happen to the tall, fair-haired Guides in grey uniforms, strapping sixty-pound packs on their backs as if they were light haversacks? What would happen to the little round-faced Dutch Guide who came squelching through the rain to exchange an address with a Scottish Patrol Leader? "Surely," wrote Catherine Christian, editor of The Guide, "grown-ups were not going to be so crazy as to start a war, when people all over the world were so willing to be friendly, to discuss things, to be interested in each other?"

The British Guides sped home through Germany, waving to the uniformed BDM girls on railway station platforms. After three days of hot and sticky travelling, they walked into their headquarters in Buckingham Palace Road on a hot August evening. "They had sampled a lot of other nations' queer cooking," wrote

Christian, "and emphatically preferred their own. They all had noticed how the stormy gleam of sunset had struck across the World Flag that last night and how the trumpets had sounded. They couldn't explain it; but they had noticed."

In 1934, Guiders, leaders of Guide companies in Wetherby, Yorkshire, had written to Lady Baden-Powell asking her what they and their Guides should do if war broke out again. She replied:

Dear Guiders,

It is practically impossible for anyone to decide now "What we would do if England went to war". Our whole thought and work should be directed into the prevention of such a thing, and I feel too much of this discussion of war and its horrors leads people to THINK about it too much, and thus to become what has been called "war minded".

Should it ever come about that England does go to war again it would be none of OUR MAKING. This is far more difficult for MEN to consider. But for women there are always the all important matters and ways in which they can serve humanity — in peace and war — i.e. nursing, caring for children, alleviating suffering of all kinds, food production, and so on.

I also hope, MOST devoutly, that there will never come a time when you will have to face the question in earnest!. Good wishes to you, and your Brownies,

Olave Baden-Powell

★　★　★

On 3 September, a perfect Sunday morning, Guides all over Britain listened with their families to the wireless as the tired voice of Prime Minister Neville Chamberlain spoke to the nation: "This morning the British Ambassador in Berlin handed the German government a final note . . ."

CHAPTER
ONE

We are the Girl Scouts

Thirty years before Pax Ting, in 1909, there were no Guides, only a few intrepid girls who had begun to discover the excitement of the Scouting movement, which had been started that year by the distinguished Boer War hero and former spy, Robert Baden-Powell.

Conscripting soldiers for the Anglo-Boer War had revealed the poor state of health of the youth of Britain, a weakness which was interpreted by doctors, eugenicists and psychologists as both physical and moral. They decided that the country was in a state of decline, and desperately needed to be regenerated and revitalised. Foreign elements, homosexuality, mental instability and female hysterics — all had to be weeded out. Popular opinion was crying out for another war to "cleanse" Britain of its social ills and weakness.

Robert Baden-Powell had been brought up with the self-discipline of "Christian Socialism". "You must try very hard to be good," he had written at eight years old. He was a good shot, a brilliant tracker and a talented artist. Posing as a harmless tourist he could sketch a town plan, or the outline of a fort with gun emplacements, and then disguise it as a butterfly. He was a man of energy and efficiency who wanted to ensure that boys lived more fruitful lives. He believed that in order to prevent them hanging around on street corners and getting up to mischief, their aimlessness had to be replaced with a sense of "fun and excitement". In 1907, when he was already fifty years old, Baden-Powell tried out his ideas at a camp on Brownsea Island, Dorset. A mixture of private- and state-educated boys slept in bell tents, cooked over a campfire and practised woodcraft, stalking and tracking, all of which were designed to teach them new skills. When a year later Baden-Powell's book *Scouting for Boys* was published in six parts at fourpence each, it was a best-seller. The book was intended merely to offer new ideas gleaned from his life as a soldier and from the Brownsea Island camp to existing youth leaders. Baden-Powell was surprised by the reaction: immediately, thousands of boys asked how they could become Scouts or started their own groups. He had unwittingly spawned a whole new youth movement.

Unknown to Baden-Powell, by 1909 girls were forming their own Scout troops in several parts of the country, from Newcastle-upon-Tyne to Clacton-on-Sea. They too had read *Scouting for Boys*, and in response they formed patrols and marched around with staves and lanyards, their haversacks filled with bandages in case they came upon an injured person. They cobbled together their own uniforms: Miss Elise Lee, the first Girl Scout in Newcastle-upon-Tyne, wore a Boy Scout hat and her own blouse. Winnie Mason of Southsea, Hampshire, wore a Boy Scout shirt and scarf, a long straight skirt and lace-up boots, and carried a staff. The first Mayfair Group, formed by three sisters, Eleanor, Laura and Jean Trotter, wore serge skirts just below the knee, navy jerseys and shiny leather belts. In Scotland, Girl Scouts wore kilts and woollen jerseys. The thirty Gillingham Girl Scouts in Kent went on cycle outings in their uniforms in 1909. These early Girl Scouts even managed to obtain badges from Scout headquarters by indicating that they had achieved the desired standard in tests, and only giving their initials rather than their full Christian names. It was some time before the Boy Scouts noticed, and then demanded the return of the badges.

Just a year after Boy Scouts had started, Baden-Powell left the army to devote himself to the movement. The uniform worn by his waxwork in Madame Tussaud's was changed from that of a General to a Scout, in his trademark shorts and broad-brimmed hat. Baden-Powell knew that more and more boys were joining the Scouts, but he wanted to find out just how popular the movement had become. He organised a rally at the Crystal Palace for 4 September 1909, to see how many would attend. Not only did *11,000* Scouts turn up, but much to Baden-Powell's surprise, standing in the front row was a group of girls wearing Scout hats and holding staves.

"What the dickens are you doing here?" he asked.

"Oh, we are the Girl Scouts," they said. Sybil Carradine, from Peckham in South London, and her friends had seen the boys going off to have fun with the Scouts and decided to copy them. When they heard about the Crystal Palace rally they put on their uniforms and marched straight through the turnstiles.

"The devil you are!" Baden-Powell declared.

"Please, please," they replied, "we want something for the girls." To their utter amazement he said, "You'd better take part in the march-past at the end." At that moment Sybil and her friends knew they had won; and it was the girls whom the photograph of the event in the *Daily Mirror* depicted standing at the front of the crowd.

In May 1908 Baden-Powell had already rhetorically asked the question, "Can girls be Scouts?" in *The Scout* magazine. He considered that "girls can get as much healthy fun out of scouting as boys can . . . and prove themselves good Scouts in a very short time". However, while he was certainly impressed by the turn-out of the girls at Crystal Palace, his attitude towards women was typical of his time. He was not a misogynist; rather, he was a military man who just didn't quite know what to make of the female sex. In his book *Rovering to Success* (1922) he would write: "The four rocks which prevent a man from achieving happiness: Horses, wine, women and irreligion." Yet despite putting women in the same category as horses and wine, he did look up to them, and tried to resist the "temptation to forget the reverence due to women. The bright side is safe-guarding oneself against temptation through the cultivation of chivalry. Sexual temptations come from perfectly natural causes, viz *sap*."

By the end of 1908, Baden-Powell was enthusiastic about girls joining his new movement: "I've had several quite pathetic letters from little girls asking me if they can share the delights of the scouting life with the boys. But of course they may! I'm always glad to hear of girls' patrols being formed." A year later he wrote, "I have had greetings from many patrols of Girl Scouts, for which I am very grateful. They make me feel very guilty at not having yet found time to devise a scheme of Scouting better adapted to them; but I hope to get an early opportunity of starting upon it. In the meantime, they seem to get a good deal of fun and instruction out of *Scouting for Boys* and some of them are capable Scouts."

Baden-Powell was very concerned that girls should not become "coarsened" or "over-toughened" by engaging in Scouting. "You do not want to make tomboys of refined girls, yet you want to attract and thus to raise the slum girl from the gutter," he wrote in *The Scout Headquarters Gazette.* A month before the Crystal Palace rally, he decided that if there were to be Girl Scouts, they should be called something different. He chose "Guides", from the Queen's Own Corps of Guides, a regiment in the North-West Frontier whose soldiers had impressed him with their bravery and efficiency when he was in the Indian army. In 1910 the Girl Guides were formed as a separate organisation, which could develop independently from boys, for girls over the age of ten years. After their foundation, Baden Powell stated adamantly that he had not started the Girl Guides — "they started themselves".

He asked his fifty-two-year-old sister Agnes to organise the girls. The unmarried Agnes enjoyed steel engraving, ballooning, making aeroplanes and playing bicycle polo. Despite these modern hobbies, she held traditional Victorian views, and believed that a Guide would be horrified to be mistaken for an imitation Scout, or to be regarded as merely mimicking boys' activities. She warned that "violent jerks and jars" could "fatally damage a woman's interior economy", and that girls who went in for "rough games and exposure" would ruin their delicate hands. She also believed that too much exercise led to girls growing moustaches. "Silly vulgar slang" such as "topping, ripping and What ho!" was definitely to be avoided.

Respectable girls and young ladies in 1910 never went out without their mother or a chaperone. Guide meetings gave them the opportunity to gather with their peers, and as there was no danger of meeting the opposite sex, they didn't have to take their mothers. They also learned independence, self-confidence and life skills.

On 27 July 1910, *Jackson's Oxford Journal*, a weekly local paper, reported: "Since the Guide movement first originated, many have swollen its ranks. We believe that there are about 60 in the Oxford region." Many existing groups of girls, such as the Girls Friendly Society, the Catholic Women's League, and the Better Britain Brigade (BBB), changed themselves into Guide companies. "A girl came down the drive on her bicycle with all kinds of things dangling from it," wrote a new recruit in Oxford. "She told us she was a Girl Guide looking for Accidents and Good Turns. She had with her everything she thought might be useful, first-aid box, rope and frying pan. I was fascinated."

Agnes Baden-Powell, an efficient organiser, gathered round her all her doughtiest lady friends to sit on committees. She adored travelling up and down Britain inspecting groups of Guides, appointing Commissioners and being treated like minor royalty. In between all this, she set about writing, with her brother's help, a handbook which she called *How Girls can Help to Build up the Empire*. In the foreword she wrote: "The Girl Guides is an organisation for character training much on the lines of Boy Scouts. Its *Aim* is to get girls to learn how to be women — self-helpful, happy, prosperous, and capable of keeping good homes and bringing up good children. The *Method* of training is to give the girls pursuits which appeal to them, such as games and recreative exercises which lead them on to learn for themselves many useful crafts."

Agnes's book was mainly copied from *Scouting for Boys*, but it included extra chapters on nursing, childcare and housekeeping. Girls, like boys, were advised strongly against trade unions and masturbation: "When in doubt, don't," they were warned. "These bad habits can quickly lead to blindness, paralysis and loss of memory."

Baden-Powell was modern in his ideas about gender-specific jobs: Boy Scouts learned traditional women's skills such as sewing and cooking, and Guides were encouraged to learn mechanics and carpentry.

"Girls must be partners and comrades rather than dolls," said Robert Baden-Powell. Educated Guides were encouraged to become translators, pharmacists, stockbrokers, laundry managers or accountants. Their role models were Joan of Arc, Elizabeth Garrett Anderson and Marie Curie. Working-class Guides were encouraged to be efficient and honest domestic and factory workers. All Guides, it was hoped, of whatever class, would make better mothers and wives. "A Guide prides herself on being able to look after a house well," wrote Agnes. "She must be able to cook, to sew, and to do laundry work: she must know simple first-aid, sick nursing and how to look after children. Her knowledge must be sound, so that she can be counted on in an emergency to care for other people as well as herself."

The book was full of health-giving advice.

The blood to your body is what steam is to the engine. It makes it go well or badly. But also your blood is food to the body, like water to a plant; if your body doesn't get enough, it remains small and weak and often withers and dies. You must take in food that is good for making blood, and avoid sweeties. When you have taken in your food and have chewed it well and have swallowed it, it goes down to your stomach and the good parts go off into the blood, and the useless part of it passes out of you at the other end. If you let this useless part stay in you too long — that is, for more than a day — it begins to poison the blood and so to undo the good of taking in good food. So you should be very careful to get rid of the poisonous part of your food at least once a day regularly.

Unless a girl can chew her food well the goodness does not come out of it in her stomach to go to make blood. So try to keep your teeth sound and strong.

If a girl could not afford a toothbrush, she could make one, just like the children Baden-Powell had met in Africa. "Take a short stick and hammer the end of it until it is all frayed out like a paint-brush. Use it every morning and evening. Attack those germs and get them out from their hiding places between the teeth, and swill them out with mouthfuls of water, so they don't get a chance of destroying your grinders."

The book included the Guide Law:

1. A Guide's honour is to be trusted.
2. A Guide is loyal, to her King, and her Guiders, her parents, her country and her employers or employees.
3. A Guide's duty is to be useful and to help others.
4. A Guide is a friend to all, and a sister to every other Guide no matter to what social class she belongs.
5. A Guide is courteous.
6. A Guide is a friend to animals.
7. A Guide obeys orders of her parents, patrol leader, or captain without question.
8. A Guide smiles and sings under all difficulties.
9. A Guide is thrifty.
10. A Guide is pure in thought, in word and in deed.

Robert Baden-Powell sometimes added an eleventh law: "(This law is unwritten but is understood: *A Guide is not a Fool.*)"

One reviewer commented, "This book is vastly more than it professes to be. It not only teaches girls to be women of the best but is one of the best aids to nature study that we have seen." Baden-Powell, however, thought his sister's popular pocket book rather confusing, and later described it as "The Little Blue Muddly".

In 1909 it was almost twenty years before all British women were allowed to vote, and the editor of the *Spectator* wrote of the Guides that "it is time to stop this mischievous new development", while one of his readers commented, "This is a foolish and pernicious movement." But Guiding was just what girls wanted, and within months 6,000 of them had enrolled. A year later, the uniform of navy blue serge skirt, cotton multi-pocketed shirt and wide-brimmed hat had been established. "We wore ETBs," remembered Mary Allingham. "Elastic top and bottom. They were navy blue, thick worsted woollen material knickers." Baden-Powell was clear that the uniform should be smart, yet not too military — he also hoped that it "makes for equality . . . it covers the difference of country and race, and makes all feel that they are members of one organization". For girls who normally wore old or ragged clothes, to wear a uniform was empowering. "We all wore these huge floppy hats," said Eileen Mitchell, "and cotton scarves, tied at the back with a reef knot, right over left, left over right." A metal trefoil badge, always highly polished, was worn on the scarf, the three leaves representing the threefold Guide promise.

Agnes Baden-Powell told Guides, "You can wear your badge any day and any hour when you are doing what you think is right. It is only when you are doing *wrong* that you must take it off; as you would not then be keeping your Guide promise. Thus you should either take off the badge or stop doing what you think is wrong." Mary Allingham never forgot Agnes's rule: "I was on my way to a date with my boyfriend when my knicker elastic went. Scrabbling in my handbag I found my Guide badge, which worked well as a safety pin. During the film he leant over to kiss me. Then his hand began to wander up my skirt. Now I knew that this was a Wrong Thing. But if I took off my badge, the situation would become untenable. What was I to do? Luckily the film became so exciting that he became distracted and my honour was saved."

The Guides' motto was the same as the Boy Scouts' — "Be Prepared". In 1910 Captain Mrs Josephine Birch of the 1st Watford Company was so proud of two of her young Guides that she took a photograph of them with the old woman they had saved from being knocked down by a milk cart. It is subtitled "An example of Guides Being Prepared for any emergency".

To make sure that they were prepared for all eventualities, Guides learned a variety of skills; after an independent test they were awarded cloth "proficiency badges" to sew on their sleeves. Among the first badges were Farmer, Electrician, Cyclist, Surveyor, Telegraphist and Braille. Two years later Geologist, Fire Brigade, Boatswain, Signaller and Rifle Shot were added.

"The badge manual was the only reference book I owned," said Mary Allingham. "Thanks to that I learnt how to dress a wound, light a fire and do Morse code. Wrapping up a parcel was a science that if achieved culminated in another Guide badge. Getting those corners straight, like doing 'hospital corners' on a bed, and tying the correct knots. Oh the horrors that might happen to a parcel not correctly wrapped. How the Postmaster would laugh and sneer!"

Baden-Powell loved aphorisms, which often appeared in Guide diaries and magazines: "If you cannot find a bright side, then polish up the dark one".

He had a great sense of fun:

> Be kind to little animals
> Whatever sort they be,
> And give a stranded jellyfish
> A shove into the sea.

By 1912, just two years after the Guides began, the fifty-five-year-old bachelor was beginning to realise that if he didn't get married soon he would end up living with his two overbearing sisters, Agnes and Jessie, for the rest of his life. He was on a cruise to New York when he met the twenty-three-year-old Olave St Claire Soames. "The only interesting person on board is the Boy Scout man," she wrote home to her mother, playing down the fact that when she was a child, Lieutenant-General Baden-Powell had been her hero.

Romance quickly blossomed, and the thirty-two-year age difference meant little to either of them. While Baden-Powell continued on his world tour, they exchanged love letters, signed with drawings of robins. The daughter of a wealthy, poetic brewery owner, Olave had been brought up very comfortably in a series of beautiful houses. She was educated at home by a governess until she was twelve, and then learned about the world by travelling with her parents. She and her sister learned arithmetic by keeping their own hens and selling the eggs to the household. A tall, attractive, sporty girl, she enjoyed canoeing, skating, cycling, swimming and football, and teaching local boys with disabilities. She had already received several proposals of marriage, but she was looking for true love and a purpose in life. In Baden-Powell she had found both. She had no idea how to cook or sew, but she was determined to learn how, or at least how to manage servants. Baden-Powell described Olave to his mother as "very cheery and bright, a real playmate". He also recognised in her a woman who could be trained up to help with the Guide movement.

Despite the disapproval of Olave's parents, the couple married ten months later, amidst huge media interest. The Scouts gave them a twenty-horsepower Standard Laundalette car, painted in the dark-green Scout colour. The couple appeared to have little in common, apart from being madly in love, and their shared birthday — 22 February, the day they later designated Guides' Thinking Day and Founder's Day for Scouts. For their honeymoon, Baden-Powell took his new wife camping in the Atlas Mountains of Algeria, where she learned to cook on a campfire and to scrub out the single pan with earth and dried grass.

The Scouting movement was concerned that Baden-Powell would have less time to spend on it, but there was no need to worry — he remained as involved as ever. The following year, Olave gave birth to their first son, Peter, named after their favourite fictional character, Peter Pan. She was happy to produce babies, but not very keen on looking after them — she did not like small children. Leaving her own in the care of a nanny and nursery maids, Olave had time on her hands, and was thus a serious threat to her sister-in-law. When in 1914 Olave offered her services to Guiding, Agnes was determined not to be displaced from her position as Chief Guide. Undeterred, Olave trained as a Guider and became a Company Captain. With her natural common sense she had a way with the girls, and proved to be popular, which further strained her relationship with Agnes.

As soon as war was declared in August 1914, young women, many of them Girl Guides, began training as nurses with the Voluntary Aid Detachment, First-Aid Nursing Yeomanry and with the Guides themselves. Several thousand other Guides volunteered as part of a readymade workforce to replace the young men sent to the trenches, and they soon demonstrated that young women could be as brave and useful as men. They looked after children, worked on farms, practised fire-drill by carrying each other out of first-floor windows and down ladders, and demonstrated how to give artificial respiration.

By this time Guide badges had increased to include Air Mechanic, Astronomer, Bee Farmer and Dairymaid, along with Lacemaker, Interpreter, Masseuse and Poultry Farmer. The outbreak of war meant that even more badges were created: the Telegraphist's Badge required a Guide to be able to construct her own wireless receiver and to send messages in Morse code at a speed of thirty letters a minute.

As well as contributing to the war effort by working in farms and factories, Guides raised enough money with "Sales of Work" to buy a large motor ambulance built by Clement-Talbot of Wormwood Scrubs. Guides in Western Australia collected used baler twine from farmers and made fly-veils for the Light Horse Brigade in Egypt. Tasmanian Guides carried out rifle practice by shooting rabbits, then cooked them over campfires and made rabbit-skin jackets for soldiers.

At railway stations all over Britain Guides set up feeding points for returning soldiers and acted as messengers for Marconi Wireless Telegraphs. Guides in London helped to organise a sports day for wounded soldiers. In a silent film made of the event, five Australian soldiers demonstrate their prosthetic dexterity by lying on the grass and racing to see who can be the first to stand up. Soldiers stand in a line, their trousers rolled up to show their artificial limbs. A one-legged soldier executes a hop, skip and jump as a hop, hop and hop into a sandpit. Then Guides offer up their long hair for a hairdressing contest. The men have to brush and plait the hair, then pin it up neatly and quickly, causing much amusement and giggling.

Olave threw herself into Guiding during the war, and in 1916 she became Sussex County Commissioner. With her husband's encouragement she then left her two babies at home for several months while she ran a rest hut for soldiers in Calais. Relations with her sister-in-law remained difficult. Agnes, much to her annoyance, was slowly sidelined, and had to be content with the non-executive position of President of the Guides.

Guiding wasn't just for schoolgirls — the movement also helped girls once they had left school. Until 1918, education was compulsory for children only up to the age of twelve, and most teenage working-class girls found employment in domestic service or in factories. "Guiding is so vitally needed by the girls of the factories and of the alleys of the great cities, who after they leave school, get no restraining influence and who, nevertheless, should be the character trainers of the future men of our nation," wrote Agnes Baden-Powell.

Even well-educated women had no freedom of action, no training for life, and little education compared with boys; needlework, painting and music were almost the only activities considered suitable for young ladies. Years later Olave wrote, "Guiding opened up new and appealing vistas to young females, visions of a life where women could face the world on equal terms with men, where they would be trained and equipped to cope with whatever emergencies might arise." The idea chimed perfectly with the growing demand for women's suffrage. After centuries as second-class citizens, women were beginning to dream of freedom and equality with men.

The First World War provided girls with an opportunity to show that they could be as good as, if not better than, boys. At the start of the war, Boy Scouts were employed as messengers at the London headquarters of Military Intelligence, MI5. But they were soon found to be "very troublesome. The considerable periods of inactivity which fell to their share usually resulted in their getting into mischief," stated MI5 report KV/49. On 15 September 1915, MI5 replaced the Scouts with Girl Guides, aged between fourteen and sixteen, who were entrusted to carry secret counter-espionage memoranda and reports. "They proved more amenable and their methods of getting into mischief were on the whole less distressing to those who had to deal with them than were those of the boys," MI5 reported.

Within just a few months of the outbreak of war, silent films were made with such titles as *The German Spy Peril*, *Guarding Britain's Secrets* and *The Kaiser's Spies*. These featured rather stupid German villains, overcome by clever Girl Guides who trick them into giving themselves up, or falling off cliffs. Spy-mania was rife, with people looking under their beds or in woodsheds, and turning against anyone with a whiff of German ancestry.

Before a Guide could start work at MI5, she had to sign a contract confirming that she had permission from both of her parents and the Guide Captain who had recommended her. She pledged with her honour not to read the papers she carried, and was paid ten shillings a week for fifty hours of work, with only a short lunch break. The Guides' working day began at 9 a.m. and finished at 7 p.m., and as well as carrying messages they were responsible for keeping inkpots filled. Some were also trained to clean and repair typewriters. By January 1917 these select girls had been formed into a special MI5 Guide Company with its own Captain, with each Patrol assigned to a separate floor of the Military Intelligence headquarters. Every Monday afternoon they paraded across the roof of Waterloo House for inspection.

Their enthusiasm could sometimes be too much, as Miss M.S. Aslin of MI5 Registry reported after working with Guides for several days. Commenting on one of the MI5 Guides, she described how "She speeds from floor to floor, bearing messages of good will, and no obstacle is too great for her to fall over in her devotion to this happy task. Released for the moment, she retires to her attractive little sitting room, where she reads and writes or converses quietly (?) on high topics with her friends."

All the women employed by MI5, of whatever age, education or competence, had to fight to be recognised as colleagues rather than regarded as mere skivvies. In "H Branch", women were employed as secretaries (a new idea), to run the photographic section and to staff the switchboard. They also cleaned, cooked and drove cars. The Guides became so much a part of the fabric of the organisation that the journal edited by its female employees, *The Nameless Magazine*, featured a cartoon of four Guides sitting in their uniforms in a corridor captioned, "The Electric Bells having broken, the GGs (*not* the Grenadier Guards) sit outside Maj. D's door in case he wants them." From 1915 to 1918, Girl Guides even took over from Scouts in the Postal Censorship office. In less than ten years since their formation, Guides had demonstrated to the establishment that girls were reliable members of society who could play useful roles beyond the purely domestic.

It didn't take long for other employers to realise that Guides were honest, trustworthy and loyal, and soon many factories only employed them. In some munitions factories, where safety was paramount, all the workers were Guides aged from fourteen up. During their lunch hour they would assemble in the factory yard and remove their working overalls and caps to reveal their Guide uniforms and their hair in long, single plaits. Their Captain wore a long skirt, navy blouse and white kid gloves to go with her felt hat and lanyard. They practised first-aid on each other, and learned new skills towards more badges. When the factory whistle went they would put their overalls and caps back on, and return to making armaments. Some employers paid for the Guides' uniforms and outings. Even after the school-leaving age was raised to fourteen in 1918, there were still many working Guides: in 1921 the 9th Oxford Guide Company was registered in the Savernake glove factory off Botley Road.

When the First World War ended, Guides were considered so reliable by the War Office that a contingent was taken with the British delegation to France. British Guides ran errands at the Palace of Versailles for the Paris Peace Conference in June 1919, and sixteen Ranger Guides were invited to witness the signing of the treaty.

Five months later, Baden-Powell made a speech at a Guide peace rally in a packed Albert Hall. He told the 8,000 Guides present that it was small, unselfish deeds that led to peace and greater understanding between people. "Each of you can go further and take a valuable part in this great work," he said. "There is no doubt that you *can* do this. The only question is — *will* you do it?" There was a resounding cheer in response: "Yes we can!"

With so many men lost during the war, the Guide movement was a blessing for many young women who had been left with little chance of finding a husband. They had to learn to support themselves, and needed all the skills they could muster for employment. Child Nurse, Toy-Maker and Gymnast Proficiency Badges were all useful for future nannies; and before the introduction of the national driving test, Mechanic and Map-Reading Badges could lead to chauffeur or taxi-driving jobs. "The Artist's Badge helped me to get a job designing toffee papers," said former Guide Verily Anderson. Not all badges meant hard work: for the Dancer's Badge, "the Irish jig should be danced with plenty of spirit and abandon", wrote Mrs Janson Potts in *Guide Badges and How to Win Them*.

Among the proposed names for older Guides, aged sixteen to twenty-one, were "Citizen-Guides", "Torchbearers", "Eagerhearts", "Pilots", "Pioneers" and "Guidewomen". Baden-Powell had a sound sense of marketing: he pointed out that a vague name, without any historical connotations, would be best, as it could acquire its own meaning. He suggested "Rangers", and "Sea Rangers" for those who lived near the sea or rivers. These young women were at "the age of fullest sexual development", wrote Olave Baden-Powell to new Guiders, "when a real love for the out-of-doors can give her many healthy interests and a wholesome tone. Beware of any tendency of allowing the idealism of the age to be fixed on ourselves [leaders] with our human failings, which must inevitably disappoint."

Running Brownie packs and Guide companies proved an invaluable outlet for the energies of many unmarried women at a time when they were beginning to express a desire for equality. The Guide movement filled a gaping hole in contributing to social order, education and entertainment. Badges now included Landworker and International Knowledge, the latter requiring an understanding of the League of Nations and the International Labour Office. The "Badge of Fortitude" was created in honour of Nurse Edith Cavell, who had been executed by a German firing squad in October 1915 for helping British soldiers to escape. This special badge was awarded to Guides with physical disabilities who showed extra fortitude.

By the end of the war, relations between Olave and Agnes were still strained, and there was nothing Agnes could do to prevent her young sister-in-law from appointing her own secretarial staff, taking charge of the training department and writing her own book, *Training Girls as Guides*. When Olave was appointed first Chief Commissioner, and then in 1918 Chief Guide, Agnes had to throw in the towel and content herself with the title "the Grandmother of Guiding".

The following year, the Baden-Powell family settled down in Hampshire, in Pax Hill, a house big enough for entertaining, run by domestic servants, many of whom were young enough to be enrolled as Guides and Scouts. It was quite normal for the Baden-Powells to have up to 150 people to a garden party, with Guides providing country dancing. The three Baden-Powell children were allowed to come down from the nursery with their nanny and join in the fun.

"Guiding is a Game; Guiding is Fun; Guiding is an Adventure," declared Olave. In 1919 she formed the International Council, to help Guides and Scouts share their ideas around the world. Dispensing with Agnes's older friends, she rallied some well-known and influential women to join the committee. A number of them had married older men, didn't like children much and preferred uniform to civilian clothes. One of these was Violet Markham, who always used her maiden name even after she was married to a Lieutenant-Colonel. The daughter of a wealthy mine-owner, she first championed the causes of miners, and then female domestic servants. Olave's Assistant Chief Commissioner was Katherine Furse, who had been brought up in Switzerland, and was an excellent skier and keen mountaineer. During the First World War she had worked for the Red Cross, and had then started the Women's Royal Navy and the Voluntary Aid Detachment nursing service. An open-minded woman, she wanted Guides to be more socially responsible, and soon became head of the Sea Rangers, which had been started in 1920 by former Wrens. They sang shanties and learned how to handle small boats, to signal and lifesave, and to cook and keep their gear tidy in cramped quarters. Before enrolment, a Sea Ranger had to make a lanyard with at least eight different knots.

In 1926 Dame Katherine founded the World Association, and was its director for ten years. A brilliant administrator and organiser, she once joked, "If I saw a child being run over by a tram, my first reaction would be to organise somebody else to rescue it." "Dame Katherine represented sheer slogging hard work," said Olave. "There was a strange unexpected streak of intolerance in her make-up and her critical, questioning mind made her appear slightly argumentative and unbending in temperament. She was so absolutely upright, that you could not but bow to her decisions."

In July 1925 the Girl Guides held a rally in Oxford. The *Oxford Times* reported the Chief Guide's opening speech: "Our aim is to train young girls to develop themselves to be useful, loyal, honourable, capable and helpful. We want them to think not only for themselves, but of others." By then half a million girls had joined the Guides and Brownies in over thirty nations — nearly double the number of Boy Scouts and Cubs. In 1929 there were enough Guides all over the world to raise £60,000 to build substantial headquarters overlooking the Royal Stables in Buckingham Palace Road. Opening in 1931, these smart new offices housed the publisher of *The Guide* and *The Brownie*, as well as a tailoring department where uniforms were made — Guide overcoats cost two guineas.

At a time when the mortality rate was still very high, anything that helped to reduce death and disease was appreciated. Guides couldn't do much about sewers and clean water supplies, but they could learn about hygiene and be on hand for first-aid in emergencies. In 1927 the 46th Westminster Company demonstrated their skills as well-prepared first-aiders, making a 16mm film in which a woman crashes her horse cart. Luckily some passing Guides take control of the frightened horse, while others bandage up the woman's leg and carry her to the village doctor. Then, as the Guides walk along a cliff, they see a boy fall over the edge. One Guide climbs down to him, while another swims across a river to alert a boatman. With the tide coming in, the unconscious boy is rescued in the nick of time.

Within just ten years of the movement's foundation, Guide companies had been started in penitentiaries, orphanages and care homes. Guiding was a way in which "the poor and needy" could be encouraged to help themselves, and the better-off could learn to help others. When a Colonel Strover organised "The Woodlarks Camp for Cripples", over a thousand children suffering from club feet, polio and TB of the spine arrived for a holiday in their wheelchairs or on crutches, and were cared for by eager Guides. Before the Welfare State or the National Health Service, disabled children had to rely on charities and volunteers. Extension Guides began in 1909 in St Mary's Hospital, Surrey, then the largest children's hospital in Europe. "The aim of Extension Guiding is to bring the blind, the crippled, the deaf and the mentally defective girl into closer touch with normal life," wrote the editor of *The Extension Guide*. Old-fashioned words, but modern ideas. "If we try do everything for the handicapped girl, we only increase her dependence on other people. If we do too little we miss the chance of helping her to find a way round the limitations of her disability." Proficiency badges were adapted to all abilities. Blind Guides were encouraged to take part in sports day and make dampers on campfires. Fire-lighting tests could be taken in bed with asbestos sheets laid over the counterpane.

In 1921 "Post" or "Lone" Guides were set up for girls who were housebound, lived in isolated places or were at boarding schools where Guides were forbidden. They held "meetings" by post: the Guide would post her reef knot and her "Second Class Useful Article" to her Captain, and it would be returned with comments for the next "meeting". At the age of sixteen a Lone Guide could become a Lone Ranger.

In June 1941 Mrs Brash put on an exhibition at Guide headquarters of handicrafts made by "crippled and invalid Guides from all over the country". She was a tough judge, and firmly told a Scottish Post Guide, "I would have passed that needlework from an ordinary Guide, Elspeth, but in the Extension branch we have especially high standards. You'll have to do better than that."

Guiding pioneered the now-accepted attitude to children with disabilities: whatever her disability, no girl was ever turned away from Brownies or Guides. Kathleen Barlow belonged to an Extension company when she was a patient in a TB sanatorium. "Most of us were lying in bed, yet full of happiness. The walking Guides took the little ones for walks in the fields, the little children pretending they were with their own mummies. The Guides grew marigolds in pots from their beds and wheelchairs. The flagpole could be carried into the ward and Colours hoisted."

The Nuffield Orthopaedic Centre in Oxford had a hospital Guide company for long-stay patients. Children's orthopaedic problems often entailed months of treatment lying flat in bed. The girls wore their Guide ties, badges and hats over their nightclothes for meetings held in wards. On sunny days they were pushed outdoors in basket-weave beds on wheels, and able-bodied Guides came to the hospital to work with them. When some Norfolk Guides discovered that many of the fifteen Guides of the Kelling Sanatorium Extension Company could not read, they paid for a teacher.

In Scotland, the Guides set up the Trefoil School for disabled children who would otherwise have received no education at all. Whether in callipers or wheelchairs, the children received a full education at the boarding school, whose motto was "Undaunted". The Trefoil School closed in 1975, by which time all disabled children were accepted in mainstream schools.

Across the globe, the Guide movement was spreading fast — by 1920 there were Guides in North America, Egypt, Palestine, Armenia and France. In 1929 Guides were established in Italy. But in 1933 Mussolini closed down all youth movements and set up his own organisation, *Balilla*, which he claimed was an improvement on Guiding and Scouting. Baden-Powell met Mussolini and pointed out that *Balilla* was compulsory rather than voluntary, super-nationalistic rather than international, and was intended to mould a uniform character rather than encouraging individualism. He also said that although the Scouting and Guiding movement encouraged service to one's nation, it never condoned the use of this for militaristic aggression. Guiding and Scouting had begun in Germany in 1914, and like Mussolini, Hitler banned them in 1933. Baden-Powell never met him to point out the deficiencies of *Hitler-Jugend* or the *Bund Deutscher Mädel*.

There was a perception that Guides and Scouts were connected to Christianity, and this was compounded by the parades that often took place in churches of the established Church of England. But Baden-Powell always insisted that they were non-denominational. "The movement is based on faith but not a particular faith," he said.

Joan Collinson was born in 1922 in Gateshead, where her Catholic father worked in the gasworks and led family prayers every night before bedtime. There was a Guide company nearby, but she never joined because its meetings were held in the Church of England church hall. "It wasn't so much rivalry," she said, "as both sides felt we were the chosen ones, and that was that. As a Roman Catholic I never dreamed of going into a different church. I don't think my parents forbade me to join, it just never came up." In fact Guides met in church halls simply because they were the cheapest or only available places to rent.

While the movement was designed to be based on neither creed nor race, Baden-Powell protested that in some countries, such as Barbados and South Africa, Guides and Scouts were organised in separate white and black companies and troops. Despite his early career as a soldier fighting in Africa and India, and his exposure to the army's institutional racism, over the years his ideas had progressed. He insisted on "One Nation, One Movement", and wanted complete racial integration. In India by 1920 there were several separate Scouting organizations — Muslim, Hindu, Seva-Samiti and "Mrs Annie Besant's" — none of them affiliated to each other or to London. In 1921 the Baden-Powells were invited to India to discuss the problem with Scout and Guide leaders. They travelled all over the country in a special carriage attached to the back of any train going in the right direction. At every station, enthusiastic Guides and Scouts greeted them, whatever the time of day or night: "We hung out of the train to talk to them and clasp their hands — and I hope that they did not notice we were both wearing uniform jackets and hats over our pyjamas." Olave met Hindu, Parsee, Anglo-Indian and European Guides, who all agreed to work together. "Once the Indian women took it up," she wrote, "the barriers between the races began to come down. Guiding could help break down the traditional conventions that kept Indian women in the background." By the end of the tour, the rival factions had all agreed to unite.

In South Africa, by contrast, Baden-Powell only managed to persuade the organisers to agree that Guides and Scouts would form one movement and wear the same uniform. They were still split into separate companies and troops for Africans, Europeans and Indians. It was not until 1936 that the Wayfarers — black South African Guides — were accepted into the Guide Association of South Africa. "At last," wrote Olave in 1973, "white had joined hands with black on equal terms. It was a giant stride for South Africa, even if it has taken several steps backwards since!"

By 1931, worldwide membership of the Guides was over a million, and in 1932 the first World Centre — "Our Chalet" in Switzerland — was opened. Olave was delighted when she was appointed the World Chief Guide in 1930, and in 1932 she was awarded the Grand Cross of the British Empire. By the late 1930s

Guiding had become international rather than Imperial, though Britain still had the largest number, with 525,276 Guides enrolled. Poland was next with 62,857, and in France there were 24,087. On the Atlantic island of St Helena there were 140 Guides to the sixty Scouts.

CHAPTER
TWO

Brownies and
Bluebirds

Younger girls had not been forgotten, and "Brownies", for girls aged from seven to eleven, were formed in July 1914, just before war broke out. Each Brownie pack was divided into "Sixes" of up to six girls, named after Fairies, Goblins and other phantasmagoria. From the age of about eight a Brownie could assume responsibility as a Seconder, second-in-command of her Six, and then work her way up to lead it as a Sixer. The pack's leaders were called Brown Owl, assisted by Tawny Owl, to continue the woodland theme.

Baden-Powell had always been keen on small people. "In our army we have a battalion of very small men called Bantams who were not big enough for the ordinary regiments," he wrote in *The Handbook for Brownies*. "They very soon showed that at fighting they were as good as anybody else. A small man can have a big heart and plenty of pluck in him. So even though a Brownie is small, she too can be just as brave and strong as a bigger girl if she likes to make herself so. The Brownies are little people who do good to Big people. Boggarts are little people who do no good — they are ugly and noisy and dirty and selfish — so we have no use for Boggarts among the Brownies."

Baden-Powell realised that the name Brownies "might be incongruous in some parts of the Empire", and suggested the alternative "Bluebirds" in parts of the world where girls had darker skin. However, in southern Africa they were called Brownies, whatever their race.

Baden-Powell suggested that each Brownie pack make a toadstool as their totem. "Like true fairies, Brownies can make their ring anywhere, not only in the woods or out on the grass, but even in the town and in a room." Toadstools were easy to make out of papier-mâché, and could be stored in a cupboard. "We all joined hands round the toadstool and danced around it singing," remembered Mary Allingham, a former Brownie. "'We're the Brownies. Here's our Aim: Lend a hand and Play the Game.' Then everyone shouted LAH, LAH, LAH, and saluted. It all seemed magic to me."

Baden-Powell took on the important job of writing *The Handbook for Brownies* himself. His understanding of tracking animals was better than his knowledge of biology, and he was very worried about germs: "There are little beasts floating about in the air called Germs. They are squirmy-looking little beggars, and very dangerous, because if they get inside you they will give you an illness of one kind or another." These squirmy-looking little beggars were more likely to attack Brownies who breathed with their mouths:

"Nose Breathing, with real cold fresh air out of doors, alone will help you to grow and to be strong."

Brownies were encouraged to exercise their imaginations, but only within limits — too much imagination might lead them astray. Good Brown Owls had read Esterel Pelly's *Brownie Games*: "Brown Owl must keep the games going and never for a minute let the pack come back to earth with a bump," she wrote. "Brown Owl must lead her Brownies from one excitement to another, and they will follow her blissfully, and she will keep the right atmosphere to the very end of the game."

At her enrolment, each new Brownie makes the Brownie promise while saluting with her right hand vertical, the palm facing outwards. Pointing to the sky, the two middle fingers represent the two promises. "The first law is that Brownies give in to Older Folk," said Baden-Powell. "The second is that a Brownie does not give in to Herself."

This two-fingered salute came long before Churchill's V-for-victory sign, and many Brownies confused it with the ruder version with the palm facing inwards.

Each Six then danced round the toadstool singing its own special song. The Pixies sing: "Look out! We're the jolly Pixies, Helping people when in fixes." The Imps: "We're the ever helpful Imps, Quick and quiet as any shrimps." There were also Welsh fairies: "We're the Bwbachod from Wales, Filling farmers' milking pails."

For great occasions, such as visits from the District Commissioner, there was a Grand Salute. "The Brownies form a circle and squat on their heels," wrote Baden-Powell, "with both hands on the ground between their feet. When the important person comes in, they howl very gently all together. 'Tu-whit-to-who-oo-ooo. Tu-whit-to-who-oo-ooo,' the second time raising the voice and gradually rising to a standing position. 'Tu-whit-to-who-oo-ooo.' The third time it is louder and the forefinger of the right hand is placed to the lips and made to revolve, the noise getting louder and louder until it ends in a shriek, a leap in the air, and a clap of the hands. The clap comes as the feet reach the ground. This action will slay the Boggarts. Then the Brownies are absolutely silent, and raise their right hands to the full salute." The Baden-Powells advised Brown Owls that a pack was "not a family, but a *happy* family", and that "laughter counteracts most of the evils of the very young and makes for cheery companionship and open-mindedness. The one who laughs much, lies little."

Once enrolled, a Brownie began her Second-Class Test, for which she was expected to know the history of the Union Jack, tie four complicated knots, make a useful article with a hem and decorative tacking, sew on two types of buttons, understand the importance of clean teeth, bowl a hoop, skip twenty times backwards, catch a ball six times and lay a table for dinner. Quite an accomplishment for an eight-year-old.

To attain First-Class standard, a Brownie had to understand semaphore, have grown a bulb, tie up a parcel, knit a jumper, lay and light a fire, cook a milk pudding, make tea, memorise a message, fold clothes neatly, skip with her feet crossing, bandage a grazed knee, know how to put out a person on fire, throw a ball accurately overarm and sing "God Save the King".

From the start, all Brownies wore the same basic uniform, wherever they were in the world, so that they could be "One Sisterhood". Brownie uniform included a knitted beret or woven rush hat, brown leather belt, brown shoes, brown hair ribbons and brown cotton knickers. The brown cotton shift-dress was designed to accommodate the growth of both the legs and bosom. In India, "Bluebirds" wore thick black stockings and white sola topees. Taking into account the fact that many families had little money, girls were allowed to wear their Brownie uniforms for up to a year after becoming Guides. Brownies were often photographed in their uniform — the only presentable outfit they owned.

Not everyone approved of Brownie uniforms. "In the pack, no element of individuality was entertained," wrote Kate Adie in *Corsets to Camouflage*, a history of women in uniform. "All Brownies wore turd-coloured bag-like shifts, with a leather belt and custard-yellow tie. Fatter Brownies looked like hamsters feeding permanently on bananas. The outfit was surmounted by a chocolate-coloured knitted Thing, which slid off your head the moment you had to do some Brownie ritual, usually involving imaginary toadstools. If you were diligent your sleeve was peppered with weird symbols, proclaiming your status as a girl well-versed in raffia craft or whatever. The good aspect of the uniform was that it blended into the dust and dirt which was swirled up by Brownie games in dingy huts. In other words, it worked, but did nothing for you."

Many Brownies loved their yellow triangular ties. "Learning how to make a yellow triangle into a tie was an art that, once achieved, felt unique," recalled Mary Allingham. "First there was the folding, to make it as thin as possible. Then that special knot that could look like a messy bunch if you weren't careful, then you had to tie it with a reef knot. This was an extraordinary piece of manual engineering — done at the back of your neck, without being able to see it. Brown Owl always checked for granny knots, which were somehow rather immoral. Why grannies were given this insult, I never knew." The Brownie tie was designed to do many things. "It was comforting to know that at any time, around your neck was an arm sling, a bandage for cut legs, a sieve for dirty water; you could even carry your rabbit in it or boil up a pudding."

In August 1914, only a month after Brownies began, Miss Richenda Gurney set up a Brownie pack for her many nieces and cousins holidaying in north Norfolk. She wore a uniform made for her by Stones & Sons, the Norwich military tailor. The day after their first meeting, war with Germany was declared and the 1st Northrepps Brownie Pack practised bandaging their uncles and the gardener, using their triangular ties as slings. During the General Strike of 1926, Brownies collected clothes for striking miners, and they would later knit blankets in squares for families hit by the Great Depression. Christine Hinkley, the daughter of a Scoutmaster in Ruislip, Middlesex, became a Brownie when she was eight: "I joined the Little People Six. We sang as we danced around our toadstool: 'We though known as little people, aim as high as any steeple.' We played feet-off-ground games, Kim's game, stepping-stones with newspaper. We learned how to make cups of tea and set a table for our Hostess Badge. For Homemaker Badge we kept our rooms tidy, dusted, swept, washed a tea towel and washed up. We had an annual get-together in Ruislip called Brownie Revels, held in the gardens of a very large house, with woodland around; about a hundred of us. We played lots of games in the woods, culminating in a wonderful picnic tea."

The transition from Brownies to Guides was marked at the "Flying-Up" ceremony, at which eleven-year-old Brownies who had achieved the First Class Test jumped off a bench to "fly up" to Guides. The Chorlton-cum-Hardy pack had a Fly-Up on 1 November 1926. "Had any strangers peeped into our clubroom they would have watched one of the nicest of all ceremonies, a 'Brownie Fly-Up'," reported their log book. "While the Brownie Pack stand in the Fairy Ring round their Totem, and the Guide company in Horse-shoe formation, four Brownies leave the pack and fly to Guides. Brown Owl fastens on their wings, then bids them go forward and do well. Then each Brownie gives the salute and handshake, and the whole pack give the Grand Howl." Less-qualified Brownies were only allowed to walk up to Guides. Christine Hinkley remembered: "I tried to get my Brownie Wings, but could not get enough badges. Much to my father's disappointment, I failed my Semaphore Badge. So I could not fly up to Guides with that special ceremony." Christine would have been less downhearted if she had known that Baden-Powell once said, "It is a greater thing to try without succeeding than to succeed without trying."

In 1920 the Princess Royal, Princess Mary, only daughter of George V, became President of the Girl Guide Association. This was no nominal title — she insisted on being properly enrolled by Olave Baden-Powell and making her Guide Promise, and she took her role seriously, travelling all over the country visiting Brownies and Guides. On May Day 1930 she found herself in a field in Kingston Maurward, Dorset, inspecting several thousand Brownies. Each pack had to welcome the Princess into a "Brownie Land Flower Garden". The 1st Swanage chose to be delphiniums and poppies, with nine-year-old Irene Makin as one of two raindrops, wearing a gauze veil over her head. "Irene was so excited she couldn't keep still," wrote her friend Audrey Pembroke. "Not many little girls got to meet a real live princess. Irene kept jumping about in her headdress in the hallway, and singing until her father had had enough. 'If you don't dry up,' he told her, 'this little raindrop won't be going!'" Irene went with her pack in a charabanc. After a grand march-past, accompanied by the Dorchester town band, the Brownies danced up to the Princess Royal to the tune of "Pop Goes the Weasel". They were led by the "Spirit of the Garden", a sixteen-year-old Ranger dressed in white, and when each Brownie reached the princess, she had to stop and curtsey. "Irene found herself gazing down at a smart pair of brown lace-up shoes. Shyly she lifted her eyes, to look up through her veil at the tall figure of the Princess." Princess Mary was wearing her navy-blue uniform, belted at the waist, the white cords of office held up with the Guide badge on her lapel, and on her felt hat was a gold cockade. She smiled at Irene and whispered, "Hello."

When Irene got home her mother asked her if she had seen the Princess.

"Oh yes," said Irene, "she looked just like Brown Owl."

When the girls of Herstmonceux village in East Sussex wanted to start a Brownie pack in 1934, a notice was read out in church that the first meeting would be held at the rectory the following Saturday morning. "Twenty little girls turned up mostly with their mothers who, when told about the uniform, shook their heads," remembered their Brown Owl. "'All right then,' I said, 'we will start the pack without uniforms and think of a way of raising the funds.'" So the would-be Brownies organised a concert, and charged a penny a peep to look at *The Brownie* magazine. With the proceeds, they bought a paper dress-making pattern for sixpence and brown cotton curtain material at 9d a yard. "Already a dab hand at making my sisters' party dresses from Woolworth patterns, I set about cutting out and machining twenty little uniforms. The most expensive parts were the Brownie belts, and these we persuaded the saddler to cut up out of old but well-polished leading reins. After a pathetic attempt to embroider the badges myself, we had to buy them from Guide Headquarters." The toadstool was made of papier mâché from old copies of *The Times* donated by the local rector.

Not all Brown Owls were perfect. Carol Snape was seven years old when she became a Brownie in Albrighton, near Wolverhampton. "My Brownie uniform was handed down from my elder sister — everything was, in spite of her being smaller than me," she recalls. "As it was rather short it showed my large brown inter-lock knickers. My brown beret soon got lost. I was always being told off by Brown Owl, who was Doctor's wife — a very bossy lady. We assembled in the yard outside the surgery. One day she was very cross indeed because I had got ice-cream all down my front. She held me under the pump because we were going on parade in the village." Despite these horrors, Carol was enrolled as a Girl Guide twice. "I liked the enrolment ceremony so much that when we moved house, I never let on I had done it before."

Some Brownies, such as Lucy Worthing from Sussex, felt the pressure to do Good Deeds could be too strong:

Before I was enrolled as a Brownie, my fellow candidates and I were each given a paper cat with a string tail about six inches long. We had to tie a knot in the string every time we did a Good Deed. One Good Deed a day was the recommended aim.

A week later we brought our crumpled cats to the Brownie meeting and we compared knotted cats' tails. I was proud to show Brown Owl that I'd achieved six deeds, mostly on my grandmother who lived next door. She had happily accepted my tepid cups of tea and efforts to untangle her knitting bag. I even picked her a fistful of buttercups from the verge. But one girl had surpassed us all. Molly had added an arm's length of string to her cat's tail, all tightly knotted. "How did you do it?" we asked in awe. "Mummy helped me," she gloated. "She found me lots of good deeds to do, like cleaning the silver napkin rings, and tidying the fish fork drawer. Daddy gave me his best shoes to polish." I felt that this did not count — you had to spot your own Good Deeds, and anyway being quite so competitive annulled them altogether.

From the start, Baden-Powell made it clear that in addition to doing Good Deeds, it was the duty of every Brownie and Guide to "Keep Smiling". To illustrate this, he told the story of Francis Palmer. "He was a very young boy belonging to the Wolf Cubs of the 18th Bristol troop, who was knocked down by a motor-car. His left leg was broken in two places, and the side of his face badly cut. The boy was naturally in great pain; but to the astonishment of the doctors and nurses, never cried or complained. One of the doctors asked him why he was so brave, and his answer was: 'I am a Wolf Cub, and so must not cry.' So whenever you break your leg just smile if you can. If you cannot — well — then grin!"

Although Baden-Powell had emphasised the importance of adaptability, and that a Brownie pack could meet anywhere, and under any circumstances, by the late 1930s rules had crept in. The outbreak of war changed everything. "We used to think you need a hall or roomy headquarters, we now know that anywhere will do, even Brown Owl's home, or sitting under a tree," wrote Violet Smith, the Chief Brown Owl, in 1940. "Recipe for being a Brown Owl: Take the *Brownie Handbook*, a limited number of girls aged 7 to 10 years old, consider their needs and, using your own commonsense, carry on. Your Commissioner will back you up, but will not always be available."

CHAPTER
THREE

Marching in
Gas Masks

As Neville Chamberlain attempted to negotiate with Hitler in September 1938 to prevent the outbreak of war, the real possibility of hostilities was brought home to ordinary British people when "respirators" or gas masks were made available to the public. Despite Chamberlain's promise of "peace in our time", the government began to plan "Operation Pied Piper" to evacuate children from cities. It was expected that the Germans would attack from the air with bombs and biological or poison gas, so as soon as war seemed imminent, the plans were put into action.

In church halls, Guides began to learn how to put on and march in gas masks, and what to do during an air raid. "Guide meetings were dominated by putting our gas masks on with our eyes shut, in case it was dark when the time came," said Lucy Worthing. "Our Captain seemed to be obsessed with our houses catching fire. We were always rolling each other up in hearth rugs or blankets." Guides also helped to distribute gas masks. As well as adjusting the devices to fit correctly, they had to reassure anxious mothers who feared that the masks would introduce head lice into their homes, and frightened children who believed that the smell of Izal disinfectant was poison gas. The number of mothers who appeared with previously unregistered illegitimate children surprised the Guides. They also noticed that some Christians were reluctant to use masks that might have been touched by Jews.

Iris O'Dell was a Brownie living at Hitchin, Hertfordshire, with her younger brothers Bill and Bob. "At St John's Hall gas masks were allotted — it was chaos! We each had to be fitted and tested. Bill had a Mickey Mouse gas mask, which used to send Mum off into peels of laughter, and baby Bob had a huge contraption to put him in. School was strict about bringing one's gas mask and you were sent home to get it if forgotten. All of them started off in very smart boxes, but the original boxes in pretty covers gave way to all manner of new covers including those which looked like a horse's nose-bag. At school we were given gas-mask drill where we were timed to see how quickly they could be put on. The teachers came around the desks with a piece of paper and you breathed in and hoped the paper stuck on the end of the mask."

Guides and Rangers across the country also offered their services to the newly formed city Air-Raid Precautions (ARP) organisation. When the North Berkshire Rangers joined the ARP, their canvas latrine cubicles were commandeered as "Decontamination Cubicles" in case of gas attacks. The Rangers Decontamination Squad had to be prepared to erect them in two minutes. "At the practice sessions," wrote one Ranger, "we each put on a huge overall, rubber gloves, Wellington boots and a gas mask." They had to stand inside the cubicle armed with a bucket of whitewash and a massive decorating brush. They were not told what real casualties would have been painted with, though they knew it would not be whitewash. "As each mock casualty arrived, we had to instruct him (they were all men) to strip off his clothing, which was bagged up and would have been burnt in a real attack. Then we had to cover the 'casualty' from head to foot with whitewash." One Ranger was horrified to find that her first "casualty" was the local curate. She reported, "He kept his underpants on but I was scarlet with embarrassment. Goodness knows how I would have coped had we done it in earnest on naked bodies."

In September 1938, Guiders working at headquarters in Buckingham Palace Road started to dig bomb shelters in nearby St James's and Green Park. "Everyone did two hours' digging a day," remembered Verily Anderson. "One hour came out of our lunch break." As a Guide in Sussex working for the Authoress Badge which had been introduced in 1920, she had followed the rules set out in *Hints on Girl Guide Badges*: "Know what you've driving at; mean what you say; never use a long word where a short one will do." Having "successfully written a dramatic sketch", "expressed her own personal thoughts in an essay" and "written an account of an event in her life" she had passed the badge, which featured an inkstand, and was now employed as sub-editor of *The Guide*. As a Girl

Guide Association employee Verily had to wear uniform at all times. She even wore it to meet her boyfriend in the pub for a beer after work.

"Christian names were forbidden but nicknames were acceptable," she remembered. "The editor, a large, dark-haired woman called Miss Christian, decided that because my maiden name was Bruce, I should be called 'Spider'. The senior editors were romantic novelists. Their salaries were so low that it was written into their contracts that, if time lay heavy, they could write their novels in the office."

Like many Guiders in early 1939, Verily decided to graduate to a more adult uniformed service. She joined the First-Aid Nursing Yeomanry, or FANYs, as a part-time trainee ambulance driver. "Once a week I scrambled out of the blue Guide uniform and into khaki. We had to march up and down Birdcage Walk beside Wellington Barracks, overseen by a Guards Sergeant." The FANYs had begun in the Boer War, consisting of young ladies who drove horse-drawn ambulances. "Our training was more like a debutante's tea-party," said Verily, who soon discovered that FANYs who had been Guides were at a distinct advantage. "We met in an Eaton Square drawing room, where those of us who had passed our Second-Class Guide Badge could advise on first-aid. We were told that the Cyclist's Badge would come in handy for mending punctures on ambulances. A cabby was brought in from the local taxi rank to enlighten us further over inflating flat tyres. 'Yer sticks a li'll nozzle in yer nipp'll and wiv one o'yer plates o'meat in yer strr'p, yer keeps at it.' When it came to training under canvas at Aldershot, those of us who were former Guides beat the rest in tent jargon — we tossed off our brailing strings and fouled our guys as we pitched and struck the Bells. We were all treated as officers, and wore Sam Browne belts, which we were told to take off when we went out dancing."

At the end of August 1939 Verily Anderson took her first annual holiday from *The Guide*. She and two girlfriends, and their brothers who were on leave from the navy, went on a cycling tour of Brittany. As soon as they heard on the French news that war was imminent, they phoned home. Their parents told them that telegrams had already arrived demanding that they join their units forthwith. "After a night sleeping on the beach at St Malo, we boarded an overladen ferry, all ready to use our Life-Saving Guide Badge. Back in London I struggled into my Guider's uniform to hand in my resignation at Guide HQ. Then I changed my mind and put on my FANY uniform, feeling that khaki would be more dramatic for the romantic novelists."

The 1st Eynsham Brownie Pack also went on holiday in August 1939 — to Swanage in Dorset. "We went down on the shore and we dug. We ate some ices," wrote Sheila Harris in their Pack Holiday Log Book. She practised semaphore with Sonia Horwood for their Golden Hand Badge, while Brown Owl, a teacher called Miss Mary Oakley, held a skipping rope for their friends Joan and Audrey to jump over for their Athlete's Badge, their uniforms tucked into their knickers. "Then we had our tea and played on the hill and went to bed." The Brownies were accompanied by Mrs Perkins, Miss

Gibbons and Miss Betterton, who wore their coats on the beach as they watched the girls swimming in their knitted woollen costumes.

On Monday, 28 August, Gwyneth Batts of the Gnome Six wrote: "We went in the sea. It was nice and wet and we tried to swim. We went to the top of a long hill to see a monument. It was a very long way and we became very hot."

On Tuesday, 29 August, Patsy Harling of the Fairy Six wrote: "We went to buy our presents. I got a vase for mummy, a shaving stick for daddy and a stick of rock for grandpa. When we got back we had Diana to tea. We met her on the beach in the morning. We did not like her much. She did not say thank you for her tea."

On Wednesday, 30 August, Joan Brookes of the Gnome Six wrote: "It was a nasty morning and the sea was so rough we could not bathe. We found a lot of seaweed. We saw two funny poodles." Doreen Bray of the Fairy Six wrote: "After dinner we got ready to go down to the beach. We had a sandcastle competition which was won by Sylvia. We had a lovely bathe because it was so rough. It was fun jumping the waves. We played hide and seek and we sang God Save are [sic] King."

On Thursday, 31 August, Joyce Betterton of the Elf Six wrote: "The sea was calm and we went on a boat. We had sausages for dinner and apple and custard. Then we did handstands." Sonia Horwood of the Sprite Six added: "The boat rocked. We picked some blackberries to eat. We sang in the boat coming home."

Joan Winterbourne of the Sprite Six was the last Brownie to write, on Friday, 1 September: "While we were having our breakfast Brown Owl told us we were going home. We packed all our clothes and emptied all our beds."

The Brownies spent the four-hour bus journey home singing songs such as "Rolling Down to Rio" and "The Jolly Waggoner". "We arrived back in Eynsham late on Saturday night," Brown Owl wrote in the log book. "Everyone was very glad to see us and we were only sorry we had missed one day of such a lovely holiday. The next day war broke out." Even so, some of the mothers complained that by coming home a day early, their daughters did not get their full fifteen shillings' worth of holiday.

During the last week of August the 1st Kennington Girl Guide Company in Oxfordshire were looking forward to camping in the New Forest. "Our Captain, Miss Gandy, was excited too," said Sylvia Rivers, then aged thirteen. "She had cooked a ham for our first meal." However, just as they were about to set off Miss Gandy received a telegram advising them not to go because of the possibility of war: "She was almost in tears." Instead, the Guides took their packed lunches to nearby Bagley Wood and practised tracking. Then they set up camp in a field next to the Captain's house in Kennington.

On Friday, 1 September, Germany invaded Poland, and it appeared inevitable that Britain would declare war on Germany. "By the Friday," said Sylvia, "as things were beginning to look dark in the Country, we were asked if some of us would go to Abingdon to help run messages to people preparing to take in evacuees." She and her patrol cycled the five miles to help prepare for children being evacuated to Abingdon from London: "We delivered notes to the families who were to care for the children." On the night of 2 September, trains travelled with no lights in the carriages, and families with relations in the country began to leave the capital. The following morning Britons sat by their radios waiting to hear Chamberlain's broadcast on the BBC Home Service at 11.15 a.m.

Mary Yates was a Guide, a leader of her local Brownie pack and a choirgirl in a village in Oxfordshire. The vicar asked her to sit in his rectory and listen to the wireless. "I then had to hurry to church and hand to the vicar one or other order of service, depending on the news." Mary heard the tired voice of Chamberlain speaking to Britain: "This morning the British Ambassador in Berlin handed the German government a final note stating that unless we heard from them by eleven o'clock that they were prepared at once to withdraw their troops from Poland a state of war would exist between us. I have to tell you now that no such undertaking has been received, and that consequently this country is at war with Germany."

"I hurried down the church drive," remembered Mary. "As I moved from the vestry into the church I felt the atmosphere — the congregation seemed to be holding their breath waiting for the vicar's words — 'The Country is at War.'"

Edna Gertrude Cole was a sixteen-year-old Guide living in Davenport, ten miles south of Manchester. "We were in the process of building an air-raid shelter in the garden when we went indoors to hear the broadcast. War had been declared. Then we went out and got on with digging the shelter. It was a hole, propped up with railway sleepers. As fast as we dug, it filled with water."

"On the Sunday morning," said Sylvia Rivers, "my Patrol Leader and I cycled to Abingdon again and helped until afternoon. When we arrived back at camp there was no one there, an empty space. War had been declared. Captain had struck camp straight away. She had already lived through the First World War and had lost her brother."

That evening, BBC radio announcer Bruce Belfrage read the nine o'clock news: "The following advice is given: to keep off the streets as much as possible; to carry a gas mask always; to make sure all members of the household have on them their name and address clearly written; to sew a label on children's clothing so that they cannot pull it off . . ." Up until then, all newsreaders had been anonymous, but now they were told to announce their names so that listeners would learn their voices and be able to tell if they were being impersonated by the enemy and giving false information. Guides invented a new game — who could name the newsreader quickest before he identified himself?

Iris O'Dell was shopping with her mother and her brothers in Hitchin when the announcement of war was made. "Mum was wearing a dark green coat with a fur collar and a green velvet hat when she went into Timothy White's to buy a jar of cod-liver oil and malt. We were outside minding Bob in the brown pram. When she popped the big jar under the pram cover, she whispered, 'We are at war.' That night I laid awake straining my ears to hear the tramp of Germans marching up our lane."

Many adults also believed that war would begin immediately, and there were rumours that the Germans would launch gas attacks from the air. Guides all over Great Britain rushed to find their gas masks and to help other people get theirs together. They knew from the news that in Poland aerial bombing had rained down explosives on small wooden villages and beautiful towns, and thousands of people had been killed or wounded. On the first day of the war, Guides all over Britain braced themselves against the feeling of panic that was in the air. They were determined that whatever lay ahead they were going to think of others, remain cheerful and set a good example of courage to other people. As Baden-Powell said, "Look up and not down, look forward and not back. Look out, not in — and lend a hand."

Operation Pied Piper was set in motion. A poster produced by the Ministry of Health Evacuation Scheme depicted a boy and girl looking miserable, and the words: "Mothers — let them go — give them a chance of greater safety and health." Every city railway station was soon crowded with children, some with their parents, some from homes and orphanages. There was plenty for Guides to do. Those in cities helped children leave, and those in safe areas helped to entertain them when they arrived. "In Ilford, Guides are 'keeping school' for the infants," wrote *The Guide*. "Left behind by the tide of evacuation which had swept the teachers along, they were having dull days with no teachers." "Our Guide company had to clean out empty houses to take evacuees," said Iris O'Dell. "Mothers and children from Manchester. It was quite dirty, but we had fun. The billeting officer came and sorted the families out, and children were taken round private houses."

Margaret Collins was a keen Guide living in Maidstone, Kent.

The actual moment that war was declared, I was helping out in the Town Hall. We listened in the Mayor's parlour to the declaration of war and immediately afterwards the air-raid sirens all went. The Mayor got very agitated and sent us down to the cellar. He dashed out onto the Town Hall steps and directed people furiously to "get under cover" but everyone was just gazing around. The sirens had gone off by mistake.

Various information offices were set up and I helped direct the evacuees. First, we Guides scrubbed the large old houses along the London Road, which had stood empty because of the Depression. They were taken over by the council and we got them ready for pregnant mothers.

We hardly went to school at all, even though it was my last year. Once air-raid shelters had been dug and blast walls put up, then we got back to school. Then we welcomed an evacuated school from Plumstead. We had three little boys to live with us: Alfie, Eric and Ernie Bell. They arrived with hardly any clothing, and were very unused to baths. The countryside was quite new to them, and they soon enjoyed apple scrumping. Their billeting fee was paid by the government but after things got better organised, their families were required to pay towards this. Then a lot of them went home to their parents.

A Kensington Brown Owl accompanied her Brownies when they were evacuated to Sussex by bus.

We loaded up with picnic food. The Brownies also took dressing-up clothes and a wind-up gramophone so that they could give a performance of their latest concert once they got there. The Brownies sang their songs, but travel sickness overcame Alice, one of the liveliest and naughtiest Brownies. A more pathetically deflated sight I never saw. She lay back green and limp and for once almost silent. "Never no more," she groaned, "will I roam." Barley sugar, a reminder of the Brownie smile in time of trouble, and an assurance that I didn't mind a bit if she was sick, helped a little. For these things, when she recovered, she was touchingly grateful. She was led away by the billeting officer, a little less green.

During this turbulent time, children could see the distress, upheavals and deprivations that their parents were coping with. But older Brownies and Guides had the advantage that they could see how to make themselves useful, which also alleviated their own feelings of helplessness. Families were separated and children sent to live with strangers, often of a different class, creed or culture, perhaps hundreds of miles from home. The children had to undergo long journeys to unknown destinations on overcrowded trains and buses. The younger ones had no idea why they had been wrenched from their mothers' arms; the older ones had to cope with their own homesickness and the distress of their younger siblings. Unqualified adults, often not parents themselves, became surrogate mothers and fathers overnight to severely homesick children.

There was no time to match children and foster parents — the evacuees were simply handed out by billeting officers at railway stations, or driven around and deposited on doorsteps. The countryside was filled with urban children wearing labels and carrying their gas masks. Rumours circulated about the horrors of children who knew nothing about closing farm gates, were covered in lice, wet their beds and never stopped crying for their mothers. Local Guides came to the rescue by helping to bath and feed evacuated babies, playing with toddlers and organising games for older children. Evacuee girls over seven became Brownies in their local packs, and the older girls became Guides; both organisations provided instant friends. Small village companies with only eight or ten girls were suddenly swelled to fifty or sixty. Most of the evacuated children were young, so Brownie packs grew overnight. "Life was disorganised for everyone," wrote *The Guide*'s Miss Christian. "Schools took place in shifts, so that in many cases there was half a day's holiday at least every day in the week." With children spending less time at school, Guide meetings could be held more often than once a week.

In addition to their gas masks, evacuees were expected to bring with them "a change of underclothing, night clothes, house shoes or plimsolls, spare stockings or socks, a toothbrush, a comb, towel, soap and face cloth, handkerchiefs and, if possible, a warm coat or mackintosh". Many children were too poor to own half of these things, and their foster parents had to find clothes for them too.

Within a few days 660,000 children and carers were evacuated from London, and 1,220,000 from other towns and cities. By the end of the war the General Post Office had registered thirty-nine million changes of address — for a total population of forty-seven million. Never before had so many people from different backgrounds — the country and the city, the rich and the poor — been thrown so closely together.

The war against Germany changed the role of Britain's Guides in other, more profound ways. As well as assisting evacuated children, those Guides who had left school were called up to military service: they were ideal recruits for WAAFs, NAAFI (the Navy, Army and

Air Force Institute, which provided the armed services with shops, restaurants and other facilities) and the FANYs. At the start of 1939 *The Guide* had featured a series called "What Shall I Be?" By September of that year the series had reached "No. 9 — Domestic Servant". The photo shows a pretty young woman with beautifully coiffed hair, ironing a shirt. "Cheery and trim," says the caption, "the domestic servant of today finds the varied work of a house gives her scope that is lacking in more mechanical occupations." The next month's cover showed a female soldier apparently changing the track of a tank using a small spanner. Domestic service was off the agenda, and the Girl Guide Association now encouraged working Guides to join up. Over 1,000 Sea Rangers enlisted with the Wrens.

With many Guide Captains and Commissioners being called up as ambulance drivers, Air-Raid Wardens, nurses or into factories, thousands of Guide companies all over the country found themselves with no Captains. Patrol Leaders stepped into the breach, even though most of them were no more than fifteen years old. They offered their companies' services to the billeting authorities, to town halls and air-raid posts, asking, "Can you use us?"

People who had never heard of Guides before, suddenly realised how useful they could be. Guides carried messages, wrote down timetables, helped officials at railway stations. They waited on railway platforms all over the country. "Quiet, friendly, smiling figures in blue," wrote Miss Christian in *The Guide*, "waiting to meet the trains, to carry luggage for tired mothers, to take charge of crying toddlers, to give a friendly, reassuring greeting to the boys and girls of their own age, arriving lonely, homesick and perhaps scared, in utterly new surroundings." "I have never had much to do with girls," said a billeting officer, "but I find these Guides most level-headed and sensible. When you ask them to do a job they do get on with it, and they do it thoroughly."

They tidied up rest centres in village halls and schools, and cleaned houses that evacuated families would live in. In Glasgow, the hostel for servicewomen was in such a dreadful state that the local Guides had to clean it from top to bottom before they could start running it. "They only acquired it a few days before the opening," reported *The Guide*. "Guides got down to it and scrubbed and scoured every evening after work to get it ready in time. The running of it in voluntary shifts entails more than would appear, for the trains deposit girls for interviews in the very early morning. It means an all-night shift of Guides every night. The Brownies are knitting dishcloths and intend to keep them steadily supplied."

In Eastbourne, a large empty house was taken for fifty girls expected from London. The local Guides set to work scrubbing it. Then they went round to everyone they knew and begged for food, cooking pots, crockery and bedding. They even scrounged hessian to cut up and make into blackout blinds for the many windows. After ten hours' hard work there was a knock at the door. There, standing on the pavement were not the fifty girls they expected, but seventy-one mothers and babies. "Never mind," said the Guides, "we know what to do." Kettles were boiled, tea made, bottles prepared for babies, and by midnight the new arrivals had settled down for the night.

Pamela Ruth Lawton was a Guide in Congleton, Cheshire. "On Saturday afternoons, two Guides had to walk the three miles to Astbury Vicarage to play with the evacuees and help with the teas. These were usually a large slice of bread ('door-steps') covered in rhubarb and ginger jam, which ran all over it. We enjoyed a cup of tea and a bun."

The skills that Guides had learned for their proficiency badges, some of which may have seemed utterly useless before the war, were now invaluable. By 1939, badges covered Air Mechanic, Bee Farmer, Carpenter, Boatswain, Interpreter and Surveyor. Suddenly, efficient camp organisation, cooking on campfires, knotting and remembering messages were vitally important. Guides with Child Nurse Badges turned up as willing helpers at evacuated nursery schools, which were often short-staffed and overcrowded. They bathed as many as eighty babies every morning, while those with a Needlewoman Badge mended the babies' clothes. The badges worn on the arms of Guides were not just a way of showing off their achievements: they were the proof of their skills. Wherever Guides went, the people in charge could immediately see what they were capable of: Sick Nurse, First-Aid, Cook, Games, Entertainers, Friend to the Deaf — all were useful.

By Monday, 4 September, barrage balloons were hovering above cities, homes were prepared with blackout curtains and windows were sealed with paper sticky-tape and strips of blankets against gas attacks. A new 11th Guide Law was made: "A Guide always carries her gas mask." Guides all over Britain helped the ARP by acting as patients for first-aid exercises.

While Guide companies in the countryside expanded, in the towns and cities many vanished overnight or dwindled to just a few members. Church halls where Guide meetings were formerly held were taken over as gas-mask distribution centres and first-aid posts. The blackout meant that going out after dark became almost impossible. There was a solid, absolute darkness in even the biggest cities: the only light was from slowly moving cars' headlights, covered in black paper apart from a small slit. People walking at night had to be careful not to bump into things, so Guides went out with whitewash and painted trees, lamp posts, kerbs and gateposts. Somehow Guide meetings carried on, the small groups often staying overnight at each other's houses.

The 1st Langton Matravers Guide Company, near Swanage in Dorset, had been formed in 1925; by 1939 it had only a dozen members. Faced with the influx of evacuees, anyone in Langton with a spare room, even a front room, gave it up. Soon the Guide company had more than doubled in size. The Guides held a "penny party", and made enough money to provide a filled Christmas stocking for every evacuee child under five years old in the village. When the RAF took over the local prep school, the Guides were invited to lay on games and sandwiches for children's parties at Christmas. Together, the Guides and the RAF men went around the village singing carols with a portable organ.

Guides had never been trained for war or fighting, but like the skills they had acquired for their proficiency badges, the training they had received in their ordinary meetings and camps soon proved invaluable. During the past year, much had been done to prepare for war conditions. Now Guides came into their own, as men had to leave home to join the armed forces, and mothers who had stayed at home to look after their families had to work in factories to help the war effort. Overnight, the skills that Brownies and Guides had been learning became imperative for the survival of Britain. The school leaving age was fourteen years, so membership of the Guides was important for many young women who would otherwise never have learned dressmaking, carpentry and cooking. For the first month of war, everything closed down — from theatres to Brownie and Guide meetings. But after a month it was realised that these meetings were very important and should continue as normal, with extra care at night for the blackout.

Surprisingly, unemployment among women actually rose after the outbreak of war. Those women in "light or inessential" industries were laid off, and the Women's Land Army and the Auxiliary Territorial Service could not cope with the huge numbers of applicants. Although 30,000 young women volunteered to join the Land Army, by January 1940 only 2,000 were employed in it. This gave Guiders a few more months to train Patrol Leaders, ready for when they had to take over running companies.

As the months went by, the gas attacks, aerial bombing and invasion that the British people had feared were imminent, did not come. For many people this period, known as the Phoney War, was an anticlimax, and some thought they had been deceived by the government. By Easter 1940 a feeling of security had returned, and not only did parents fetch their children home, but whole schools returned to the cities. A few Guiders carried on as if nothing had happened. In December 1939 the Oxford City Guide Commissioners held a badge meeting at which the Needlework Examiner complained that the standard of needlework was falling. She also objected to the use of French seams in garments, but the other commissioners decided that tidiness of sewing was more important than the type of seams.

Like many evacuee children, Alice the travel-sick Brownie was soon back at home. "When I saw her again, she would walk along with me, her hand tucked in mine," said her Brown Owl. "One day she announced perkily: 'I've got to be good till tomorrow, Miss.' I expressed my pleasure and relief. 'Till after my mother's funeral at eleven,' she said. It turned out that she had been living with what she described as a 'wicked step-aunt'."

A week later, Brown Owl met Alice in the street when it was nearly dark. "I shan't be coming to

Brownies no more," the child said. "Brownies often said this, perhaps to get extra attention, but they did not usually mean it. One Brownie, who never missed a meeting in three years, said it frequently, giving such excuses as 'because we're getting a built-in fireplace' or 'because Dad might be coming home.' But Alice, who was wearing her usual fur-lined boots and a coat but no frock, explained: 'Auntie's washing my frock, for going back to my dad. She's putting me on the Glasgow bus tonight.'"

Brown Owl was appalled, and went home to find some barley sugar to give Alice for the journey. But she was too late. "Alice had already gone and I knew I should never see her again. I lay awake that night thinking of the bus creeping up England and Scotland with my naughtiest little Brownie slumped in a corner, moaning her vows never to go roaming no more."

A few days later a letter came with a Glasgow postmark. The note inside was a bit sticky, but the message was a joy: "Dear Brown-Owl dear," Alice had written. "There was a woman on the bus worsen me. She felt a lot better when I gave her an emergency smile and told her I didn't mind a wee bit if she threw up."

CHAPTER
FOUR

Kinder-Guides

While people in Britain were living through the Phoney War, in Germany Jewish people had been suffering horrendous persecution since the start of the 1930s. Their shops were plagued by pickets, and in September 1935 Hitler had passed the Nuremburg Laws, depriving "non-Aryans" of citizenship. Jews' passports were marked with a large "J", and they were forced to wear a yellow star as a means of identification. Jews were banned from public places and schools and had their property confiscated. In 1935 Samuel Hoare, the British Foreign Secretary, made it clear that Britain would be hospitable to individual Jewish refugees with sponsors, but not to Jews *en masse*. However, after the events of 9 November 1938 he rethought his policy.

On that night "The entire Jewish population of Germany was subjected to a reign of terror," reported the *Daily Telegraph*. "No attempt was made by the police to restrain the savagery of the mob. Almost every synagogue in the country was burnt to the ground. Scarcely a Jewish shop escaped being wrecked. Looting occurred on a great scale. Jews of all ages, of both sexes, were beaten in the streets and in their homes.

Jewish patients in hospitals were dragged outside in their nightclothes." The Nazis imprisoned 30,000 Jewish men on what became known as "Kristallnacht", or the Night of Broken Glass.

Two weeks later, Hoare, now Home Secretary, held a breakfast meeting with Jewish, Quaker and other religious leaders, and the Committee for the Care of Children from Germany was formed. He proposed that Britain should admit European Jewish children as long as organisations or families agreed to sponsor them once they arrived. He had been assured by Jewish organisations that in order to save their children from the Nazis, Jewish parents in Germany, Austria and Czechoslovakia were prepared to send their children to a strange country and an uncertain future.

Later that evening, a full-scale debate on refugee policy took place in the House of Commons. Hoare announced that the Home Office would allow entry to all child refugees whose maintenance could be guaranteed. The Commons resolved "That this House notes with profound concern the deplorable treatment suffered by certain racial, religious, and political minorities in Europe, and, in view of the growing gravity of the refugee problem, would welcome an immediate concerted effort amongst the nations."

Hoare agreed immediately that in order to speed up the immigration process, travel documents would be issued on the basis of group lists rather than individual applications, and from December 1938 Jewish children began to arrive in Britain from Germany, Austria and Czechoslovakia. Their parents had taken the agonising decision to send them away, not knowing what the future held. The Nazi authorities decreed that leave-takings must happen quickly and without fuss, so farewells were brief. The trains carrying the children often left at night, and while some children saw the journey as an adventure, most were frightened and distressed. Few would see their parents again.

The first two hundred children of the "Kindertransport" departed from Berlin on 1 December 1938. After that, an average of 250 children aged between four and seventeen left Germany and Austria every week, arriving by train at the Hook of Holland, where they were despatched onto night ferries to Harwich in Essex. A few travelled on to stay with relatives in America, others went to Paraguay, but the majority remained in Britain. Some went to live with Jewish relatives; others were offered homes with families of other religions, often Quakers. Upon arrival, many of them stayed in wooden chalets in Warner's Holiday Camp at Dovercourt near Harwich. "The whole camp was charged with anxiety and fear," wrote Hugh Barret, a volunteer student. "It was there I first heard the word 'angst' and appreciated what it meant." When the children heard a rumour about a pogrom in Vienna, they started wailing, and panic soon spread among the Viennese staff. Shouting above the noise that it was only a rumour did not help, and the refugees only calmed down when one of the older Jewish helpers started to sing a Hebrew song of courage and hope, that every child knew. Within minutes, the camp hall was filled with the sound of soothed voices, united in song.

Ingrid Jacoby, an eleven-year-old growing up in Vienna, was not a Guide, but her diary reveals the painful and challenging experiences endured by many Kindertransport girls. On 11 March 1938 she wrote: "My father is in a terrible state because Hitler has marched into Austria. It happened two days after my eleventh birthday and I couldn't have my party. I cried. Still no period. I pray for it, but Granny says it's wicked to think of God in the lavatory." Just over a year later, her aunt had secured visas for her and her older sister Lieselotte to go to England, and in a matter of days the girls were taken to a station in Vienna. "We were each given a cardboard number on a string, to hang round our necks. As I lay in Mummy's arms, saying goodbye to her for heaven knows how long, I still didn't realise what was happening. We joined a queue with hundreds of other children, and stood about for a very long time. Then suddenly we were on the train and waved to Mummy until the train took us out of sight. The other children were all talking and shouting and running about. We sang Viennese songs and some of the children cried. When we crossed the border into Holland and freedom, a great cheer went up. Some Dutch people handed each child a bar of Nestlé's milk chocolate through the train windows." The children were all sick on the overnight Channel crossing. They then took a train from Harwich to London, where Ingrid and her sister were put on another train on their own to Exeter.

Three weeks later, now living in Falmouth with a solicitor's family, Ingrid confessed to her diary in German: "I'm tortured by homesickness. If only I could be back in Vienna, going for walks with my parents. I wish Austria was a monarchy and that Hitler didn't exist. Everything is destroyed. But I must keep telling myself that everything will be all right in the end. Now I must explain to you the meaning of the word 'melancholy'. It is when one doesn't feel like doing anything any more and believes that nothing will ever make one happy again. It is wanting to cry all the time. It is looking forward to nothing and suffering from homesickness and memories of the past." A week later: "Homesickness is terrible. I used to pray and pray and long and long for my visa to come to England. My wish was granted. Now I pray and long to be back in Vienna. To think I may be here for months, years! I feel I shall die of misery. If Mummy had the slightest suspicion, how upset and unhappy she'd be. She must never, never know!"

Unfortunately, Ingrid's foster parents, Mr and Mrs Robins, never recognised this melancholy; they saw only a lazy girl who didn't tidy her room, and wrote to her parents to tell them they preferred her older sister. They told the girls how to stand, sit, throw a ball and breathe; and then went on holiday for three weeks without them. On their return they announced that if Ingrid's English didn't improve they would send her away. "It seems I can't do anything right," poor Ingrid wrote. On 2 September 1939 she wrote in her diary, "Hitler, I hate you even more than I hate Mrs Robins!"

On 18 April 1939, Ruth Wassermann, aged twelve, said goodbye to her family in Germany. Her father had been imprisoned on Kristallnacht, and her mother hoped to save their daughter's life. She joined several hundred other children at Berlin station, each carrying one small suitcase. After arriving in Britain, Ruth lived with a Jewish family, but their children did not treat her well, and in July the Committee moved her to a hostel for refugee girls in Hackney run by B'nai B'rith — "Children of the Covenant" — a Jewish welfare organisation set up in New York in 1843. The girls all went to Lauriston Road School in Hackney. Ruth shared a room with Gretel Heller from Berlin, also twelve years old, who had arrived in London in June 1939. Her father had also been imprisoned on Kristallnacht. Gretel had lived with a German Jewish family for a month, but then they had emigrated to the USA.

By the end of August 1939, over 10,000 children had come to Britain on the Kindertransport scheme. The last train left Germany a few days before war broke out, and from that moment the British government cancelled all outstanding visas, and borders were closed. The last children arrived in England on 2 September. Another train, containing 250 children, was about to leave Prague on 3 September, but the Germans did not let it leave the station. In future, for Kinder-transport children in Britain, communication with their parents was limited to twenty-five-word Red Cross postcards.

As soon as war seemed inevitable, the Committee for the Care of Children from Germany made plans to evacuate all the girls in the B'nai B'rith hostel out of London. They left on the morning of Saturday, 2 September with other children from Hackney. It took them all day to reach Swaffham in Norfolk, a journey that normally took about two hours. With two million children being evacuated from cities all over Britain and thousands of soldiers returning to their posts, the nation's transport system was in chaos.

Village halls all over the country became billeting stations where anyone with a spare room or a warm heart turned up to collect as many children as they could manage. Not many people wanted children who spoke the language of the enemy, but in rural Norfolk lived a landowner who understood their predicament and wanted to help. Sir Samuel Roberts owned the small feudal village of Cockley Cley, close to Thetford Forest, and employed everyone who lived there apart from the postmistress.

"It seemed to take forever, sitting on railway platforms," recalled Gretel Heller. "We finally arrived in Cockley Cley village hall, along with some English children also evacuated from Lauriston Road School, Hackney. We were lined up and the villagers of Cockley Cley picked the children they wanted to take home. They were looking for children who spoke English, and who could be useful." This left a dozen girls from the B'nai B'rith hostel who spoke little or no English, including best friends Ruth Wassermann and Gretel Heller.

The Robertses had been expecting twenty-five children, but by the time Lady Roberts arrived at the corrugated-iron village hall, she found that most of them had already been billeted around the village. She took nine of the Kindertransport girls, aged eight to thirteen, back to Cockley Cley Hall, a four-storey Victorian house where she and her husband lived with the ancient Dowager Lady Roberts and their son Peter, who worked on the farm. Working for them were a butler, two teenage footmen, a lady's maid, a cook, a scullery maid and a head housemaid with several maids under her.

Sir Samuel and Lady Roberts welcomed "the Jewish girls", as they called them. Escorting them was their rather bossy matron, Miss Kohn, who had been a teacher in Germany, Mrs Reissner the cook, and her twelve-year-old daughter Hanna. Both women had arrived in London in early 1939 and found refuge in the B'nai B'rith hostel. Lady Roberts understood that they would need a special kosher kitchen, and gave them the scullery. "We had our own kitchen downstairs," said Gretel, "and the top floor for our bedrooms — five to a room — and a sitting room. We were not permitted to go into the Roberts family part of the house."

"We kept kosher in the sense that we did not eat any meat," said Ruth, "except on the rare occasions when it was sent from London. By the time it arrived in unrefrigerated trains, it was not the freshest, but 'waste not want not' was the motto." The girls ate mainly turnips, potatoes, cabbages and greens grown in the

Hall garden. In the summer, Lady Roberts treated them to baskets of soft fruit. "Lady Roberts was very elegant looking," said Gretel, "very stately, tall, always neat and properly dressed. She came into our sitting room about once a week and would pat a girl on the head." All the girls were homesick, but during the day they never showed it: they were expected to be grateful. At night their bedrooms were filled with the sound of muffled sobs as they cried into their pillows.

Not all the Kindertransport girls lived in the Hall. Mr and Mrs Howard, the cowman and the dairymaid of the Cockley Cley estate farm, picked twelve-year-old Cilly-Jutta Horwitz from Hamburg and Lotte Levy from Cologne. In the Howards' cottage, water came from a well in the garden, the floors were made of stone and there was no electricity. Cilly-Jutta, later known as Celia, and Lotte were both used to living in middle-class urban homes. Celia had been learning English at grammar school in Hamburg for two years, and had arrived on the first Kindertransport train in December 1938, so her English was already good, but even so, things were very difficult. "Living with the Howards in a small village in Norfolk was a real culture shock," she remembered. "Everything was a blur. You no sooner seemed to have settled somewhere than you were off again. My first homes in Britain were two holiday camps in the south-east. After three cold months I was taken in by a Jewish family in Hackney and then by a hostel for young refugees."

Lotte was braver than Celia, and told the cook, Mrs Reisner, that she was unhappy at the Howards'. The girls at the Hall were asked if any of them would swap places. "I was very stupid," said Gretel. "I said yes." Gretel, brought up in Berlin, found life with the Howards no easier than Lotte had: "There were paraffin lamps and we went to bed with a candle. Mrs Howard treated me and Celia like servants. There was no heating and I had perpetual colds living there. I soon regretted it, especially when winter came and it was so cold." The winter of 1939–40 was the coldest for decades: even the River Thames froze for the first time in over fifty years. "Mrs Howard cooked a delicious dumpling stew on our first night; she was a good plain cook," remembered Celia. "But after that she was quite mean with the bread and margarine. I liked the countryside, but not the outside toilets." Exiled from Germany for being Jewish, she was now taunted by some of the other refugee girls for being only half-Jewish — her mother had converted to Judaism before marrying her father. "That counted as Jewish to Hitler," she said. "When my parents divorced, my father insisted that my mother renounced being a Jew to save herself. In addition, standing up in class in England was agony when I had to say my name, 'Cilly-Jutta'. The children always laughed." After she was married she changed her first name to Celia. Mr and Mrs Howard had two teenage sons — the oldest was Nigel, aged fifteen, who looked after the pigs and had a slight squint; his younger brother Geoffrey, who was fourteen, sometimes took Celia around the village on the horse-drawn milk cart, doling out fresh milk into housewives' jugs. "I had a bit of a crush on Geoffrey," said Celia, "so that was always fun."

Cockley Cley village school had closed down a few years earlier due to a shortage of children. The few local children went to school in Swaffham, three miles away, and did not mix much with the evacuees. The village school was reopened for the British children from Hackney and the eighteen Kindertransport girls. Two teachers were drafted in from London — Miss Gadsby and Miss Payne — one for the five-to-eight-year-olds, the other for nine-to-fourteen-year-olds. "They had to cope with a wide range of children," said Gretel, "including some very naughty London evacuee boys. One was beaten with a cane often."

The teachers had to deal with both homesick London evacuees and girls who spoke little or no English and had even more reason to be homesick. "Miss Payne was a very good English teacher, especially for poetry," said Celia. Ruth described how the teachers "taught us songs and poetry by rote. Arithmetic was easier since they could use the blackboard. They also taught us drawing." Ruth enjoyed art: her grandfather had been a folk poet, and encouraged her to embellish his poetry with drawings while listening to music. The children learned English quickly: "The teachers took an interest in us, and found creative ways of teaching. We wrote essays, read English books and got a good appreciation of English songs, poetry and literature."

Miss Gadsby had been a Guide, and after a couple of months she suggested starting a Guide company in Cockley Cley. "Those of us from Germany had never heard of such a thing," said Gretel Heller. "Miss Gadsby explained to us that Guides were about doing daily Good Deeds, and taking badges. We thought this all sounded like a good idea. But we couldn't afford a full uniform." Each girl was issued with a hat, a maroon scarf and a Guide belt, donated by Lady Roberts. "The best part was learning Morse code and being able to signal secret messages to each other. We did a lot of stalking in the woods. We would have used these skills if the Germans had invaded."

The 1st Cockley Cley Guide company had two patrols — the Sky Larks and the Swallows. Ruth was Patrol Leader of the Larks, with Gretel as her Second; Celia was in the Swallows. Miss Gadsby acknowledged that the Cockley Cley Guides were not British by amending part of their Guide promise from "To do my duty to God and the King" to "To do my duty to God and the country in which I am a guest." "We enjoyed doing the Guide salute," said Gretel. "It helped us to connect to Britain, and to what was going on elsewhere in the country."

Miss Gadsby was not alone: running companies near her in Norfolk were other Guide Captains such as Miss Twiddy, Miss Jolly, Miss Cocks, Miss Flowerday, Miss Sparrow and Miss Capon. One day the President of the Guides, the Princess Royal, came to Cockley Cley on her way to Sandringham. The Guides polished their badges and belts to perfection. "We knew she was the sister of King George," said Gretel. "We all lined up and curtsied to her."

Lady Roberts had given the Guides a wind-up gramophone and a few records. Their favourite was Beethoven's Fifth Symphony. "Dot-dot-dot-dash, the Morse code V for Victory opening, became a code of hope for victory throughout England," Ruth said. "We played it constantly; it gave us courage as well as an appreciation of classical music, which most of us had been accustomed to at home."

The teachers started a Victory Garden at the school, where the Guides grew vegetables for themselves and to sell to the villagers. "I got terrible blisters," said Celia, "but it was a joy growing things like carrots." Ruth, Celia and Gretel made up a song, in English, which they sang while working in the garden:

> For days work and weeks work,
> As we go on and on,
> Digging many trenches
> Which is not much fun.
>
> Teacher saw as lazy
> She thought we never knew.
> Oh teachers who like gardening.
> You can do ours too.

"We knew that the teachers were watching us and yet, apparently, we were lazy and did not care," said Gretel. "We also made up a lot of secret sentences, in German, that concerned our matron." Matron was not very popular, especially as she told the other girls not to talk to Celia because she was "not really Jewish".

"The Guides taught us self-discipline, responsibility, provided adventure, a good respect for self-reliance, and to be helpful to others," said Ruth. "It helped us to cope. We also learned path-finding, knotting and semaphore with flags. The Guide principles played a big role in our formative years, especially since we had no parents to guide us." "I was very proud of being a Guide," said Celia. Guide meetings were among the few times when she was happy, and she was delighted to be photographed giving her three-fingered promise salute in her uniform.

Lady Roberts' lady's maid was Ellen Richardson. She looked after her mistress's clothes, and due to her well-corseted body she bent down with an absolutely straight back. She insisted that the Kinder-transport Guides did their housework properly, but also invited them into her parlour for tea and to listen to her wireless. "That was the only way we could hear the news," said Ruth. "When we needed advice, which we were afraid to ask matron, we went to Miss Richardson. She never divulged our secrets. Whenever she needed to correct us, she came to us directly; we were fond of her and trusted her." She also gave them scraps of wool and cloth with which they could make presents. "She showed us how to make small mending bags with a crocheted thimble-cover attached, a most useless but unique gift."

None of the Kinder Guides had lived in the country before, but they came to appreciate the beauty of Norfolk. "Near the village were the Spring Woods," remembered Ruth, "with their early splendour of blooms. The Hall had a beautiful formal garden, leading to a lake with swans, where I learnt Wordsworth's 'I wandered lonely as a cloud . . .'"

With the fall of France in May 1940, the British public, encouraged by newspapers and Churchill, began to panic about "fifth columnists" — saboteurs and spies in their midst. Guides all over the country were on full alert, watching for flashing torches that could be German spies sending Morse messages to each other: the BBC warned Germany that any parachutists not wearing uniform would be shot on sight, rather than taken as prisoners of war.

As Britain prepared for invasion, the Prime Minister issued a leaflet which declared: "STAND FIRM. Do not run away, or stop work. Do the shopping, send the children to school, do not evacuate to other areas . . . With a bit of common sense you can tell whether a soldier is really British or only pretending to be so. If in doubt, ask a policeman. Disable or hide your bicycle, destroy your maps."

The fear was so great that 27,000 German and Austrian refugees were interned on the Isle of Man, many of them Jews who had only recently fled from their homes. "We were not aware that we were enemy aliens," said Gretel, "until the British government started to intern the men, and announced that no 'enemy alien' women over the age of sixteen years could live anywhere near the south or east coast. Miss Kohn and Mrs Reissner had to go back to London." Mrs Reissner's daughter Hanna remained at Cockley Cley, and took over the cooking.

All refugees were subjected to tribunals at which they had to prove their allegiance to Britain. The Germans had overrun Belgium and Holland with ease, and the girls remembered that when they had left Germany the Nazi guards had told them, "You can go now, but we'll get you in the end." When Holland was invaded, Germans who had lived there for years rose up to support the Nazis. Would the same thing happen in Britain?

For their own protection, the girls at the Hall were told to destroy all letters from their parents written in German. "For me it felt like cutting out a part of my life," said Ruth. "I always carried these letters with me in my gas mask case. Once war started we seldom got word from our parents. We could receive messages of twenty-five words via the Swiss Red Cross. These came seldom and usually were very carefully worded because of the German censor. Even before the war, all letters were opened by the Nazis."

Celia had to do any household chores that her hosts required. Only girls who had already left school had the protection of the Home Office ruling which stated that refugee girls under eighteen could only work as domestic staff "where there are trained domestic servants, so that they can receive proper training". This was intended to prevent exploitation by hosts who could not afford to pay domestic staff. But it did not apply to refugees who were still at school. Celia had some respite from the Howards' cottage when she caught ringworm from the cows. "It was very contagious, and Peter Roberts' young wife, Judith, took me into the Dower House where she lived in the village. She was very kind to me, something I had not felt since I left home." When Judith Roberts' first daughter, Jane, was born in October 1940, the Kinder Guides presented her with crocheted clothes-hangers. "Getting to see the new-born baby was a great event for us," said Ruth. This tiny new life brought them some hope for the future.

With so many farm workers serving in the forces, the Guides at Cockley Cley weeded sugar-beet fields to help with the war effort. They were paid 1½ pence an hour — worth about 25p in today's money. Even though nearly all the land in Britain was by now under the plough, Cockley Cley still had woods and thick hedges. "There were gorgeous old trees," remembered Ruth. "We could climb to a comfortable spot in the low branches of the beech trees where we could read. Privacy was a very precious commodity for us who lived dormitory style." The Guides received sixpence a week pocket money, which they could spend in the village post office. "I splurged my chocolate ration on a Milky Way. I would take a bite a day to make it last longer." Ruth saved up enough of her sugar-beet earnings to buy wool to knit herself a jersey, which lasted the entire war. She was also working hard at her Guide badges. By the summer of 1941 she had learned the names of thirty-two English wild flowers she had spotted in the Norfolk meadows. They included Viper's Bugloss, hare's foot clover and the ubiquitous stinging nettle. She also learned to identify wild fruit that could be eaten, including the gooseberries and beech nuts that grew along the road to the Hall.

After Hitler's Deputy Führer Rudolf Hess parachuted into Scotland in May 1941, the fear of invasion grew amongst the girls. "The Germans had been so successful at invading France, Poland and the Netherlands. Why would the English Channel stop them?" said Gretel. "We knew we would have been the first to be imprisoned if the Germans came." "It affected us refugees especially," explained Ruth. "We Jewish, we feared that we would be the first victims and be caught. We started preparing ourselves to cope, defend ourselves and fight."

The Swallow patrol decided that they must Be Prepared, so they worked out a plan: as soon as they heard that the invasion of Britain had started, the younger Guides would climb trees. If they saw the enemy approaching they would signal in Morse with their torches to the older Guides, including Ruth, waiting nearby. The older Guides would then lure the enemy soldiers into the stinging-nettle fields by running ahead of them. "When we had them in the field we would hit them in the face with the stinging nettles," said Ruth, "and then cut them with our Girl Guide penknives, which had blades about one inch long. In order to prepare for this grand plan we needed to make ourselves immune to the nettles' sting. We began to run though the fields with our bare legs, and fought each other with the nettles. When we all came home with swollen legs, arms and faces, matron was very angry with us. We never revealed to her that all we really wanted to do was to protect England and ourselves."

One day while Gretel and Ruth were hoeing a field they saw something that terrified them. "A white half-round shape appeared on the horizon," said Ruth. She and Gretel were sure it was a parachute, and that they would have to put their plan into action. "A few minutes later a man clad in khaki, with a gun slung over his shoulder, came by on a bicycle." The girls were certain that the invasion had begun. Panicked, they ran to the nearest house, which happened to be where Sir Samuel's son Peter and his wife Judith lived. The door was answered by the butler, Arthur, a handsome young man, small, thin and dark-haired. "We told him what we had seen, and immediately he hurried with us back to the field with his Charlie-Chaplin-like stride. We arrived breathlessly at the field, to discover that our parachute had risen to become a bright, full moon. We were embarrassed. The man on the bicycle was a rabbit hunter coming home from a hunt. How could we have known?"

"To begin with, the English evacuees stood apart, but once our English improved, we all mixed together," said Gretel. "But we foreign evacuees were quite a tight bunch. All of us had left our parents behind, so we stayed close together." The older girls — aged twelve or thirteen — set standards and tried to guide the younger ones. "We told the younger ones how to behave: we told them off if their behaviour was wrong. For example, all our possessions were kept in our suitcases under our beds. One by one we noticed that our underwear was going missing. One girl was very poor and had few clothes. When we asked her to open her suitcase, she had taken our knickers. We knew that her father had been deported from Germany to Poland, so we didn't punish her, we just took the underwear back."

"Whining was not tolerated," said Ruth. "We were all in the same boat and knew how the others felt. Our youth was over, and we had to look out for each other, like a family."

In May 1941 Ruth led a discussion at a Guide meeting on "How do you think we the Guides can help win the war?" She then taught the Sky Lark patrol the art of square-lashing two poles together with string, part of her Second-Class Test, which she completed later that year. The Guides put on entertainments in the Village Hall, including a ballet choreographed by Ruth. "Whenever I see a simplistically poorly performed ballet I think they must have seen mine."

Even though they wore their Guide uniform and were learning English fast, the Kindertransport girls were constantly reminded that they were foreigners in a remote part of Britain. Some of the adult villagers made it very clear that they were not sure about these foreign children. When Miss Payne asked the senior class to sing the hymn "Glorious things of thee are spoken", the girls refused. It wasn't because they were Jews, but because the hymn shared the tune with the German national anthem. Only when the teacher threatened them with punishment did they comply. When a passerby heard them singing, he complained: "First the British children sing God Save the King, and then the Germans sing their national anthem. Are they spies?" One of the London evacuee children called the girls "Nazis", and others followed his taunting. "We just ignored them," said Celia, "but it hurt." The path the girls took to school ran through a wood in which a Scottish army battalion was camping. When the soldiers heard them speak in a mixture of broken English and German, Ruth felt even more alien when she heard one say, "Who are these children?" His friend replied, "Oh, they're prisoners of war."

As the girls grew, they handed their clothes on to the younger ones. Harry Watts, a member of B'nai B'rith in London, brought them gym-dresses "which seemed to grow with us". One memorable day, when all their shoes were worn out, he brought them each a pair of Wellington boots.

After 1941 any "enemy aliens" over sixteen years of age with no passports could not live in Norfolk, which was considered too close to Germany for comfort. In August of that year, when Ruth, Gretel and Celia were fifteen, the Committee decided that it was time they left school and returned to London to begin work. The trio became such close friends that they were known as "the Clover Leaf" — also the symbol of the Girl Guides. The Clover Leaf girls shared a room in a North London hostel. "Ruth had an older sister in London and she told us useful things like the facts of life," said Gretel. They volunteered as Air-Raid Wardens, and their friends were fellow refugees, musicians, artists and writers. Celia started work as a junior clerk in Marshall and Snelgrove's department store in Oxford Street, but was soon trained to use a capstan lathe and found herself in an ammunitions factory. "I made the screws for the end of bombs," she said. "I had nightmares, because although I wanted Britain to win the war, I knew that any one of those bombs could have killed my parents. I wanted Germany to be taken off the map but not with my parents in it. I missed them terribly. I used to have this recurring dream where I was on one side of the road and they were on the other and this Doodlebug was going down the road on legs."

Celia last heard of her father in 1941, when he was deported to the Minsk ghetto as slave labour — but he never returned. Her mother kept in touch with Red Cross letters. One day in 1945, as Celia was getting off a London bus, she met and instantly fell in love with Ken Lee, a British soldier on leave from serving in Germany. Ken later found her mother in Hamburg, but it was not until 1949, when they were married with a daughter, that Celia visited her for the first time in eleven years. She realised then how much living in Britain had changed her. "I was embarrassed by the big emotional show when I arrived," she recalls. "I'd become pretty English by then. That sort of thing wasn't done." Although she continued to visit her mother, she never wanted to stay in Germany. "I felt horrible the first time I went back. I looked at everyone and wondered what the hell they had been doing during the war." Celia Lee now says emphatically, with a slight accent from her childhood, that her nationality is definitely British.

After the war, Ruth Wassermann settled and married in America, where she studied art in Chicago and worked with problem children. In late 1941, just before Pearl Harbor, Gretel Heller received word that her parents had managed to emigrate to the United States. She never saw her father again — he died two years later — but she met up with her brother and mother in the USA in 1946, and married a Kindertransport man originally from Austria.

On the night of 27 April 1942 the Luftwaffe bombed Norwich, destroying thousands of buildings and killing hundreds of people. Even Cockley Cley, thirty miles away, was not spared when an incendiary bomb dropped on the Hall roof. The remaining refugee girls were woken up and shepherded to the back staircase while the local Air-Raid Warden put it out.

By the end of 1942 only the oldest servants were left at Cockley Cley Hall; the Guides had all gone. Sir Samuel closed up his home and moved into a smaller house in the village. He wrote, "We are beaten. The army is all around us every day. We have hardly any servants left, and next winter it will be impossible to get fuel to heat this very large house . . . the little German Jewish girls have gone." The Hall became the headquarters of the 22nd Armoured Brigade in preparation for D-Day.

Another German refugee who benefited from joining the Guides was Iris Calmann. She had arrived in London from Hamburg with her two older sisters and her parents in 1937, when she was nine years old. Iris and her sisters attended South Hampstead High School for Girls, and were soon fluent in English.

On 1 September 1939, Berkhamsted High School for Girls in Hertfordshire was informed that the entire staff and 256 girls of South Hampstead High were on their way from London. They arrived two days later in a fleet of buses, having been incorrectly sent to Northampton railway station, forty-five miles north of Berkhamsted. The two schools managed to maintain separate identities, coming together only for concerts and sports. "They had lessons in the mornings and we used the classrooms in the afternoons," remembered Iris. "Our teachers kept us busy after school, collecting rose-hips and foxgloves for medicines." The three Calmann sisters were initially billeted together, but after their foster father died, Iris was sent on her own to an evacuation hostel. "The first thing they did was strip me and scrub me all over, searching for lice. Then they put me in a hospital gown, with tapes down the back, so humiliating." She was then sent to another foster home. "As an evacuee I was so unhappy and homesick. At home I had no religious upbringing, but because we were known as Jews, suddenly we had to practise Judaism. It was very strange, being told that we could not read the back of the Bible."

After June 1940, when her father was interned on the Isle of Man, life became much worse for Iris. "No one wanted the daughter of an internee, an enemy alien who was Jewish. I spoke fluent English with no accent, which made it worse as the foster families didn't realise where I came from." When they learned the truth, she would be moved to another foster home, with no explanation. "Imagine the pain of being both a refugee and then an evacuee. And then nobody wants you because you are German *and* Jewish."

Help came for Iris when a Guide company was started in the school.

Being a Girl Guide was the one place where I could forget about it all. It was a blessed relief for one afternoon a week, an escape from being an unhappy refugee.

I loved stalking among the gorse on Berkhamsted Common. I'd never been camping before and I enjoyed being in the countryside. We only went as far as the common for camping, but it was a little bit of freedom. Guides was the one consolation for being evacuated. At school there was no encouragement — it was all very negative. We marched to school in a long crocodile, and marched back to our foster homes as a crocodile. It was suffocating, so different from our own loving home life with liberal, educated parents. We were constantly reminded that we were not at home, and that our home country was at war with Britain.

At Guides, we were encouraged to learn new things. I became quite ambitious about badges, and ended up with an arm full of them! Tying knots was important — not only because knots are always useful but also the picture of knots was beautiful, and it was something that had to be done right, and only you could do it.

Iris found refuge even in the Guide uniform. "They were inspected every week and we took a pride in being smart. Making sure that your badge was polished, *even on the back*, gave one a feeling of achievement. A polished badge was only a small thing, but it was something, in a chaotic and frightening world." Through being a Patrol Leader, Iris learned responsibility for her future work.

When her father was released from internment, Iris joined her parents in a village outside Oxford. From 1943 she had to cycle six miles each way to and from school, and so had no more time for Guides. But in her last year at school she helped with Cubs and Brownies for the children of aeroplane-factory workers in Cowley, Oxford. When she left school she trained as a social worker in London. "I used the skills I had learnt as a Guide — how to take children camping, making fires, playing games."

Over 10,000 children — probably 10 per cent of all Jewish children living in Germany and Austria at the time — were saved from the gas chambers by the Kindertransport, despite the fact that the scheme only ran from December 1938 to September 1939. The impact of forced emigration without their parents differed from child to child; many of them never overcame the shock and disorientation from the separation. Those who had some form of family —

98

whether a foster family, a caring hostel or the Guide movement — fared the best. Guides became a family to many of the girls, providing them with structure in the form of patrols, achievements in the form of proficiency badges, and friendships that often lasted their whole lives. World War II is remembered for physical horrors such as the Blitz, food rationing, concentration camps and death. But there was also a huge, invisible cloud hanging over Britain and Europe, of "attachment disorder", the problems that children often carry into adulthood from instability and lack of parental love, that would be described by the child psychiatrist John Bowlby in the 1950s.

The few Kindertransport children who were reunited with their parents after the war found they had lost siblings, grandparents, aunts, uncles or cousins. Amongst the majority who never saw their parents again, there were those who felt rage towards their mothers and fathers for abandoning them, although this had saved their lives. "Kinder-terror, Kindertransports, Kindertrauma," wrote Fred Barschak, forty-five years after coming to England on the Kindertransport. "A chain of events linking these stages in the odyssey of the children of 1938–9. Kristallnacht, the night of broken glass and broken lives. The trauma of re-establishing some infrastructure of normality in a strange land, with new families, however sympathetic and kind, with the children enjoying a dubious status, neither as temporary guests nor adopted, a sort of twilight world of not knowing where she belonged." Joining the Guides helped give girls a focus and a sense of belonging, and offered them a creative way of helping with the war effort. "Human beings, and especially children, have an infinite capacity to adapt to their surroundings," wrote Ingrid Jacoby. "And so the misery and homesickness were gradually overlaid by an enjoyment of new friends, and ultimately, even by a superficial feeling of belonging." The Guide movement made this possible.

CHAPTER
FIVE

Golondrinas

The German army invaded Holland in tanks on 10 May 1940. "We saw an aeroplane swooping over Amsterdam that Friday morning," remembered Josephine Klein, then aged thirteen. "Everybody knew this was deadly serious. Rotterdam had already been flattened by German bombs."

Josephine's father, Simon Klein, had already been a refugee once. He was born in the Austro-Hungarian Empire, and at fourteen his parents sent him away to escape conscription. He stayed with relations in Leipzig until he was seventeen, when they told him to "Go to Holland, it is the land of the free." When he first arrived there in the early 1920s he worked in a Jewish psychiatric hospital not far from the border with Germany, later moving to Amsterdam, where he worked as a general office boy in a small firm that made tailors' accessories. "There he met and married my mother, whose brother ran the firm. They were good, honest bourgeois people."

Soon after their first son, Eli, was born, the Kleins moved to Germany, where Simon became a sales representative for "Interlock" woollen underwear.

Josephine was born in 1926. "My parents began to see things going wrong for Jews in Germany, even in 1930." So the Kleins returned to Holland. "In Holland nobody took any notice what religion you were. It was no big thing. Holland has no underclass — you were either in trade or farming. Whether you were Jewish or gentile didn't make any difference. It wasn't a matter of interest."

Josephine joined a Girl Guide company in Amsterdam. "We were totally the same as British Guides. We wore the same uniforms, had the same rituals, and the same patrol system. When we went camping, in heath-covered parkland, we had to track coloured embroidery threads. I got several badges but was no good at knots. Throughout the 1930s cousins kept coming from Germany to Holland. They would stay with us and tell us the horrors of what was happening to Jews in Germany, and then go on to America. We saw people wandering around Amsterdam behaving strangely, making funny noises or with tics. My parents told me they had escaped from concentration camps. My mother, Maria, was an exceptionally sensible woman, she knew what would happen if we stayed."

After the invasion of Holland, most people who wanted to leave went south through Belgium to France. But when Germany invaded France too, there were terrible stories of roads packed with refugees. Catherine Christian described the scene in France: "Long roads, poplar trees shivering in the breeze, white dust rising from the feet of marching soldiers going up to the front line. Guns, tanks, mechanised columns. All going northward. And southward, down the same roads, thousands and thousands of poor people, old women, mothers with children, cripples being pushed in bath chairs, invalids on stretchers — the refugees!"

News of the fleeing populace travelled through France. There were Guiders who remembered the last time this had happened only twenty-five years before, in the "War to End all Wars". They would never forget the wave of panic then, as people fled from their homes, and their misery as they wandered aimlessly around the country. The French Guides and Rangers were soon mobilised. In their khaki and blue uniforms the Catholic Guides de France and the non-denominational Éclaireuses worked shoulder-to-shoulder at canteens and trestle tables set up beside the roads. In a world of chaos and cruelty, it made all the difference to have blistered feet and grazes cared for at first-aid posts. Hot drinks and the Guides' smiles gave families the strength to continue. The Guides had been trained to keep their heads, and however terrible the despair around them, they served the refugees from barrows or borrowed tents. One Guide found a blackboard and wrote on it: "We have found George Ducleaux, aged three. He is here if his family want him. Grandmother Camillion is at the first-aid post. Will her daughters join her there? Half the family of Petion from St Marie-le-Bec have gone on by train to Paris, if the other half comes through, please call at the Guide canteen for a message . . ." The idea soon caught on, and all along the road at canteens or first-aid posts, notices were put up to help reunite families separated by the confusion.

A newsreel shown in cinemas all over London depicted a long line of terrified people plodding through France. Among the driven herd is a girl of about fifteen, barefoot in a ragged dress, carrying a bundle for an old woman beside her. Behind them the crowd surges, and a lame child is knocked over. He lies screaming while adults run past. They have heard the drone of bombers approaching overhead. The girl looks back, hesitates for a moment, and returns to pick up the child. As she walks out of the picture, one arm around the child, the other dragging the bundle, her face shows her tiredness and misery. Her ragged dress reveals, by the badge that holds it together, that she is a Girl Guide. What happened to her, nobody will ever know. But Guides who saw the film knew that she was a symbol of Guides not only in France, but all over the world.

Similar stories came from Holland, Belgium and Luxembourg. "Like a great thunderstorm, spreading out to darken the whole sky, the German armies swept over Europe," wrote Miss Christian. "The same tale of pitiless bombing, machine gunning, firing from passing tanks, bombardment from the big guns. There was no safety for civilians, whether women or children or tiny babies. The Germans believed terror might shorten the war. They took terror with them on a scale no one had ever pictured before."

The Klein family in Amsterdam had heard the stories and were determined not to get caught by the

Nazis. Maria Klein was a hardworking housewife, who supplemented her husband's meagre earnings by letting out two rooms of their second-floor apartment to lodgers. Josephine, their only daughter, was small and immature for her thirteen years. On the night of 14 May 1940 she had gone to bed as usual in the attic, when her parents heard that the Germans were only a few miles away. Maria woke Josephine and told her to hurry: there was no time to do anything but dress and grab a few clothes. She had already phoned her brother and two brothers-in-law to ask if they wanted to join them. A taxi was ordered. "Two of the uncles could not imagine leaving so quickly," remembered Josephine. "They did not realise the risk — only one of them survived the war." Uncle Ralph arrived, and the family made their way through the dark streets of Amsterdam and twenty miles west to the fishing town of Ijmuiden.

"People were milling about, having hopes that there might be ships to take them out of reach of the advancing German army." But there were no ships. "Father realised this and found a man who owned a large rowing boat. They struck a bargain and shared the cost of the boat with some other people."

It was after midnight when the Klein family climbed quickly on board, followed by six other adults, including an old man. Josephine and her older brother Eli were the only children. The boat was about fifteen foot long, and there was just enough room for everyone to sit down. The rumour in Ijmuiden harbour was that British ships were just over the horizon, waiting to pick up Dutch refugees. Mr Klein's plan was to row out to sea, where they would be picked up. But there were no ships over the horizon either.

"None of us knew anything about boats or sailing," said Josephine. There was just enough room for her to lie down, but not the adults. The weather turned rough. Day came, and night again, and another day, with a rising wind at night and big waves that crashed against the boat. There was no food and very little water on board — they had only expected to be at sea for a few hours. They found some water in a tank under a seat, but there was no pump or even a pipe to get it out of the small hole. One woman had a thimble, another had some thread. They attached the thimble to the thread, and scooped up one thimbleful of water at a time, which was poured into a tobacco tin. "The water tasted brackish, but at least it wasn't salt water," remembered Josephine. "The tobacco tin was passed round for each person to sip from."

On the third morning Josephine cried a little, but with another tobacco tin she helped to bail out water that had spilled into the boat. "When we needed to complete our ablutions, someone held a coat up at one end of the boat and we took it in turns to go behind it. The next day we sighted land. Wonderful — we had rowed the hundred miles to the east coast of England! But no — terribly disappointed, we realised we had drifted down the coast of Holland. We were approaching a port and we knew that by now it must be occupied by the Germans." They were right: the Germans had arrived at The Hague on 15 May, the day after the Kleins left Amsterdam.

In London on 13 May, the House of Commons had heard Winston Churchill make his first speech as leader of the coalition government: "I have nothing to offer but blood, toil, tears and sweat. We have before us an ordeal of the most grievous kind. We have before us many, many long months of struggle and of suffering. You ask, what is our aim? I can answer in one word: Victory. Victory at all costs — Victory in spite of all terror — Victory, however long and hard the road may be, for without victory there is no survival."

As the House debated the state of the war, Benjamin Smith, Labour MP for Rotherhithe, said, "When I was at sea we had an old story of a parson who went to the skipper of a ship which was foundering and asked, 'What shall I do to be saved?' The skipper said, 'Jump into the long-boat and pull like blazes.' It seems to me that we have jumped into the long-boat and, having jumped into the long-boat, I want to see the Government 'pull like blazes,' for the successful prosecution of the war." In the North Sea, Josephine and her family were pulling like blazes in their longboat. Starving and parched with thirst, the refugees turned towards the open sea once again.

"We had to keep on bailing out the sea water. When it got dark, my brother and I worked out where north was because of the Great Bear. I'd learned some of the stars at Guides. For days nothing much happened and there were pitch-dark nights. Twice we saw aeroplanes. From one open plane, the pilot pointed with his arm which way we should go. The weather was wonderful for May. I can only remember one orange which we shared. There may have been some rusks already on the boat. When the bottom of the boat got damp with sea water, we couldn't lie down." None of the refugees had the energy to row, as they drifted in the English Channel. "It was as if we were all sitting on a bus. The adults were polite to each other, but didn't chat or make friends. The old man sometimes sang psalms. Everyone was thirsty."

More than a week after they left Holland, a British destroyer sighted the small boat. By then Josephine was semi-conscious. Having been sitting in sea water for so long, the refugees' feet were so swollen they could not walk. The British sailors carried them on board the destroyer, where they were taken care of. "The destroyer took us to Dover, but there was a fear that Dover would be shelled by Germans, so we were evacuated to Maidstone. The hospitals in Kent were all on stand-by for the evacuation from Dunkirk. They were fully equipped but with nothing to do."

Josephine and her family were soon recovering in Maidstone Hospital. "Our feet had become infected, and were very painful." They had all succumbed to "trench foot", a bacterial infection caused by prolonged immersion in water, which can lead to gangrene and even amputation. "Everybody was tremendously kind. My feet hurt and a nurse put cream on them, but it didn't help. I cried a lot because no one could understand me. I didn't have the language. In some ways I was fortunate: my mother was with me and my brother and father were not far away in the men's ward." Josephine never saw the other passengers again. "I don't know where they went, they just dispersed."

A few days passed. Josephine's mother began to worry about her daughter not talking and looking so miserable. Then one afternoon some girls of her age came to visit the ward. They were dressed in blue uniforms and had made up bags for the refugee patients, each one containing a comb, scissors, sewing materials, coloured crayons, safety pins and soap. Maria Klein was very happy to receive such sensible presents, but still Josephine lay very quietly. Eventually she whispered "Thank you" to the Guides who stood round her bed. Her spirits were coming back. As they turned away, her face lit up, she sat up and gave them a Guide salute. "What a reunion that was, between sisters who had never met!" wrote Catherine Christian, who met her later. "Josephine had lost her home and everything she owned, even her Guide badge, but she was never to lack for friends in her new country. Soon she had a uniform, and a place in an English Guide company, and was beginning her new life as if it was a great adventure."

When Maidstone Hospital was needed for the evacuation from Dunkirk, the Klein family was sent to a refugee hostel in London. "It seemed very luxurious, an old children's hospital in Cheyne Walk, Chelsea," said Josephine. Next door was Crosby Hall, the University Women's Club which was now used as a store for shoes and clothes for Blitzed families.

My feet were still sore and they found me some slippers. The people in the hostel were poorer than we were used to, mainly Belgian fishermen. This was a great worry for my parents because we had to be protected from their rough language. I went to Fulham Central School for Girls, and soon my English was quite good. The hostel was run by incredibly English institutions — rich ladies living in Sloane Square, such as Lady Lubbock, the Earl of Derbyshire's daughter, and well-to-do American ladies, including Mrs Martineau, who everyone believed was the sister of Mrs Roosevelt. She worried that the Germans would invade very soon. Everybody fell over themselves to be good to us. We had to be rescued from London before the Germans came to England. We needed three different passports — Father could never get one, my mother and brother were Dutch, and I needed a German one.

In the autumn of 1940, Josephine's mother decided that they should live near Liverpool to be ready for a boat to the United States. Her father chose to stay in London. "We came out of Chester railway station, and landed up with the Women's Voluntary Service, by the cathedral," said Josephine. "The lady who ran the WVS was a notable in the town." Her retired cook and butler had returned to work for her for the duration of the war, so she arranged for the Klein family to move into their council house just outside Chester. "The day after we arrived, we found some beetroots and cabbages outside our back door. They had been thrown over the fence by our neighbour. Their daughter was called Josephine too!" Josephine soon joined the local Guides. "The Guider, Miss Blakeney, showed up and I enrolled. They found me a new uniform. It was very like the Guides I was used to. By now there were no language problems. We met on Thursday evenings and I was in the Cornflower patrol. We had to go school, so the WVS rang up the Queen's School in Chester and told them, 'You must take these refugee children.' They equipped us with secondhand uniforms and a Bible each." Then the ships that had been carrying refugees and evacuees to North America stopped because of German U-boat attacks. "So then we knew we would never get to the USA."

Soon after the Kleins moved to Chester, a doctor's wife from a small village in Derbyshire wrote to Guide HQ. She had a thirteen-year-old daughter, and asked if there were any refugee Guides of her age who would like a holiday. "Guide headquarters sent her my name," said Josephine, "and off I went to Derbyshire, to stay with them. I spent two happy weeks there and fell in love with their dachshund. I went every summer for several years."

One of the refugees who arrived in London in May 1940, after the fall of France, Belgium and the Netherlands, was Thérèse, aged thirteen, the eldest daughter of a big family from a small Belgian town. She had struggled to save up for the blue uniform, wide hat and blue cloak of a Belgian Guide. On the night she and her family escaped from the advancing Germans, Thérèse ran upstairs and grabbed her precious uniform. "This they shall not have!" she said to herself, changing into it at lightning speed.

A week later she was still wearing it as the family, tired out but at last safe, walked into Wembley Stadium, where many refugees were taken on their arrival in the capital. She shepherded her tribe of little brothers in their black pinafores, her three great-uncles and her mother leaning on her arm. There in the stadium were British Guides to provide tea, food and a warm greeting, while other Guides helped to sort out accommodation. Thérèse knew that she had found some friends, and with other Guides from all over Europe she was soon incorporated into the Girl Guide Association. Some nationalities formed their own companies — Polish, Belgian and French.

International Commissioner Rose Kerr wrote in *The Guide* in 1941:

Gone are the days when I always had in prospect some delightful visit to Guides in distant countries; or arranging a stay in this country for our friends from other lands. And yet — there is something real and enduring in the world-wide friendship which we succeeded in establishing through the Guide movement.

For many, Guiding was the central pivot of their lives. It was linked up in Poland and Czechoslovakia with the newly found freedom of their people. In these dark and despairing days, Guiding is helping them to live. From Belgium, from France and from the Netherlands, messages have reached us to say "We are carrying on . . ."

There are two concrete and practical pieces of service which Guides can do. The first of these is to do all they can — and *more* than they can — for the strangers within their gates. The British Guides have a heaven-sent opportunity of showing forth the true meaning of the 4th Guide law ["A Guide is a friend to all, and a sister to every other Guide"]. Thousands of people who have lost their homes have come to this country. Among these — Czechs, Poles, Belgians, Dutch, French — some are Guides. We have put them in touch with local British Guides. Are the Guides in all these places welcoming them into their hearts and homes — not as "refugees", not as objects of charity, but as real friends and sisters?

These Guides have chosen the word "Golondrinas" which in Spanish means "swallows". Now you must all look for a golondrina in your town or village. When you have found her, cherish her, warm and comfort her throughout the hard winter, so that when sunshine comes again to Europe, she may fly back to her home unharmed and happy. A good Guide is not one who has an armful of badges, a good Guide is one who is really helpful, cheerful and friendly.

"They are dear to us like swallows," she said, "these sister Guides from across the sea. Like swallows, we must enjoy them and get to know them while they are with us because soon they will fly home again. They are only birds of passage."

Anna from Warsaw, a dainty and pretty Ranger of seventeen, was one of the many Golondrinas who arrived in Britain. At a training camp at Waddow in Lancashire in 1942 she proved excellent at stalking. When praised for this, she laughed, saying "If I could not stalk, I would not be here. My father escaped from Poland in 1939 while I and my mother and sisters remained there. Word was passed to us that he was ill and fretting for news. We arranged that I, as a Guide, must be the one to go to him. So I managed to escape over three frontiers and came here. You see it was very easy, the snow was on the ground, and I wrapped myself in a white blanket. Twice I had no difficulty. The third frontier I had to pass so near the German sentry I could hear him breathing. If I had not learnt in Guides to stalk, I would not be here. You do see that?"

CHAPTER
SIX

The Clover Union
of Poland

In 1910 Olga Drahonowska, a handsome, well-educated Polish woman, met Andrzej Małkowski, the founder of Scouting in Poland, who introduced her to Scouting and then married her. The following year she became the first Chief of Girl Guides in Poland, and co-wrote the lyrics to the Polish Scout anthem "*Wszystko co nasze*": "We will give to Poland everything we have". The only difference between British and Polish Guides Law was the addition at the end of the 10th Law, "A Guide is clean in thought, word and deed", of the words "does not smoke cigarettes and does not drink alcohol". Olga Małkowska organised the first national Guide camp in Poland in July 1914. Guides from the Russian, Austrian and German territories of Poland attended. Baden-Powell thoroughly approved — he believed that they all belonged to one nation called Poland, not to three separate countries. During the camp Germany declared war on Poland. The borders closed, and three hundred Guides were unable to return home. So in the nearby town of Zakopane they ran the postal service, organised a children's home, helped with the harvest, and opened a café to support themselves.

In 1915 the Małkowskas fled to the USA, where their son was born. Andrzej Małkowski returned to Europe in 1919 and died fighting with the Polish Army, and in 1921 Olga returned to Poland as a Guide trainer. Guiding continued to flourish into the next decade, and in 1937 Polish Guides opened a sanatorium for children with tuberculosis, run on Guiding principles with patrols doing the housework. From 1938 the 65,000 Guides in Poland began preparing for the possibility of war by training in first-aid, signalling, running canteens and air-raid practice.

On 1 September 1939, Hitler's army and air force invaded Poland. Thousands of tanks tore across the cornfields of the Polish plains, bombs were dropped and refugees were machine-gunned from the air. Guides dug trenches, prepared gas masks and sealed rooms against gas attacks. Poland is an intensely patriotic country, and most of the Guides joined the Home Army, the underground movement that defied the Germans. They were here, there and everywhere, at one moment teaching younger Guides how to tie a reef knot, the next derailing a train. As men were recruited to defend their country, Girl Guides were among the women who replaced them as telephone operators, in post offices and as messengers in the army. With so many families separated or destroyed, to many girls the Guides became their family.

Since 1925 Olga Małkowska had been running a boarding school and an orphanage on the southern frontier of Poland, a centre of modern education based on Guiding principles. In August 1939 she sent all the school children home, except the twelve Rangers on the staff and two orphans, aged nine and seven. On 1 September she was staying in the nearest town, fourteen miles away, where she had gone to buy provisions. She was woken at dawn by heavy gunfire, and found the town under bombardment as the Germans attacked. There were no trains, so she decided to walk back to the school, but was forced to crawl through ditches, dodging the fire of the German columns. When she reached the school she found it deserted and partly destroyed. The Rangers and the two orphans were hiding at a secret meeting place in the woods, carrying out a plan they had trained for at the Pax Ting camp in Hungary a few weeks earlier. Only now they had to leave their country, not get back in. For the next few days they headed towards the frontier, walking through the woods to avoid German tanks on the roads, and sleeping under hedges.

"All went well until they had to cross the frontier," reported *The Guide*. "Madam Małkowska thought the best thing was to board one of the evacuation trains. German aeroplanes flew over the train, bombing it." The terrified passengers, most of whom were peasants, fled into the fields, where they crowded together in a huddle. "Madam ordered her Rangers to scatter and lie flat. She lay with the two children under a haystack. The bombers flew so low that the faces of the airmen could be clearly seen. Young faces. They deliberately machine-gunned the herd of peasants — an easy and terribly vulnerable target." When the planes finally flew off, the Rangers gave the injured survivors first-aid, but could do no more. They continued their journey south along the Czechoslovakia — Ukraine border until they reached the home of a friend of Madam Małkowska just inside Romania. There they heard of a convent orphanage from which the nuns had been recalled, and offered to look after the children. Madam Małkowska left her Rangers to care for the Romanian orphans, and set off through Italy, Yugoslavia and France by train, heading for Britain.

Madam Małkowska's many friends in England had been growing increasingly anxious about her. Then, on a grey afternoon in October 1939, a small woman with a tired face, wearing a brown coat, walked into Guide headquarters in London and asked for the editor of *The Guide*. Despite what she had seen during her long and difficult journey, Madam Małkowska was confident and unshaken. "We must go on," she said. "Guiding must go on. We must hold steady and work for the future." She described the situation when Warsaw was under attack the previous month: "The Guides in Poland have been doing splendid work ever since war began. You could see them everywhere helping courageously, doing their duty."

Poland's Scouts and Guides were branded as criminals by the Nazi Party, but carried on as a clandestine organisation, nicknamed the *Szare Szeregi* (Grey Ranks), operating with the Polish underground.

They worked in children's homes, as nurses, provided bandages made from old linen, and gave out food and drink at railway stations. They acted as guards stationed in towers, listening out for enemy bombers. Trained to recognise different types of aeroplanes by the sound of their engines, when they heard a raid approaching they would radio the report centres.

One Guide company set up a first-aid station in a school; each classroom was looked after by one patrol, the Guides working in three-hour shifts. The girls helped to organise over fifteen auxiliary hospitals, several of which were destroyed by bombs and had to be evacuated repeatedly, as well as refugee shelters in schools, cinemas, offices and centres for lost children. During one air raid on Warsaw the Guides rushed into a collapsing hospital ward, picked up the patients and carried them on their backs to the cellar.

Guides stationed on the roofs of Warsaw shovelled off incendiary bombs while others in the streets below put them out with sand. As the siege closed in on the doomed city, Guides from farms in the neighbouring countryside made their way through enemy lines with potatoes, eggs and any other food that could be found. One group of Rangers made a home among the ruins for orphaned toddlers. Some were severely wounded, and were too young to know their own names. As hundreds starved all around them, the Rangers took care of these children throughout the German occupation.

One of the most dangerous tasks undertaken by Poland's Guides was delivering food to the front line.

"We pulled trolleys filled with bread over a one-kilometre bridge on the Vistula river to get to the kitchen at the railway station. The air-raid siren would sound in the middle of the bridge, and then we had to run," remembered a Guider from Torun.

One morning Guide Zina Schuch-Nikiel went out with her first-aid bag to see if anyone needed help. "By the gate I saw some soldiers with a light field gun, and a Lieutenant. A soldier approached the Lieutenant and asked where he could have his wound dressed — he had hurt himself when building a barricade. The Lieutenant looked at him helplessly. 'We have not a nurse yet or any first-aid kit.' I dressed his wound and ten minutes later I was accepted as a nurse."

Cecylia Skrzypczak, a seventeen-year-old Guide in Bydgoszcz, northern Poland, was looking after the children of unemployed people when Germany invaded. "On Sunday 3rd I had to report for duty at the barracks at nine o'clock in the morning," she remembered. While she was on her way, an air-raid siren sounded. "I went into the cellar in the main street and waited there, but nobody knew what was happening. From the cellar window I could see everything. The Polish army was retreating on their horses. Germans were gathering in the woods outside the town, helped by the local Polish Germans. I knew them, they were my neighbours. I could see them shooting from the church tower with rifles." There was general confusion, shooting, and sniping from all sides. "Later one of the Germans who had lived in the same house as me was taken away and shot — he was about twenty. Then the local Poles were looking for me." Her neighbours thought she was German too, because her father had fought with the Germans in the First World War and half of her family lived in Germany. She feared that she would be found and executed, although she felt "I am Polish and they are invading my country."

The day after "Bloody Sunday" — 10 October 1939, when Warsaw suffered seventeen consecutive German air raids — Cecylia, her brother and her mother found a boat and began to travel down the Vistula towards Warsaw. When they saw that the Germans were shooting people from Stukas, they turned back. "So we stayed with some friends for two weeks, and then when the Germans had come there too, we went back to Bydgoszcz." Cecylia's brother was arrested in October, as part of the German reprisals against Bloody Sunday. "He was loaded onto a cattle train to be deported to Dachau. But the Polish railway workers attached two of the cattle trucks to the wrong steam engine, so that instead of going to Dachau it went to Warsaw, where he escaped."

Germany had defeated Poland by 23 September, and this posed a huge challenge for the Guides. "When the war started we were very proud to do our duty," wrote K. Popiwniak-Gburek. "We stood up ready to work, sure of the victory. This mood changed quickly. Defeated retreating soldiers and refugees woke us up from our dream about heroism."

Guiding was no longer a game, it was a banned, illegal movement. After a few weeks Cecylia heard the Germans were looking for her too, "Just because I was a Girl Guide. All Guides and Scouts were under suspicion because it was a patriotic youth movement." German spies all over Poland had identified the country's senior Guides, and they began to be arrested. As a result, the Polish government ordered adult Guiders not to stay and fight, but to retreat to save themselves from betrayal and execution. Reluctantly they obeyed, but this meant leaving younger Guides behind. "One of my brother's friends brought me false papers so that I could travel to Warsaw," said Cecylia. "There were trains, all very full. There was nowhere to live in Warsaw — my brother and I lived in a bombed-out house for the winter." The only thing they had to eat was potato soup. "We were very hungry. The Germans were catching people from the streets, taking them to slave labour in the trucks."

Guides and Scouts wanted to wear their uniforms to show their allegiance, but they soon realised this was too dangerous. In the face of the Nazi threat Guides hid their uniforms and became part of the wider Polish underground movement, using the codename "Clover Union" and later "Be Prepared". In order to prevent their arrest and deportation to labour camps, the Home Nursing Council (*Rada Glowna Opiekuncza*) issued Guides with identity cards stating that they were their employees. Guides then worked in day-care centres, open-air kindergartens and summer camps. Those who completed a Red Cross course were permitted by the Germans to keep a first-aid kit and to move around during the air raids. Doctors and nurses from hospitals including Ujazdowski Hospital and the Central

Pharmacy handed over medications and dressing materials for the Guides to hide in their homes and use to treat resistance workers.

Despite the nightmare of Nazi occupation, the Guides carried on helping others. They were prepared to die for their country, but meanwhile they would live for it too. Their responsibilities included caring for their own and other people's families, continuing their own and others' education, and coping with occupation while preparing for freedom. But when they got together they also played games, sang songs and enjoyed the countryside. "Through camping we could rediscover youth and joy," said a Guide from Silesia, "in spite of what was happening around." To show their dislike of the Nazis' destruction of the forests, Guides planted new trees.

Forced to take place in secret, Guide meetings were now often held at night, even after curfew. "We would do our activities until midnight and then sleep on the floor," said Irena Leparczyk. The Guides were very patriotic: they celebrated national anniversaries, read books about Polish history, tended the graves of soldiers and those murdered by the Nazis. "We were looking for the lost sense of life," said Guide Maria Kann. In October 1939 the Guides from Tarnow decided to record as much as they could about the graves of soldiers scattered in Poland's fields. They walked from village to village drawing plans, describing the graves and collecting documents and information from local people about the circumstances in which the soldiers had died. These reports became a valuable basis for exhumations and identifications after the war.

Things did not get any easier for Poland's Guides. The winter of 1939–40 was particularly cold: temperatures plummeted to minus 32°C, and there was not enough food or fuel to go round. In Warsaw, Guides ran a kitchen for children, cooking five hundred to six hundred lunches every day, and smuggled what food they could into the ghetto for children there. They rescued as many Jewish children from extermination as they could, by removing them from the Warsaw Ghetto, Vilnius and Bialystok, and taking them to the suburbs. A dozen Jewish children were taken by Guides to live in three convents in Warsaw. Guide Maria Jirska visited them once a week, supplying them with oil, eggs and sugar.

The Guides did what they could to help the many thousands of people taken prisoner by the Nazis. As well as organising escapes from prison camps and hospitals, they kept prisoners in hiding until they could be reunited with their families. "Every Sunday . . . we loaded our sleigh with food and clothes. Then in a group of four or five we walked 7 km along the frozen Vistula River and to the prison fort to bring those poor locked-up people a bit of relief."

After Warsaw had fallen, Olga Małkowska wrote in *The Guide*: "If we want our civilisation to survive, we must build it on love and not on hate, on goodwill and trust and not on suspicion. In short, we must build it on our Law and Promise. This must become part of our lives, whether we are active members of the Movement

124

or are temporarily, or definitely, outside of it. Aren't we lucky to live in such times when our 'Guidiness' is continually tried and tested! Thank God, we can show our Chief that he can count on us, that his life's work was not in vain." In December 1939, Queen Elizabeth crossed the road from Buckingham Palace to the Guide headquarters and pinned the Bronze Cross, the very highest Guide award for gallantry, on Madam Małkowska's grey Polish uniform. "I give you this for the Guides of Poland," she said, "but no one has earned it more than you."

Just before Christmas 1939, a young mother arrived in London from Poland with her baby. "Peter was tiny, pale, and delicate, with big brown eyes and an aggrieved expression," wrote Catherine Christian in *The Guide*. "His mother was a Polish Ranger not yet twenty years old who had escaped from Warsaw. Peter had been born in a field on her flight north. His father was a sailor and no one knew where he might be. After a short rest, Peter's mother made her way to the coast with her new-born baby, hoping to find a passage to England. Walking wearily, with Peter rolled in a blanket, she heard a shout — her husband came running towards her. His ship had put in for repairs at that very port. It was a small cargo ship but room was made for the young woman and her baby." Peter was wrapped in an old flannel shirt, and when the ship arrived in London his mother found her way to Guide headquarters. The Guides found Peter a crib and some blankets: he was the first refugee baby that they had seen, and he gave them an inkling of the horrors being experienced in Poland. The Guides quickly realised that this was a very real war, and that to "Be Prepared" might become necessary for them too.

The Germans not only wanted to occupy Polish land; they were also determined to destroy Polish culture. Secondary and university education were abolished. University professors were arrested and laboratory equipment was confiscated. Thousands of Polish books were destroyed, but Guides collected those that they could and hid them. They copied out textbooks, and made new ones with pictures cut from magazines. "I taught young children," said Anna Pigoń. "My school was the garden. My educational equipment consisted of a stick, a stone, a tree and the paths." Many Guide Captains were teachers or students under thirty years old, and they set up secret schools in each other's homes. Groups of more than three people were forbidden by the Nazis, and if they were caught, teachers and children alike were deported to labour camps. Two members of each class stayed on sentry duty, watching for approaching Germans. One child would try to engage the soldier in conversation while the other would warn the teacher with a prearranged signal, such as throwing a stone. If German soldiers did discover a class, they would be told that the children were learning German and arithmetic, as these were the only officially required skills for Poles, who had to be employed as menial labourers by the age of twelve. "It was enough for the Germans if we could read and count," said Cecylia Skrzypczak, "because we were supposed to be the workers, not the intelligentsia. So there were only vocational schools for dressmaking, or hat-making. We had secret schools; my younger brother and younger sister went into manual work at ten, when they could read."

Learning became an act of patriotism and part of the fight against the Nazis. Every child was keen to be educated, and everyone had something they could teach someone else. Older Guides taught younger Guides, and younger ones taught children. By 1942 over a million Polish children attended underground primary schools and just two years later there were more than a million secondary school students. At least 18,000 students passed their final school exams and received certificates from officially non-existent schools to enter officially non-existent universities. Schools weren't the only Polish institutions closed down: theatres and art galleries were closed, and Polish music was banned. Only propaganda films chosen by the Germans were permitted.

Cecylia Skrzypczak lived on one side of Warsaw, and attended a secret school on the other. "The tram went through the Jewish quarter, so when we approached the Ghetto the German soldiers came on the train to stop us contacting any Jews, and to stop them jumping on the tram. The ghetto was horrid, horrible, people looking like skeletons, people lying around with just newspaper to cover themselves. I saw them being deported in cattle wagons, skeletal hands coming out of the small windows, and we tried to bring them bread. There were Germans everywhere looking for food parcels."

As the Nazi stranglehold on their country grew stronger, Polish Guides had to develop their skills in orienteering, moving around without attracting attention, selecting the best routes, organising alarm networks and signalling with Morse, flags or secret codes. With the increasing demand for helpers in the resistance, even younger Guides became involved as messengers. They had to locate safe border-crossing points, keep information and arrange contacts, as well as find food and accommodation, and if necessary a change of clothes so they would be able to disguise themselves. By the end of 1941 over a hundred Guides had been trained as decoders, able to identify weapons and the enemy's army ranks, and capable of coping with interrogation and imprisonment if arrested.

In Poznan, Girl Guides helped a group of British soldiers to escape from a prisoner-of-war camp. Unfortunately the men were caught on the Yugoslavian border, and two Guides were arrested: Olga Prokopowa was beheaded in Berlin and Maria E. Jasinska was hanged in Łodź. In Chojnice, Pomerania, Guides provided British prisoners of war with warm clothes and gloves. They left food parcels in secret places close to where the prisoners worked. To ensure that the men had received the goods they left a note asking for them to confirm it by whistling "It's a Long Way to Tipperary". They were delighted when the soldiers whistled not only that tune on their way back from work to the camp, but also two Polish songs in thanks.

Guide Captain Helena Danielewiczowa looked after prisoners in Pawiak, the notorious political prison in

Warsaw in which 80,000 people died during the war. Despite the risk of arrest, she visited every day from March 1940 until August 1944. In December 1943 the Nazis ordered that all the children in the prison aged from one to five had to be taken from their mothers; Helena helped find them their families or new foster homes.

Cecylia Skrzypczak soon became involved in the underground resistance. A friend of hers took her to the home of her headmistress. "But when we got there we got such a dressing down, because they said, 'We should find *you*, you are not supposed to track us down! How could you do this?'" The headmistress was the leader of Intelligence Liaison, and put Cecylia in charge of a group of young people aged between sixteen and twenty-one. "Couriers came from all over, and collected the messages. We had to get intelligence records to Britain on the 20th of every month — they usually went by plane. I collected the messages, and somebody else took them to the plane in the countryside. We didn't think about the danger of knowing such valuable things. The messages were written in code on tissue paper. I was not allowed to read them. If the Germans stopped you, you had to eat it. All of us had secret places where we could keep messages overnight." Cecylia hid her messages in an ironing pad which was filled with sawdust. "We just accepted that we might be killed. We had to be approved, and if we were trusted we could go up higher." They had to be ready for orders at any time. "There was a man who was very nervous, because he had been caught once, and his courier failed to turn up because she was ill with TB. So they sent me to the church to meet him, knowing that I would calm him down."

Cecylia was sent to Rosolinksy to take messages to the wife of one of the top intelligence officers, who received information from the Eastern Front. "One of their couriers was a beautiful young person, and then they found out she was actually Gestapo and the whole family was killed. And my head of liaison, she too was executed after a trial in Germany."

Possession of an identity card, or "*Ausweis*", showing that the holder was employed by a German company or government agency such as the railways, was the only safeguard to prevent young people from being arrested. Cecylia was very good at faking signatures for identity cards, and had several identities.

In autumn 1943 she moved to Krakow so she could attend university. Officially she was a secretary in the veterinary labs, but her friends were teaching her veterinary research. "We made rabies vaccine and fowl pest vaccine. In Krakow I was organising underground schools. It was still illegal work. All young people were involved, but we never talked about it, we didn't know who did what." One day she was carrying a mechanical part in her briefcase through Warsaw in a tram. "It was very full when Germans boarded. The front part was always for the Germans and I was sitting there, and the people said, 'Oh there is *lapanka*,' which meant that random civilians would be arrested. I was by the barrier near the front of the tram. I couldn't get out. So I put the briefcase on the German side under a German lady. When they came to check me I didn't have any luggage. I was never caught."

Over 50,000 copies of *Biuletyn Informacyjny* (Information Bulletin), the underground newspaper of the resistance Home Army, were distributed all over Poland, mainly by Guides and Scouts. They had to be collected at an appointed time and then delivered without the Nazis noticing. Irena Bobowska of the 6th Poznan Guide Company was paralysed, and hid the newspapers in a secret box in her wheelchair. The Guides wore their badges under their jacket collars, which they could turn up as a sign.

One day in July 1943, Scouter Wojtek heard that a *lapanka* had begun in Kowelska Street in Warsaw. He knew that the Gestapo would search his flat, where copies of *Biuletyn Informacyjny* were stored. The newspaper's liaison officer, a Guide called Gena, was very nervous, and told him that the Gestapo had already arrested three lorry-loads of people. Knowing that they would reach his flat in half an hour, Wojtek summoned a fourteen-year-old Scout called Edek, and told him to buy a bunch of flowers and two apples, and then to take a taxi as quickly as possible to the flat. Edek went to the shops, while Gena and Wojtek went to the flat. They had no difficulty in getting into the cordoned-off area: the Nazis were only concerned with those trying to leave. They quickly packed the newspapers into two large suitcases, and had just finished when the taxi arrived with Edek, who rushed up the stairs. Gena and Wojtek emerged from the flat, each carrying a suitcase and casually munching the apples Edek had brought with him. "You must remember," whispered Wojtek, "we are just married and are now going on honeymoon. How happy we are." They hoisted the suitcases into the taxi, and climbed on board to the cheers of their neighbours, Gena clutching the bunch of flowers. Five German soldiers appeared at that moment. Wojtek explained, "These suitcases have already been searched. We are off on honeymoon. Surely you have not the heart . . ." The Germans waved them on, and that evening the newspapers were distributed as usual. Gena and Wojtek married for real just before wojtek was arrested in 1944. He did not meet their son Chris until the war ended. Between 1942 and 1944 the Nazis took approximately four hundred people from Warsaw to concentration camps every day. In September 1942, 3,000 were rounded up in just two days and transported by cattle train to Germany.

Guides undertook very dangerous activities in their attempts to stand up to the Nazi regime. In December 1940, five Ranger Guides carried out a "small sabotage" or "*Wawer*", smashing the windows of a photography studio which displayed pictures of German soldiers. Another Guide, Danuta Kaczyńska, commanded a special "*Wawer*" Guide company. "We scattered leaflets in cinemas, threw tear gas or vomiting stimulants into restaurants used by Germans and removed Nazi flags. At night we would connect to the German loudspeakers in the streets and broadcast the Polish National Anthem or the Polish news from the front." They sold false editions of the official newspaper *Goniec Krakowski*, and on 28 January 1941 they stamped the official newspapers with birthday wishes for the President of the Polish Republic, Wladyslaw Rackiewicz. "Just before the anniversary of Polish independence we painted the date of it — 11.XI — on walls." This was reported in London newspapers as an example of the defiant attitude of Warsaw's people. The saboteurs could not be given medals or certificates, so they were rewarded for their work with new surnames chosen from among their heroes. Danuta Kaczyńska became "Kinowska" after an attack on a cinema.

Whether Jewish or Christian, many Guides involved in sabotage or intelligence worked for "Zegota", the codename for the underground Council to Aid Jews (Rada Pomocy Zydom). Teresa Bogusawska was one of them. Aged just fifteen, she was the youngest Girl Guide arrested in Warsaw for sabotage. Despite being beaten during interrogation, she did not give anyone away. Many others were either executed or died in Auschwitz.

Wherever they were, Guides took part in small acts of industrial sabotage. In Pomerania, Guides working as mechanics purposefully delayed repairs to cars belonging to Nazis. In the German uniform factory they did sloppy work, damaged machines and stole fabric to make gloves for prisoners working on roads. In Łódź, Guides working in shops and pharmacies were forbidden to sell certain goods to Poles, so they gave them away. In Chelm, the Guides ran a bakery shop as cover for their underground activities. In Lublin they had a workshop for making brooms, in which messages could be hidden. Guides employed in German offices destroyed files and warned people who were on the lists of those to be sent to labour camps. They also obtained and delivered illegal identity cards.

The number of Guides caught was relatively small because of their quick wits, efficient alarm network and ability to remember names and addresses, rather than writing them down. Those Guides who were arrested, usually in random round-ups, faced atrocious investigations, long periods in prison, and almost certain execution. But the Gestapo never managed to work out the Guides' secret communication system, and no Guides are known to have broken under torture.

Guides involved in intelligence services were at greatest risk, though little is know about their work, only their fate. Izabela Lopuska from Warsaw was executed in 1944; Helena Dobrzycka, known as "Lena", from northern Poland, was arrested in 1942, imprisoned in Danzig, then moved to Berlin, where she was tortured and sentenced to death. When Berlin was bombed she was evacuated to another prison, and escaped. Sisters Caban and Poborc were executed in Ravensbrück for stealing German military plans. Halina Grabowska, "Zeta", died during an unsuccessful assassination attempt on the hated German commander Wilhelm Koppe in Krakow in July 1944.

CHAPTER
SEVEN

Blackout Blues

In August 1940 *The Guider* printed a letter from an Extension Guide in the north-east of England. She was fourteen years old and totally bedridden. "The night that we had the raid, my young sister and I had Mother for casualty number one. She bled profusely, and we were thoroughly glad of our combined first-aid knowledge. Emma did the running about, and I produced the equipment." Although she was lying helpless in bed in the midst of a bombing raid, while her mother lay wounded, blood streaming from a deep shrapnel cut, her training as a Guide allowed her to keep her head and instruct her younger sister to dress the wound and stop the bleeding. Raids like this tore into Britain every night during the Blitz. The Guides, as ever, remained level-headed and helped to boost morale amongst the terrified population.

A month before the Blitz began, the Luftwaffe attacked airfields and aircraft factories all over Britain in preparation for Germany's planned invasion. Despite having fewer aircraft, the Royal Air Force fought back. "The Battle of Britain took place right over our heads, in the summer of 1940," remembered Sally Half, a

Guide from Maidstone, Kent. "A German plane and a Spitfire fought over our house. The Spitfire had run out of ammunition but he forced the German down by getting very, very close to his tail and gradually brought him down into a field not far away. We all went to have a look. We saw one of our pilots bailing out and parachuting down but he was shot at as he dangled there helplessly. At Detling aerodrome, we could see the planes dive-bombing and great palls of black oily smoke. One felt so helpless — there was nothing we could do to help while this dreadful thing went on. The plan for Maidstone was to fight to the last man, because it was the bridging point towards London."

On the afternoon of 7 September, 348 German bombers, escorted by 617 fighters, bombed the docks and industrial areas of east London. Four hours later, another wave of bombers, guided by the fires set by the first wave, began another attack which lasted until dawn. This was the start of the Blitz, the sustained period of the bombing of Britain. For most British people, this was when the Second World War truly began. From now on, few people got enough sleep: "Everywhere you went during the day there were people having little catnaps to catch up — in the parks, on the buses and tubes, in the corners of tea-shops," wrote Judith Kerr, a teenager at the time. A night in bed between sheets, wearing a nightdress or pyjamas, was out of the question for Guides in London and many other big cities. Somehow or other, when the air-raid sirens sounded in the middle of the night, families had to get into their Anderson shelter — a tin-covered hole in the garden — or a public shelter. Everyone went to bed in their clothes, in case they were roused during the night. Many Guides slept in their uniforms.

Judith Kerr described a raid she witnessed in London: "The sky was red, reflecting the fires on the ground, and in it hung clusters of orange flares which lit up everything for miles around. They looked like gigantic Christmas decorations floating slowly, slowly down through the night air. In the distance, yellow flashes like lightning were followed by muffled bangs — the anti-aircraft guns in Hyde Park. Suddenly a searchlight swept across the sky. It was joined by another and another, crossing and re-crossing each other, and then a great orange flash blotted out everything else. A bomb or a plane exploding in mid-air."

"Air raids at home always seemed quite interesting down in the garden shelter," remembered Iris O'Dell. "I hated Dad marching about outside looking up at the sky and saying, 'There goes Gerry.' I was sure he was going to be killed! There was the fun of going back to the house late at night and having cocoa and, once, hot apple pie. For a while we slept in the wash-house — Dad constructed a bedding area in an alcove."

Dorothy Eagleton was a Ranger in the 7th North Lewisham Company in Surrey when her home was wrecked during the Blitz. "Micky our cat is a real beauty with long black hair and amber eyes. We couldn't find him after the crash but the next day I had a brainwave. I crawled on my tummy over plaster and under roof supports, and there he was, poor little frightened beast, crouched right at the farthest corner under the bed, too scared to move."

The Streatham Hill ambulance station in south London was manned by Lilian Epcott, Brown Owl of the 7th Streatham Hill Brownie Pack. One night she was on telephone duty when a bomb fell behind the building and the ceiling caved in on her. She crawled under a table with the telephone, but it wasn't working. So she crawled out again, and in complete darkness felt her way through the shattered building until she found a phone that worked. There she stayed for the entire night taking messages and directing ambulances to where they were needed. Without Lilian, the ambulances would have had no idea where to go on that terrible night.

On 15 October, the BBC began to broadcast the latest news: "This is the BBC Home and Forces Programme. Here is the news, and this is Bruce Belfrage reading it." As he said these words there was a loud crash, and the sound of shouting in the background. Belfrage continued to read as if nothing had happened: "There has been some success in the Mediterranean . . ." A delayed-action bomb had crashed through a window on the seventh floor of Broadcasting House, and landed two floors below in the music library. Moments later, as firemen rushed to the scene, it exploded, killing seven people. But Belfrage, covered in dust and soot, continued to read the report of attacks in which nineteen enemy aircraft had been destroyed. It was BBC policy not to comment on such interruptions while on air.

Since the Nazi occupation of western Europe, German bombers could fly from the islands off Holland to attack the Thames Estuary and East Anglia; from the Somme to the south coast and on to London; from the Channel Islands to the Dorset coast and as far as Birmingham and Coventry. The British did what they could to put up a fight: old bedsteads and cars without wheels began to appear in the middle of London's squares, to deter German parachutists from landing on the grass.

When Coventry was bombed in November 1940, the Guides of nearby Leamington put their trek cart to good use. First they collected two hundredweight of clothes, forty pairs of shoes and fifty pounds of toys, and pushed them to the bombed-out people of the city who were now patients in Warwick Hospital. They then they set off for Coventry itself, where they distributed blankets, socks, hats and mittens they had knitted, along with 2,500 cigarettes.

In between the bombing raids, there was still school to be attended, money to be earned for good causes and badges to be achieved. One mother told how her daughter, a Guide, sat sewing placidly through a particularly bad evening. Suddenly, there was a shattering crash and the rest of the family dived under the solid dining-room table. When they emerged, the Guide was still sewing. "I've got to finish it or I shan't be ready for the badge exam on Saturday," she explained. "And if I don't pass Needlewoman, I shall never get my First Class!"

With the start of the Blitz, the British Guides' work really began. Those who had learned first-aid and how to put out incendiary devices now had to put their lessons into practice. Blitz first-aid for Guides included the instructions: "When carrying patients out of a bombed building, one puts joined arms over neck and other person holds under legs and then both walk in same step. Patient with bowels protruding: do not talk to patient. Soak towel in salt and warm water (blood heat) and place across wound."

Guides helped keep up the morale of frightened people huddled into bomb shelters. They served tea and cakes and organised "Blackout Blues" sing-songs. The government recognised that Guides had skills they could pass on to adult citizens, and the Ministry of Food asked them to demonstrate "Blitz cooking" to Londoners by constructing emergency ovens from the bricks of bombed houses. Suggested recipes included "mock fish-cakes" made from potato and anchovy sauce, sandwiches filled with bacon rinds and cold mashed potato, and vegetable broth. For a treat, "Swiss milk" could be boiled in its tin until it turned into caramel.

After food rationing was introduced in January 1940, Guides with a Gardener's Badge threw themselves into the Dig for Victory campaign, in which the Ministry of Food exhorted everyone to grow vegetables on every available piece of land. Some companies took on their own allotments, and encouraged the growing of larger crops with competitions. One company issued each patrol with six seed potatoes, and *The Guide* reported: "The patrol that grows the largest weight in potatoes gets the honour of carrying the colours at the next Harvest festival." Guides took their vegetables to hospitals and evacuee hostels, or sold them to raise funds for refugees.

"We had all been issued with ration books," said Julie Ashworth of Cheltenham. "Everyone had to be registered with a shop and collect their rations from the same shop each week. If you were a loyal customer, sometimes you were lucky enough to get a little extra. But those who kept changing their supplier by re-registering were not looked on very kindly. Long queues would form at fish shops, or when word got around that some unrationed foods had been delivered, and tempers got frayed when there was not enough to go around. The field in front of the school was given over to producing hay, and after it had been cut, in warm weather we were allowed to play out there and make dens with the leavings. Dutch troops were billeted in my street. One day as they marched by, Prince Bernhard of the Netherlands took the salute from the steps of the Lion and Swan pub. They kept the downstairs windows open and I was amazed at the amount of food they had, especially butter, when it was on ration. I used to walk past like a 'Bisto kid', sniffing at the aroma of well-cooked food."

Iris O'Dell and her Guide friend Rita were thrilled when they found a sachet of custard powder in Mrs Pratt's corner shop in Hitchin. "It was lovely when

Mum brought home some little day-old chicks, which she kept in a box in the hearth. I think only Gert and Daisy survived, but we had eggs. Chickens got their own ration of grain, but then you had to give up your egg ration. We gathered greenery food from the countryside for the rabbits. When we killed a rabbit for Christmas dinner, I stoutly refused to eat it, so for Christmas dinner I had an egg." Iris remembered the fun: "Gleaning for the hens and coming home laughing with bundles and sacks of wheat ears." Those without chickens to provide garden manure collected pigeon droppings from municipal parks or statues.

Mothers of growing children had to be especially inventive with food, but families with Brownies and Guides were often at an advantage. "Joining the Brownies, we took over an allotment beside St John's church and grew mainly radishes," said Iris. Posters proclaimed: "Turn over a new leaf — Eat vegetables to enjoy good health". The cartoon characters Potato Pete and Doctor Carrot appeared on leaflets with affordable recipes, and every morning housewives listened to *The Kitchen Front* on the radio. They learned how to make pastry using mashed potato and less fat, and cakes with neither butter nor eggs.

"A Sharp's toffee tin is a nice size for two people to make a good tin-can stove," the Lewisham Guides wrote in their log book. "Cut a door in one side and make holes on the other for the smoke. You have now a very good stove which needs little fuel and is safe in the wind. Carry your food in it to the site. Turn it upside down, when hot smear the bottom with grease and cook on it or fry your egg on it. When finished, it must be battered and buried deeply, or wrapped in paper and taken HOME. Birch bark is best for punk [tinder] and beech wood is best for heat."

The 5th East Oxford Company saved fuel by cooking meals in a "hay box". They brought a lidded pan of soup or stew to the boil, then tucked it into a wooden box full of hay, with more on top. A few hours later, the food was cooked.

In September and October 1940 London was bombed on fifty-seven consecutive nights. Fires destroyed much of the city, and people had to seek shelter wherever they could find it — Underground stations were used by nearly 180,000 people during night raids. "We had plenty of air-raid practice," said Gillian White, a London Guide, "with a fair number of signals using a whistle. Our Captain would blow her whistle loud and long, and we had to act as though it was an air raid. We all had to assemble by the door, very quickly, and then march down to the air-raid shelter."

Guides who had passed their Pathfinder Badge had "an intimate knowledge of the locality including hospitals, telegraph offices, omnibus and tram routes, livery stables, cycle repairers, bridle paths, blacksmiths and cab ranks". They were especially useful in helping people to air-raid shelters in the blackout, and even more so when whole streets were destroyed. Guides' tracking and map-reading skills were important after all the signposts had been removed in order to confuse Germans, whether spies or invaders. Guides acted as messengers for the Home Guard, who depended on their ability to memorise complicated messages and their speed at reaching men in outlying farms and cottages. They made sure their bicycles were always in tiptop condition: a flat tyre would waste valuable time when the local Home Guard depended on being informed quickly of the need to defend a strategic spot. To win the Cyclist Badge, a Guide had to own, or at least "part-own in the same house", a bicycle in good working order which she was prepared to use in any emergency. Broken saddle springs could be mended with cork or grass; punctured tyres could be removed with the aid of a penny. For the blackout, Guides covered their bicycle lamps with black paper, leaving a small pinhole of light. Had the Germans invaded, the Guides' cycling skills would have saved many people. One night, ten Guides, aged from twelve to sixteen, called out over two hundred Home Guards in only two hours. When the commanding officer saw the men on parade, he said, "Good heavens! How on earth did you get here so soon?" "The Guides have done it again, sir!" was the answer.

In 1940 the Home Emergency Service was set up to enable Guides and Rangers to gain a mastery of first-aid, nursing and signalling — Morse, semaphore and radiography. As disciplined, fit and ready-for-any-emergency volunteers, their job was to cooperate with the local Air Raid Wardens, Home Guard and Red Cross, and to be ready to put out incendiary bombs with foot-operated stirrup pumps.

First-aid instructions for Guides during a bombing raid were simple, practical and firm:

CLOTHES ON FIRE
1. Throw person on the floor, flames uppermost.
2. Roll in blanket, rug or curtains.
3. Take care you do not catch fire yourself.

HYSTERIA
1. Avoid sympathy and speak firmly.
2. Threaten with a cold water douche, and sprinkle with water if this has no effect.
3. Encourage sleep, but watch the breathing.

The Guides of the 5th East Oxford Company acted as patients in air-raid exercises involving the local emergency services. "I was hoisted to the top of one of the chimneys at Morris Motors," recalls one Guide, "to give the fire service practice in getting down a badly injured person. I wore a label which said I had major internal injuries and two broken legs. This sort of injury was the most popular since it meant a ride in an ambulance. I'd only ever been in Captain's car before, if she had petrol."

By the time the Blitz reached its height, former Guide Verily Anderson was married and living in a luxurious flat in Mayfair, central London, which due to the air raids she and her husband were able to rent for only £2 a week, about £50 today. One night they were especially thankful for the shelters in St James's Park that she had dug as a Guide. "When a delayed-action bomb fell in our street, we were turned out of the cellar of our flat in our dressing gowns. We felt disinclined to follow the policeman and his flock to the cellars of the American Embassy in Grosvenor Square." Instead, they walked towards a friend's house beyond Oxford Street. "To our right John Lewis's store blazed with giant fingers of red and yellow reaching to the sky. The Westbourne River had burst from its tunnel and was pouring into a bombed shoe-shop. All the side streets were impassable with curtains of flame." They turned back, and headed towards some other friends' in Victoria. "Firelight and moonlight made the night as bright as day. Over Piccadilly Circus we saw a wave of enemy aircraft crossing the moon. Then a bomb whistled. We jumped into a porch and then laughed when we saw both its roof and its walls were glass." They reached a church further up the street as more bombs fell nearby. "When the aircraft passed, we came out from our guardian church. The glass porch had disappeared beneath a pile of rubble. We reached Green Park and searched for the shelters I had dug with the Guides. As the next wave of planes came over we shot into one, barely disturbing two bus drivers and a very old lady Air-Raid Warden. Safe at last, and grateful for our pre-war efforts, we went straight to sleep." The Blitz was providing plenty of opportunities for taking Baden-Powell's advice: "Smile if you can. If you cannot — well — then grin!"

Just before Christmas 1940, a house in a poor quarter of Manchester was bombed to the ground and completely destroyed. The Air-Raid Wardens began to

146

dig furiously in search of survivors, but without much hope. Suddenly, out of the great mound of rubble, a small, grimy figure, hauling a still smaller figure up by the hand, appeared. "Here we are, man!" announced Brownie Gladys Hulme. She and her small brother had been separated from the rest of the family and then trapped in the corner of the cellar. Somehow she had managed to scrabble her way up and out, pulling the little boy with her. A kind neighbour tucked them both up in bed. At the next Brownie meeting, Gladys confessed to Brown Owl that it was only later that evening, when the siren went again and she was blown out of the neighbour's bed, that she cried, "just a bit".

During Christmas the Newdigate Guides in Surrey entertained Guides evacuated from Poland and Danzig with Christmas carols played on bagpipes. "They also entertained evacuated mothers and children from Tottenham," reported *The Guide*, "and they cycled to a large house which is now accommodating invalid and crippled evacuees. One of these cripples was carried down to an Anderson shelter during the Blitz. She was obliged to live in it for three months, as it was impossible to lift her up and down. She is one of the cheeriest people alive, and told the Guides how much she would have loved to play a pipe, only her hands were useless. But she sang the refrain of 'Noel' as the pipes echoed softly round the room, everyone facing the crackling logs in the huge open fireplace."

The 1940 Christmas appeal in *The Guide* was for clothing, food and toys for the bombed-out families of London. The response was so huge that the

Buckingham Palace Road headquarters were almost overwhelmed: thousands of parcels poured in containing hand-made toys, knitted woollies, blankets, and enough food to fill a grocery shop. Everyone who worked at Guide HQ helped, including the editors, who put aside their romantic novels and threw themselves into war work like everyone else. Every spare inch of every office was stacked with parcels, "pounds of tea, packets of cereals, tins of cocoa, fruit, sardines, Christmas puddings", reported *The Guide*. "Every chair was draped by a gay knitted blanket, and the floor was covered in neat piles of clothing and woolly toys."

The Guiders had no time to send out the parcels which arrived on Christmas Eve, but for some East Enders this was lucky, for on 29 December the Luftwaffe set fire to the City of London. The raid was carefully planned to coincide with both the Sunday when most firefighters would still be on Christmas holiday, and a very low tide of the Thames, making access to the water almost impossible. The first bombs landed on the water mains, and then 10,000 fire bombs were dropped on the City. Firemen, soldiers and civilians rallied round, and although large areas of the City were flattened, St Paul's Cathedral was saved.

"That grim Sunday night", the editor of *The Guide* called it. "On Monday morning the editors of *The Guide* and *The Guider* arrived at work early. We filled the car to the roof with clothing, food, and toys, and off we went to one of the poorest districts." The firemen were still at work, "their hoses all over the road, and the people at the settlement wondering how on earth to

148

cope with all the pathetic families who kept coming to them for help, saying they had lost their homes last night. So the late gifts gave as much comfort as those which were distributed in shelters all over London on Christmas night." Rangers over sixteen and Guiders donated as much blood as they were allowed.

Bermondsey in the Docklands did not have enough air-raid shelters to protect everyone from the shrapnel and fire bombs that rained down from the sky every night, so people took cover where they could. One cold winter night, thirteen small children crept under a railway arch. They had no blankets, but their shelter was near a sawmill, and they burrowed into the warm sawdust. A bomb hit the bridge above them, and the arch caved in. The sawdust caught alight. Someone heard the children crying out, but there was only a very small hole through which to reach them. Marie Monk was the Captain of the 2nd Bermondsey Guides. A slightly built young woman, she crawled through the hole into the smoking, smouldering cavern and calmed the children down. She then stood up to her knees in smouldering sawdust and handed them up through the small hole. Afterwards she said, "I didn't think of being frightened. But don't you go imagining I'm a brave person. Once I had to go and unload one of those grand new American ambulances and drive it down the Old Kent Road on a Saturday. I'd only just learnt to drive. I can tell you I know about being afraid all right!" She was awarded the Guide Bronze Cross for keeping those around her calm during the dock fires of the Blitz.

In April 1941 all unmarried women were called up to either join the forces or to work in factories. "I cannot offer them a delightful life," said Ernest Bevin, Minister of Labour. "I want them to come forward in the spirit that they are going to suffer some inconvenience but with a determination to help us through." This meant that Brownies and Guides had even more work to do caring for toddlers suffering from "shelteritis" — a new form of post-traumatic stress disorder. Small children who arrived in country nurseries "wild-eyed, pale and thin from shock" were "miraculously cured with fresh air, quietness, proper feeding and patient care", reported the Ministry of Information. Guides also now not only had to run their own companies, but Brownie packs too.

Many of the Guides who had been conscripted into the services chose to wear their Guide badge under their lapel of their uniform jackets as a passport to friendship; just by turning up their lapel, they could often find another Guide who might be a support in moments of hardship or danger.

Section Officer Daphne Mary Pearson of the WAAF had been a Guide for many years in Bristol. When a plane crashed on the airstrip she rushed to the wreckage and managed to rouse the stunned pilot, knowing that bombs were on board. She dragged him out, and they were only a few hundred yards from the plane when a bomb exploded. Section Officer Pearson pushed the wounded man down onto the ground and threw herself across him. They both survived, and she was awarded the military order of the British Empire Medal.

Gillian Tanner was an ex-Guide in her early twenties from Gloucestershire with the Women's Auxiliary Fire Service. Her job was to drive a petrol tanker with reserve supplies to the fire service vehicles. The fact that houses were burning and bombs falling all around didn't stop her. One night she drove the tanker, containing 150 gallons of petrol, for three hours through a heavy raid. While she waited for the fire engines to come for their petrol, she simply carried on with her knitting. She was later awarded the George Cross.

During the eight months of the 1940–41 Blitz, 16,000 tons of high explosives were dropped on factories, warehouses, docks and homes in London. Landmarks such as Buckingham Palace, the Bank of England and the National Gallery were hit, and forty acres of the City of London flattened. Odd buildings stood in otherwise ruined streets like single rotten teeth, their inner walls revealing fireplaces, staircases and wallpaper. In midsummer the sites glowed pink with rose-bay willowherb, also known as fireweed because of its rapid invasion of fire-damaged land.

With so many injuries among the population, dressings were in short supply. "Up in the North," reported *The Guide*, "the sphagnum moss gatherers have been working overtime — a cold and a hard job. A bag of wet moss, used to dress wounds, is not a feather-weight proposition! The Guides are out to do the job that needs doing — they are out on the watch, and where something turns up, they settle on it like a flock of gulls on a new-ploughed furrow."

All over Britain, Guides were making a difference. During a bad air raid on Cardiff, Joan and Paddy Smythe, Guides aged just twelve and fourteen, spent a whole night fetching water and pumping it onto fires with stirrup pumps. The local Air-Raid Warden said afterwards, "They were a real tower of strength — both girls were so much help and I'm proud to have them in my sector." Over in Hartlepool, Margaret Sanderson was seventeen when the war began. Her skills as a First Class Brownie and a Guide helped her get a job in the Royal Observatory Corps. On the night of 10 May 1941 she was on duty watching the radar screen when she spotted a strange plane flying across the North Sea, straight for Scotland. "I was on a revolving chair, I saw it coming in, a single plane from Germany," she remembered. "Coming straight along, I'm plotting it, and I got Captain Jones to come over and listen in." She kept a careful note of its exact movements, and later discovered that she had plotted a Messerschmitt 110 on its way to Scotland after a five-hour, nine-hundred-mile flight from Germany. Seconds before the plane crashed into moorland in Lanarkshire, Hitler's deputy, Rudolf Hess, bailed out and parachuted into a field near the village of Eaglesham on Fenwick Moor. He surrendered to a ploughman named David McLean, armed with a pitchfork, and told him in English, "I have an important message for the Duke of Hamilton." Hess was then offered tea at McLean's cottage before being taken into custody by the local

152

Home Guard. He may have been on a peace mission, or he may have gone insane. After the war he was tried at Nuremberg and sentenced to life in prison in Berlin, where he committed suicide in 1987, aged ninety-three.

In streets where bombs had fallen and gas or electricity supplies had been cut off, it was impossible for people to cook. Often entire houses had been flattened; and the families were in need of a hot drink and comfort to get over the shock and help them through the next few hours. Guides designed outdoor cooking fires that they could assemble on bomb-sites or in the streets. On Merseyside, members of the 3rd Wallasey North Company found that their school was closed because of unexploded bombs, so they went along to the rest centre to see if they could be useful. Finding that there were only three small oil stoves to cook for over a hundred people, they returned to their Guide hall, fetched their camp equipment and built an outdoor kitchen, using wood from bombed houses. For the next week Guides cooked dinner and tea every day for everyone in the rest centre, entirely on their own.

A government committee was set up to discuss how to provide hot food for people who had been bombed out of their homes, but the elaborate boilers and stoves that were available took forty-eight hours to erect. At last the chairman turned to the only Guide present. "What equipment would you need?" he asked. Without hesitation she replied, "Twenty-four bricks and two door scrapers." So in early 1941 a team of Guides was sent around the country to demonstrate cooking methods to the Women's Voluntary Service. Stoves built of mud, which could be used at night without creating a glow, caused a great stir. There was no messing about in an outdoor kitchen. Everything had to be just as spick and span as in the tidiest house. Washing-up water was heated in bins using sawdust as fuel.

In Denbigh, North Wales, Rangers fitted up an emergency mobile canteen staffed by Guides. It was a converted horsebox, with just enough room for the helpers to sleep inside. The big, lumbering vehicle, painted Guide blue, travelled to Coventry and then to Manchester after major air raids. Next, it went to Chingford in Essex to feed Scouts who were demolishing buildings damaged by bombs. The Guides also sewed on buttons, mended socks, helped to write letters home and treated small ailments as well as selling hot drinks and comforts. One Yorkshireman who enjoyed the services of the canteen was heard to say, "They be'nt Girl Guides, they be mothers to us." Later the team stayed for several weeks in the Chislehurst Caves in Kent, where thousands of Londoners escaped the raids each night. A cup of tea from the canteen early each morning helped them trek back to their work.

In recognition of the new conditions, the Homemaker's Badge for Guides was revised in 1941, but still included: "Clean flues, and black lead kitchen range or stove. Mend household linen by hand. Keeping dustbin sanitary, usually emptied two or three times a week." However, there were additions, such as "Demonstrate use of telephone: 1. Don't keep saying 'hello'. 2. Speak plainly — it is not necessary to shout."

154

As the war went on, the working day grew longer for everyone, with more and more being demanded of both adults and children. Mothers had to work in factories, and Guides found that they had to take on responsibilities that before the war they would never have expected. "For years we have moaned that Guiding has become over organised," wrote Rose Kerr, "complicated, that there are too many rules. Now the organisation is in abeyance, the rules are suspended. Now is the time for the individual Guide to show what is in her. We know of such a Mary or Betty or Joan, who has helped to keep people cheerful in a shipwreck, in a shelter, in a bombed school. For each deed that is heard of, there are hundreds that never come to light, because they are taken as a matter of course by Guides." In the second year of the war, over 1,500 new Guide companies were started in Britain.

Julie Ashworth was a Guide in Cheltenham, working towards her War Service Badge at a YWCA hostel where servicemen and women went for meals. "We went up and tackled loads of washing up which was piled into a huge greasy tin sink in the basement. Several bombs were dropped around the railway area and one on the coach station. Rest-centres were opened in the church halls where we tried to make the people who had lost their homes comfortable, and served them breakfasts. Despite all this, I never completed my ninety-six hours!"

Guides could also obtain the badge by volunteering at farms, market gardens, nurseries or clothing factories. A Nottingham Guide offered her services to the local hospital. "They sent me to the men's wards. The sister asked me to give all the men a bottle. Our hot water bottles were made of stone, and I thought these were the same. But they didn't hold any water. This surprised me. After about five minutes the men called out, 'I've done with my bottle, duck.' I said to the nurse, 'The men are all warm now, they want me to collect their bottles already.'" The Nursing Badge was a practical one, even if one Guide, Irene Makin of the 1st Swanage, failed it because she did not know the answer to "What is a laxative?"

The Blitz finally ended on 11 May 1941, when Hitler called off the attacks in order to move his bombers eastwards in preparation for Operation Barbarossa — Germany's invasion of the Soviet Union. But the war was far from over.

CHAPTER EIGHT

Dampers and Doodlebugs

Three Girl Guides, three Girl Guides
See how they camp, see how they camp
They pitch their tent and hoist their flag
And think no tirade to work a fag
In fact they think it a glorious rag
Those three Girl Guides.

This was a popular round among Girl Guides, sung to the tune of "Three Blind Mice" as they sat around campfires.

Ever since Agnes Baden-Powell wrote *How Girls Can Help Build Up the Empire* in 1912, in collaboration with her brother, camping had formed a key component of Guiding. For many Guides it was an important part of their development as young women: it helped them to forge a relationship with the countryside and taught them how to cope under strain and to acquire skills such as lighting a campfire, building a den, hosting meals and inventing games.

157

The annual camp had always been a special treat for Guides, particularly for those who lived in cities and rarely had holidays or the chance to visit the countryside. Camping gave poor Guides a holiday with no cares other than keeping the campfire going. Better-off Guides had an opportunity to live independently from their mothers and servants. Digging latrines and washing up in buckets added to the fun of burned potatoes, smoky porridge and wasps. "Leaking groundsheets, whispering through the dark, stumbling through wet grass to the latrine — all added to the wonder of camping," said Lucy Worthing, a Guide in 1942. Baden-Powell believed that "A good camper does not rough it, he smoothes it." Camping did not need to be uncomfortable; it was up to the Scout or Guide to improvise.

Once World War II began, camping in the countryside, one of the great joys of Guiding, became very difficult. The blackout forbade the use of any light from dusk to dawn, which meant no torches in tents, no campfires, not even that last hot drink before creeping into a sleeping bag. Tents in fields could attract enemy planes looking for military objectives. There wasn't even much in the way of camping equipment any more — most of it had either been destroyed in the Blitz or been requisitioned by the army. By November 1940 many campsites had been commandeered by the military, but somehow most Guide companies still managed to go camping. They camped in back gardens, or on vicarage lawns; they camped in disused brickfields and gravel pits; they camped anywhere that was near home and well camouflaged from above. What mattered was the spirit of the camp, cooking out of doors and learning how to pitch and strike a tent in the dark. Stalking, tracking and signalling could be done just as well a mile or so from home as on the other side of the country. Trenches that were not just latrines had to be dug in case of air raids. "It is surprising how many quite large Guides can squeeze into the bottom of a slit trench when something unpleasant is zooming overhead!" wrote Miss Christian.

Two-thirds of the Guiders who had been qualified to take camps had now been called up or were too busy with war work. Remaining Guides decided to arrange their own, and in July 1941 headquarters announced that Patrol Leaders could earn camp permits which would allow them to take six other Guides camping. A new rule said that company camps were allowed to include up to 25 per cent of evacuee girls who were not yet Guides.

The cost for a week's camp was twelve shillings and sixpence, and before a girl left home a "Permission Form for Guide Camp" had to be signed by her parent or guardian to give consent, or not, for bathing. Preparations for camping included tying up bundles of tent poles with strips of car inner tube, putting the camp clock in a tin and making bags for underclothes out of the sleeves of old plastic macs. Lucky Guides travelled to camp sitting on their rucksacks and blankets in the back of a van with the tail lifted up and the back open, singing songs such as "She'll be coming round the mountain" with gusto.

"Is any day more thrilling than the one when we go to camp?" wrote the 1st Chorlton-cum-Hardy Guides near Manchester. "It is certainly an extremely busy one. When we arrived there was great excitement and busy time unpacking kit. We had tea and then put our store tent up." Clothes pegs were used to hang ties and berets from the tent poles. If the weather was cold, Guides tied an extra scarf round their waist to keep their chilly spots warm.

"We didn't actually go very far," said Alma Camps, a Guide from Lancashire. "Petrol was rationed. All our equipment was piled into the back of a lorry. In full uniform, we scrambled on top of the equipment, and off we went." They stayed in the grounds of Crawshaw Hall in Rawtenstall, about twelve miles from both Manchester and Liverpool. "At night we heard bombing. If you were lucky enough to have a torch, you daren't switch it on, in case anyone flying overhead could see the light. It was very frightening."

When travel by motor vehicle became both too dangerous and, with petrol rationing, extremely difficult, most Guides camped near home, travelling by "Shank's pony" — on foot, pulling their equipment on trek carts. In 1943 the 5th East Oxford Guides raised £22 to buy a new trek cart by collecting and selling jam jars and newspapers. As well as using it for camping, they rented it out by the hour.

From 1938 to 1943 the 5th North Oxford Girl Guide Company camped in the grounds of Blenheim

Palace. "I learnt to cut turf, lay and light a fire and cook on it," wrote one Guide.

Afterwards all traces of a fire had to be removed, the turf replaced and watered. Our Captain, Miss Kathleen Alden, was very strict: she could reduce us to jelly, hence her nickname, Jelly. Uniform had to be immaculate and shoes absolutely gleaming. In our pockets we had to have two pennies for the telephone, a clean hankie, paper and pencil and a safety pin. Each patrol had a special wooden box with a padlock holding rope, pencils, paper, bandages, slings, dry kindling, compass, scissors, knife, map etc., and a patrol flag attached to a patrol stick. Mapping was very important when all the signposts had been removed. We did a great deal of tracking, laying the trail with sticks and stones.

An enormous number of gadgets were made from wood which we cut and lashed together. We made tables, shoe racks, clothes hooks for the tent pole, stands for pots; you name it, we made it. Pillows were our kit bags. We took turns as the wood, water, mess or cook patrol. During the winter we hemmed squares of butter muslin in assorted sizes, sewing on china beads at intervals. These were to cover food and jugs of milk in camp. Food was cooked in huge metal dixies which quickly became blackened by smoke. Before striking camp, these had to be cleaned to their original gleaming state, very hard work with a little hot water, some wood ash and wire wool. Our fingers were often raw by the time we had finished.

Mary Yates lived not far from Alton in Staffordshire. "The army had taken over Alton Towers, a large stately home near where I lived, as an officer cadet training camp. We used to go there on Friday from school with a tent and camp for the weekend, spending all the daylight hours picking rose hips." The price paid for Vitamin C-rich rose-hips went up from tuppence to 3d a pound, and a company could pick up to fifty pounds in a day, making twelve shillings and sixpence. "Our Guide Captain could not come with us, but no one seemed to worry. The army kept an eye on us and gave us extra things to eat. They helped load our heavy sacks onto lorries to be taken off to be made into rose-hip syrup for children."

Over the New Year of 1944, the 5th East Oxford camped in the Guide cottage in Wytham Woods. "The cottage was not the warmest place to spend a weekend but we loved it," they reported. "It was very cold going to the latrine shed. The big room has a huge chimney; we could see the sky at the top." They filled the shed with firewood and wood for making gadgets from the coppiced hazels. "My mother made us banana sandwiches. It was years before I discovered that those wartime banana sandwiches were made with parsnips." In January, the cottage was surrounded by carpets of snowdrops, and later in the spring there were masses of bluebells. The Oxford Guides picked them and sent them by train to families in London whose houses had been bombed.

The 1st Chorlton-cum-Hardy Company of Manchester camped near Windermere in the grounds of Mrs Hellis, alias Beatrix Potter, who also contributed £10 towards the cost of hiring tents for them. "The camp was at the end of Troutbeck Valley, with hills all round and the river flowing nearby," one of the Guides recorded in the log book. "On Sunday it was very wet, but it cleared up a little during the afternoon. At night, we had a sing song round the fire, we made dampers. While we were having supper the moon rose over the hill. As usual the beds seemed very hard the first night. I woke up after our first night with my entire body outside the tent — we had slid down the hill and only my head, anchored by my chin, remained under canvas!" Sitting cross-legged on their rugs, Guides sang patriotic songs such as "There'll Always be an England".

"We always camped in damp fields," remembers Celia Ward. "We went by lorry with enormous tents, it was all of about four miles away. We got up early and cooked breakfast — scrambled eggs with ash in. We made washing up bowl stands that always collapsed. We made a raft out of tin petrol cans and went down the river. It was so wobbly that we didn't risk going down twice."

"We camped at Sevenoaks in Kent which was real country to London children like us," said Eileen Mitchell, leader of the Thrush patrol. "We slept in ex-army bell tents, six of us on straw palliasses, feet to the pole and in the morning had to rush out with our hats on, to salute the flag, and renew our promise: 'I promise on my honour to do my best to do my duty to God and the King, to help other people at all times and to obey the Guide law.' "

Although Guides may have shared bedrooms with their sisters at home, unless they attended boarding school, sharing a tent with up to six other girls was a novel experience for them. Some found it a damp and depressing one. Many were not used to queuing up for latrines, washing with metal bowls of lukewarm water, or eating burned sausages. They also had to cope with countryside hazards such as cows, sheep and rain. "First the cows got into the field and knocked down the tents. Then it poured with rain most days. Then while blowing the fire, I knelt on a wasp and was stung on my knee. It swelled up and Captain rubbed honey on it." Guides also had to deal with mosquitoes, for which there was no repellent: sleeping between scratchy blankets was excruciating with legs covered in festering bites. Many girls suffered from homesickness: there was usually at least one Guide in each tent who cried all night, keeping everyone else awake.

Camp kit list included a blanket, which was folded into a sleeping bag, a canvas pail, signalling flags, soap in a box, an enamel mug, two tin plates, rubber shoes and a prayer book. Each patrol had to bring an electric torch, a mirror, a billycan and kit for cleaning belts, badges and shoes so that their uniforms could be in tip-top condition at all times. When clothes rationing began in June 1941, replacing uniforms became even more difficult than before: eleven clothing coupons were required for a Guide dress, one for a Guide tie, two for stockings, and two for Brownie knickers. Captains and Brown Owls could only obtain extra coupons for their uniforms by applying to the Board of Trade.

"We had no mattresses, but it didn't matter," remembers one former Guide. "One morning I got up bright and early and made tea on the campfire for Captain. I took her a cup in her tent. Beside her was Brown Owl: they looked very cosy. All I thought was, 'Brown Owl is so short and fat, and Captain is so tall and thin, it's amazing that they both fit into one sleeping bag.'"

Uniform was always worn at camp, including either a straw hat or a navy blue felt one. Guides also took "One change of underclothes, warm pyjamas, two pairs stockings, jersey or blazer (blue if possible) and apron." "You couldn't buy anything rubber," said Alma Camps, "because rubber was needed for the war effort. So, if you hadn't got any Wellingtons, you had to take a pair of plimsolls. It rained most of the week, so my feet were wet the whole time."

Each patrol took turns to do the various jobs that ensured the smooth running of the camp — wood collecting, cooking, and latrine duties. The first job on arrival was digging the trench for the latrines. "Captain had arranged the building of the lats," remembered Eileen Mitchell from Sevenoaks. "This was a canvas arrangement over a trench with a large twig hanging over the side. You sat on a normal lav seat poised over the trench. There was a pile of earth and a trowel beside you and a card pinned to the canvas which read:

Fill in the earth till that's all you see.
Cover the seat for dry it should be.
Pull up the danger flag [the twig] over the door,
And Captain won't ask you to do any more."

Preparing and cooking food was the main task of the camp. With food hard to come by after rationing was introduced in 1940, the girls had to bring their own jam, butter and eggs, as well as their ration books. Guides always cooked on a wood fire, after sods had been cut from the turf and laid carefully to one side. Girls who had taken the Pioneer Badge knew all about starting fires with a "fuzz stick" and "punk" — dry gorse, holly or moss kindling carried in every well-prepared Guide's pocket. They constructed kitchens by lashing together sticks and string for washing-up bowl stands, and racks for pans. "There is nothing quite so good as smoky porridge cooked over a wood fire to start the camp day," recalled Eileen Mitchell. In the summer of 1940 there was still enough food for the camp menu of the 2nd Witney Guide Company to read:

Breakfast: porridge, bacon, prunes, cereal and kippers and herrings, fried bread, bread and butter.
Dinner: beef stew, boiled cod, liver and bacon, roast leg of lamb, cold lamb.
Tea: bread and butter and cake.

166

High tea: macaroni cheese, sausages, pasties.
Supper: cocoa and biscuits.

By the end of that year, things had changed. Manual workers were allowed a daily allowance of 3,900 calories, but adults and teenagers received only 2,600 calories a day. The weekly allowance included one hundred grams of bacon or ham a week, fifty grams each of butter, tea, jam and sweets, two pints of milk and one egg. Guide leaders found it increasingly difficult to feed growing girls for a whole week. Foods such as semolina, dried peas and sausages canned in brine were available with coupons. Fresh eggs and sweets were in very short supply. Most fruit went to make jam for the army. Soon there were fewer fried eggs and many more tins of corned beef and Spam.

"We had to take our food with us in a brown paper bag — our sugar ration, cereals and jam," remembered Alma Camps. "We also took our bread ration cards, so that they could buy bread for us throughout the week." "Mock sausages" were made from shredded cabbage, potatoes and wild fennel seeds, patted into sausage shapes and fried in lard. Beetroots and cornflour made a tasty crimson pudding which didn't need much sugar.

Guides also learned how to cook a hike meal without utensils, delicious treats such as fish in brown paper or a broiler chicken cooked with chocolate. For those who didn't already know, *The Guide* also gave instructions on "How to Make a Damper".

Dough can be cooked in various ways out of doors to provide a simple, satisfying, yet quick meal. A simple dough "cake" is the Damper. As you would expect, it is merely a ribbon of thick dough wound round a stick.

Take a couple of handfuls of flour, a pinch of salt, and two pinches of baking powder. Mix these ingredients well together, preferably with a clean stick rather than young hands. Add water gradually, stirring all the time, until the mixture is smooth and like thick cream in firmness. Let the mixture stand whilst you make the other preparations.

The stick should be of some sweet wood, such as birch, in length about two feet and in thickness about two inches. It should first be peeled and then heated well over the embers of your small cooking fire. Knead the dough with clean hands until it is stretchy like clay. Then pull it into long thin strips like worms, and wrap around the stick. The stick should act as a spindle as it rests in forked uprights, and should be turned constantly so that the dough cooks evenly and does not burn. When cooked, the spiral cake should slip easily off the stick.

Baden-Powell believed that a bowl was unnecessary — the ingredients for dampers could just as well be mixed in trouser pockets. What these instructions fail to mention is that in order to eat a damper, it is imperative not to have eaten any food at all for some time.

Extreme hunger is the only state in which dampers can be consumed. They also require large quantities of good jam, and strong teeth.

When whale meat was almost the only protein available, this song grew popular at camps:

There's a hole in the bottom of the sea
There's a whale in the hole
There's a tail on the whale in the hole
There's a bone in the tale on the whale in the hole
There's a nerve in the bone in the tale on the
　　whale in the hole in the bottom of the sea.

Severe food shortages forced Guides to develop skills that weren't part of their badge requirements. Many became successful rabbit trappers, breaking the animals' necks before skinning and cooking them. Squabs, or young pigeons, taken from nests were excellent roasted on a spit over a fire, washed down with sugary tea in enamel mugs. And however scarce food was, midnight feasts remained an important feature of all Guide camps. "We were always 'prepared'," said Eileen Mitchell. "We had midnight feasts in our tent and everybody brought something disgusting to eat. I took a tin of condensed milk, someone else took a tin of sardines. It was a right old mix, but though we all felt a bit sick, it was the done thing."

"The greatest excitement was being awake at night," said Lucy Worthing. "It was worth damp, cold nights in tents without groundsheets, to whisper through the dark and eat sweets hidden in rolledup knickers."

169

On Sundays at camp, Guides either attended the nearest church or an outdoor camp service taken by the local vicar. "On Sunday evening we went to church next to the farm and the congregation was only seven people beside ourselves," recorded the 4th Wood Green Company. "We managed to follow the service although it was Church of England and we were Baptists." When the Oxford Guides prepared for the local priest's visit, they made an altar out of vegetable boxes containing lettuces. "The visiting minister noticed this and we were all hard put to keep straight faces as he intoned 'Let us pray.'"

Girl Guides had their pin-ups, but they weren't always film stars. Maisie Norris was in the East Malling Guide Company, Kent. "I was in the Lily of the Valley patrol and during the summer holidays we had a summer camp in Clear Park. It was a day camp: we weren't allowed to camp overnight because of the bombs. We knew that Guy Gibson lived in Clear House with his wife."

Squadron Leader Guy Gibson was one of Britain's most celebrated war heroes. He had joined the RAF at eighteen, and by the outbreak of World War II he was a bomber pilot. After promotion to Wing Commander, he led 172 sorties in under a year, including the Dambusters raid in the Ruhr Valley in May 1943, where he drew the enemy fire to allow the destruction of two major dams. On his return he was awarded the Victoria Cross. After a lecture tour of the USA he successfully pestered Bomber Command to be allowed to return to operational duties in 1944, and was based at nearby West Malling airfield.

"The tap was opposite his house," remembered Maisie Norris, "so I was a very enthusiastic water gatherer. One day I asked him for his autograph and I got it. He was awfully nice to have taken an interest in a twelve-year-old Girl Guide. He drove a little sports car in his uniform. One time some of the girls got a lift in his car. We all admired him for his Dambusters raid, everybody knew about that."

Guy Gibson was killed only months later, in September 1944, when his de Havilland Mosquito crashed while he was returning from a bombing raid on the Netherlands.

For many Guides, summer camp was the first time they had ever seen the sea. At the first sight of it they often sang:

> We're riding along on the crest of a wave
> And the sun is in the sky.
> Keeping our eyes on the distant horizon
> Looking out for passers by.
> We'll do the hailing
> While other boats are round us sailing.
> We're rolling along on the crest of a wave
> And the world is ours.

Those who could swim would plunge into the waves in their knitted woollen swimming costumes. Those who couldn't remained in uniform on the beach playing

171

French cricket, or hoisted the union flag on a branch of driftwood. "We had a ripping time," wrote Ruby Baxter of the Croydon Girl Guides about camping in Kent. "One of the jolliest features of seaside camp life was going off for a run along the sands. We only wished the days were longer. The weather did not behave itself too badly, the sun paying us quite a lot of visits to make up for the time the rain also called. The Brownies took their part by helping peel potatoes and cleaning boots." But when invasion by the Germans looked imminent, the beaches of the south coast became out of bounds and were fenced off with barbed wire.

The 1st Woodside St Andrew's company from Luton went on camp at Cudham, near Sevenoaks in Kent, for the last week in August 1940. The company, travelling by lorry, was held up on the way by an air raid. Joan Wells, one of the trainee Guiders, had set off by bicycle, but when she heard the air-raid siren she sensibly took shelter in a hedge.

After arriving at the camp, just two miles from Biggin Hill aerodrome, they set up. "We were preparing lunch when one of the Guides heard the siren," they wrote in their log book. "As no one else heard it, we were carrying on when Muriel ran across the field with the same news. There were no aeroplanes up but our discussion was broken by a German plane which dived out of the sky." They all jumped into the shelter, where for nearly three hours they sang, getting louder when bombs fell nearby. "When they fell in the field the blast blew us into a huddle. The teapots and kettles were thrown on the floor and the butter, sugar and salt was

172

mixed together." That night they kept two-hour watch. "It was rather distracting to hear the planes and time-bombs and the telephone was out of action so that we did not know whether the Guides' parents were worrying." A month later the campsite was commandeered by the RAF.

County Commissioner Lady Evelyn Mason, of Eynsham Hall near Witney, encouraged Oxfordshire companies to camp in her park. After Pearl Harbor this meant sharing the site with the American Army. The 5th East Oxford Company found that the American soldiers would tease them by demanding to inspect their gas masks and identity cards before allowing them through the gate for a day out.

"Dear Captain," wrote a North Lewisham Guide while camping near East Grinstead in August 1942.

One wet evening we went out for what Miss Edginton called a ramble. We walked along tarred roads in a crocodile. We got wet through but were lovely and warm. Today it has not rained at all yet. I am hoping to pass my fire-lighting. There are plenty of wasps about.

We had just gone round the site when the rain simply fell — a cloudburst and soon the tents were flooding. The site was on a slope in clay soil, so the rain rushed down in streams. We ran round telling the Guides to stand up and to put on any dry clothing over their pyjamas and hold their dry bedding clear of the water on the floor of the tents.

173

Once everything had dried out, they set off to buy provisions in East Grinstead.

We arrived just before closing time. At Sainsbury's we did very well and bought 3lb of Spam and became quite friendly with the assistant who lent us scissors to cut out the coupons from twelve separate [ration] books — four per book. We walked down the street to find a newspaper, but there seemed to be a shortage of news in East Grinstead and our paper search was unlucky.

Each patrol was given its own tent identity — we were Germany and I did a dazzling impression of Hitler, "Plooking out ze enemies' fongernoils". This involved capturing the enemy and bringing her back to our tent — pinning her down and trying to pull her fingernails out — not really of course, all in jest and with much giggling. This was usually during the hour after lunch set aside for napping. "Quiet, Girls!" said the Captain from her tent.

Camping in the rain was always tough, as Christine Hinkley of the 4th Ruislip Guide Company discovered when they went to Ault Hucknall in Derbyshire. "We went by steam train with our bedding rolls and equipment all laid out on the platform ready. We had great difficulty in getting dry wood for our fires. I learned that fires had to be kept going if we needed to cook, and that water had to be fetched by bucketful after bucketful. We taught our patrol to keep warm with blankets, lots of kilt pins and a ground sheet." Fun and frolics were the order of the day, or night: "About the middle of the week the Guides bought some tarts," reported the 4th Wood Green Company in the log book. "They put some mustard in their middles and on the pretence that they wanted to take the Rangers' photo eating them, made the poor dears devour them. You should have seen their faces after they'd taken a bite! It was a treat! But the next night the Rangers sewed up the Guides' pyjamas so they had their revenge."

In some companies, new Guides had to endure camp initiation. They would be blindfolded and led through a terrifying obstacle course of worms in their faces (spaghetti), swamp (mashed potatoes), dangling skeletons (rolled-up newspaper) and spiders down their clothes (tomato tops).

Camp games included tapping Morse messages at one end of a fallen tree trunk, which could be heard by Guides lying down at the other. Throwing a Guide in the air with a blanket was also popular, especially if it was her birthday. "We played Cat and Mouse, Hunt the Thimble, and an adding game," said one Guide. "You had to add things up correctly, as practice for the Invasion."

With the fear of German invasion, there were many games involving spies and fifth columnists. In one, the Guides ran through the woods in the dark, trying to track down the "enemy", their Patrol Leader. Once caught, her "secret" — which might be a stone or a key

— had to be found, wherever it was hidden in her clothes.

One Surrey company arrived at their campsite in 1944 to find a "strange and menacing object" sitting in the field. A Patrol Leader ventured, "I think it's a dead Doodlebug, Captain." "I hope it's *very* dead," Captain remarked. With long poles they levered the twisted mass of hot wreckage into a nearby ditch and set up their camp. The patch where it had burnt itself out just hours before was ideal for their campfire.

Although Girl Guides were supposed to be "pure in mind and body", they were also teenagers full of hormones; Scout camps anywhere near Guide companies were a source of much romantic intrigue and excitement. Lucy Worthing's Guide company was not far from a woodland campsite in Norfolk that was used by Scouts. "My friends and I used to raid the Scout camps after dark, when they were sitting round the campfire. We'd put on trousers, creep through the bushes up to the camp and let down their guy lines. Then the Scouts would leap up and chase us, and we would dash through the nearest stinging-nettle bed, knowing they were in shorts. It was an odd form of flirting, but we'd soon be singing round the campfire with them. The lucky Guides might get a Scout's arm round their shoulder, or even a kiss."

Mary Pick first fell in love at Guide camp.

Captain was just divine. Her uniform was always perfect, her badge shiny, every stroke of her soft

176

wavy hair in place. She could do no wrong. There was a husband somewhere in the RAF, but I knew that he did not appreciate her the way I did. Only I could see how her delicate fingers understood every twist of a knot; how her long legs could run to catch the ball at rounders; how her pert bosom rose and fell beneath the pockets of her uniform when she sang the World Song or lifted her arm to salute. Every day I did a Good Turn in the hope that Captain would approve. The evening before weekly meeting, I polished my belt and my badge, my shoes until they almost disappeared. She always seemed to show me extra concern over my attempts to gain badges. I was convinced that everyone else in the pack noticed our special relationship. But maybe they were all in love with her too? I never loved anyone the way I loved Captain. I married a man and had four sons.

In June 1943, Barbara Henley was a fifteen-year-old Patrol Leader in Halifax, Yorkshire. "The boys' grammar school Scouts decided that they would like some co-operation between Scouts and Guides," she remembered, "so they invited us to a joint campfire. It had rained all day, but it cleared up in the evening. The Scout Senior Patrol Leader was desperately trying to light the fire but all the wood was wet and even the matches were damp and refused to strike." Luckily for the Guides and Scouts all waiting for their supper, Barbara had come prepared. "I took a small tin from my uniform pocket. In it were matches I had prepared earlier with their heads pushed into wax. They were completely dry, I handed them to the desperate Scout. They struck immediately and a fire was soon alight." Barbara was delighted when she discovered that the seventeen-year-old Scout was called Ron Fawkes, a descendant of the famous Guy. "This was my first taste of co-operation between Scouts and Guides. But a match had been struck and a fire kindled."

Ron was conscripted into the navy for the next three years, and then trained as an architect. Meanwhile, Barbara did a degree in biology. They married in 1952. Since then the Fawkeses have produced five children and twelve grandchildren. They have also kept their ties with the Scouts and the Guides. "We have both served as unit leaders, commissioners, advisers, trainers and tutors. Now, out of uniform, we are each active vice-presidents of our Guide and Scout counties. Thank you Guiding and Scouting for all the fun those dry matches brought us."

Peggy of the 4th Wood Green Company wrote her own account of "Why I like camp":

The first day with the joy of stuffing palliasses with straw which shows a contrary desire to poke out of the corners and leave a trail all over the floor.

The weird experience of sleeping on the ground with a faint gleam of the moonlight through the cracks in the tent.

The morning when the flag collapsed instead of flying bravely in the wind and we had to stifle an insane desire to giggle as we went on with prayers.

The evening when a group of Rangers suddenly started dancing a country dance to no known or recognisable tune — as an outlet for the sheer joy of living.

The night when I left the campfire and looking back caught the flicker and glow of the flame lighting up the circle of Guides sitting round and making all the rest of the world look darker. Mingling with the trees came the realisation that campfire time summed up all camp. I hope that the vitality of camp week can radiate us through the other fifty-one weeks of the year.

"There is nothing like chopping a hefty log to relieve one's feelings," said Pat of Wood Green. But her favourite time was campfire. "Where else could one find the equal to a fire out of doors, surrounded by Guides? All feeling they've had a good day, and glad now just to enjoy one another's company; spending an hour singing old favourite rhymes and songs, learning new ones, telling jokes and yarns, some jolly, others sad. And to finish the glorious day with Taps. When even the jolliest is hushed, capturing some of the wonder and peace from the surroundings. The quiet night, with nothing living stirring but themselves; with only their voices and when they finish — the echo."

When the 2nd Witney Guides camped at Eynsham Hall, they chatted in bed before "Taps", always sung last thing at night from their tents. "It sounded very nice in the still of the evening to us Guiders standing outside," wrote their Captain, "and made us realise more than ever how near God is to us all. That night an alert sounded and I dressed partly and put on my coat and rested on the bed just in case the girls had to be called but this camp slept on peacefully. It is a tremendous responsibility to take Guides to camp anytime but in wartime it can be awesome."

Day is done.
Gone the sun
From the sea
From the hills
From the sky
All is well
Safely rest.
God is nigh.

CHAPTER
NINE

Brownies in China

Just as Guides adapted to wartime conditions in Britain, they carried on as best they could wherever they were in the world. China was no exception. Guiding began in Shanghai in 1913, and within a few years there were many Brownie packs and Guide companies, both for Chinese girls and the daughters of European missionaries, diplomats and business people. In 1937 the Japanese army invaded the east coast of the country, and while the international compounds in Shanghai and Peking were left to their own devices, Japan "ate China", Churchill said, "like an artichoke, leaf by leaf". But not even the Japanese could stop the 1st Chefoo Brownies at Chefoo school.

Overlooking a sheltered bay in Shantung province, north-east China, opposite Korea, Chefoo school was founded in 1881 by Christian missionaries, and built with home-made bricks and wood from shipwrecks. The establishment of Chefoo meant that the children did not have to go to Britain for their education, and even though most boarded, they at least saw their parents once a year. By the 1930s there were 350 pupils boarding at the school, aged between seven and eighteen. Three-quarters of the pupils were the children of Christian missionaries working in western China, the rest were the children of British businessmen or civil servants. The Classics master, Gordon Martin, described the teachers as "disciplined by a life of faith, a staff somewhat Spartan, somewhat lacking in wide-world outlook or readiness for new things or ideas, but experienced in God's ways and committed to His direction".

The children of Chefoo school lived a carefree life by a beautiful beach, where the air was free from malaria and other tropical diseases. They enjoyed swimming, rowing, playing tennis and hockey; and a high standard of education based on the British curriculum, finished off with Oxford Matriculation examinations. The worst that could happen was a caning, the normal punishment for breaking school rules, or a toothbrush dipped in Lifebuoy soap for bad language. But once the teachers saw the brutality of the Japanese soldiers to the Chinese, the children noticed that the cane disappeared and the soap was rarely used.

When war in Europe broke out in September 1939, some British people in China decided that it was too dangerous to travel home by boat and impossible to do so by train through the Soviet Union; most, however, believed that the war would soon be over. The missionaries had plenty of experience of political troubles in the region: the Boxer uprising of 1899; the fall of the Qing dynasty in 1911; the Anti-Foreign movement of 1927; and since 1937, the war between

China and Japan. But Chefoo school had long been a safe haven for their children.

There had been Guides at Chefoo since 1937. Led by the art mistress, Inez Phare, a tall, regal and inspiring woman, by 1940 there were forty-eight Guides and about sixteen Rangers. Gordon Martin taught them astronomy and boating, and his wife taught baby care. Guides was so popular that there was a waiting list. Miss Elizabeth Rice, the teacher in charge of the girls' section of the school, said, "We must remember that we are a Girls' School running a Guide company, not a Guide company running a Girls' School."

"We started a knitting craze in the Chefoo Guides," remembered Estelle Cliff, the daughter of missionary pharmacists who worked in the interior of China, who was eleven at the outbreak of war. "There were very few ready-made clothes in those days — most were handmade. So we were given khaki wool and, for our Knitting Badge, we learned to knit gloves and socks for the British army during the Battle of Britain. Our reward for our first completed garment was a brass Spitfire pin."

The 1st Chefoo Brownies met once a week in "Foxglove Glade", a corner of the school grounds. Only two days after Baden-Powell died in Kenya in January 1941, they held a memorial service for him. Brown Owl wrote in the log book: "He invented us!" She noted that a chart of grins was kept by each Six. "The Grin charts are a record of when we smile, and when we are tempted to do the other thing," she wrote on thick, blue, sugar paper.

For some time the war in Europe had little impact on Europeans in China. On 29 September 1941 some new girls arrived from western China without their parents and joined the Brownies. But when the United States declared war on Japan after the attack on Pearl Harbor on 7 December, the lives of the children of Chefoo school and their teachers were to change dramatically. Japanese forces immediately took control of all international assets in China, and rounded up all Europeans except for Germans. As the Japanese soldiers entered the school, Gordon Martin said softly to his Latin class, "So, here are our new rulers." Shinto priests performed a rite, after which everything in the school, from tables to soap dishes, belonged to the Emperor of Japan. The Chinese servants were told to leave, and their work was given to the children.

The Japanese soldiers wore khaki uniforms and highly polished knee-high boots, and carried bayonets or swords. "They were quite short and sinewy with sallow skin," wrote Fred Harris, one of the pupils. "Always at hand was a fierce rifle with fixed bayonet. Spectacles and gold-filled teeth shone when they smiled." A plane dropped leaflets in Chinese explaining "The New Order in East Asia": "The Japanese Army is an army of strict discipline, protecting good citizens. Members of the community must live together peacefully and happily. Every house must fly a Japanese flag to welcome the Japanese."

Chefoo's headmaster, Patrick Bruce, was arrested and thrown into a freezing prison. "I had started knitting my first man's jumper," remembered Estelle Cliff. "At the time of Pearl Harbor, I had finished the body, but hadn't started the sleeves. I wanted to send Mr Bruce something for Christmas, so I finished it off as a sleeveless jumper, and it was parcelled up and sent to him. Later he was transferred to a Chinese prison, where a businessman died of typhus from infected fleas." Mr Bruce was returned six weeks later, with his head held high, and never mentioned his experience.

Every foreigner in China, including children, had to wear a red cloth armband stamped with his or her name and nationality. The Brownies and Guides of Chefoo embroidered over their stamps in coloured thread. "They were stamped with 'A' for American, and 'B' for British," said Kathleen Strange, a Brownie who had been at Chefoo school since she was seven. "When the teachers and the Japanese weren't looking, the American children turned the 'A' upside down, chalked out the crossbar and proudly wore a 'V'."

Gordon Martin, the Classics master, continued preparing his puppet show for Christmas. "With his puppet dancing from its strings, he went walking about the compound, in and out among the children and the Japanese sentries," wrote Mary Taylor, aged seven at the time. "And the Japanese laughed. The tension among the children eased after that, for who could be truly terrified of a sentry who could laugh at a puppet?" Mary was at the school with her eleven-year-old sister Kathleen, and their brothers Jamie, aged ten, and

Johnny, aged six. The starving Chinese outside often broke into the school looking for food. One night they stole all the girls' overcoats. After that, the women teachers slept with their hockey sticks under their pillows. While many Chefoo children had now left China with their parents, those from missionary families hundreds of miles away in the west of the country, could not leave. There was nothing the parents of those children could do, except pray.

By May 1942, Hong Kong, Singapore, Malaya, and the Philippines had been overrun by the Japanese. Finally the Japanese navy commandeered the school, giving the teachers only days to pack. Each person was allowed to take only a mattress and whatever they could carry. Brown Owl packed Guide and Brownie uniforms. Teachers filled their tin trunks with textbooks, exercise books and past examination papers. Musical instruments were hidden inside mattresses.

The entire school, every member of staff and all the children, were marched off to the Temple Hill section of Chefoo city. "We were a long, snaking line of children, teachers, and retired missionaries marching along the road by the ocean to the prison camp. Our Chinese friends wept as we marched away," remembered Mary Taylor. "As 'enemy aliens' we were now prisoners of war."

The Japanese had summoned crowds of Chinese citizens to ridicule, spit and curse at the pale-faced Europeans, but they just stood open-mouthed as the procession of children marched past pushing handcarts, pulling rickshaws and carrying as much as they could on their backs. They all sang, in strong clear voices, Psalm 46, "God is our refuge, our refuge and our strength. In trouble, in trouble, a very present help . . ."

They were taken to a compound of missionaries' houses, now commandeered as an internment camp. Seventy of the younger children were packed into one family house, the fifty-two boy pupils and two teachers' families into another, while a third house held the families of interned European businessmen who believed the war would be over in a few months, and had brought only packs of cards, tennis racquets and bottles of gin. The thirty-three Chefoo schoolgirls, aged ten to sixteen, their teachers and some nurses lived in a four-bedroom house, sleeping on mattresses on the floor of the loft.

One of the teachers was twenty-five-year-old Evelyn Davey, who had arrived from Liverpool in October 1940. "I thought God wanted me in China," she remembered. "My family told me not to go, they said I was too young. But I wanted to go out and teach for a year. I had been teaching in nursery and primary schools in Liverpool. It took me three weeks to get to China through German U-boats across the Atlantic, then train across Canada and another boat to China." Evelyn had been a Brownie in Liverpool, so she suggested starting an additional Brownie pack, the 2nd Chefoo Brownies. "I loved the toadstool in the centre, dancing round it and singing, and I had been a Girl Guide. I wasn't trained as a Brown Owl, but I remembered what we had done as a Brownie myself. I didn't really know what to do — there were no books

— so I just made it up as I went along. The headmistress said I could only do it if I didn't stop. Mostly I was interested in having fun, and the idea of helping other people. We did a Good Turn every day — it was more difficult because the children weren't with their families. They couldn't go home and offer to wash the dishes, but they found helpful things to do every day. They ran errands, getting the food for people who were sick."

Jenny Bevan and her sisters had been at Chefoo school since 1940. She remembers the excitement of becoming a Brownie on 15 December 1942, a month after arriving at Temple Hill. "Our older sisters were already Girl Guides so we knew what to expect. We were all delighted with our uniform of brown dresses and soon learnt to tie our yellow scarves properly and pin the Brownie brooch in the right place, topped with a brown cotton hat. We were all starting out from scratch and the place was ahum with us all learning the promise and motto — in readiness for the grand enrolment. Brown Owl, Miss Davey, was one of our teachers, and had one of the senior girls as Tawny Owl. The Guide Captain and other Brown Owl Miss Inez Phare, of whom we were in great awe, came to the enrolment ceremony to see that all was done properly. I was made Sixer of the Elves and wore my two stripes with pride."

On the same day, Elizabeth Hoyte was enrolled as Sixer of the Kelpies. She kept a neat log book, and wrote up each meeting in pencil; she had not yet learned joined-up writing.

We're the little Scottish Kelpies,
Quick and quiet ready helpers.
A Brownie gives in to the older folk
A Brownie does not give in to herself.

They started each Brownie meeting with the fairy ring, six songs and inspection of hands and uniforms. Then they played games reinforcing the Brownie laws, promise and health rules. Next came badge and test work, such as learning the names of trees and birds. They always finished with a story from Brown Owl, who then awarded points for the creativity and tidiness of their log books.

The emblem of the winning Six was put on the toadstool at the start of the next meeting.

"At Brownies," said Mary Taylor, "we learnt how to tie knots: reef, granny, bowline, round turn-two half hitches. We practised for First-aid — washing a wound, wrapping a figure-eight bandage around a sprained ankle. A pair of us knotted our hands to make a carriage to transport someone who was injured." They learned signalling, semaphore, and Morse code. "We did lots of badges," said Evelyn, "including Toymaker, Writer, Needlewoman, Minstrel, Knitter and Gardener. We just used whatever we could find — sugar paper, string, grass, old sheets. We had taken uniforms with us, but the Brownies soon grew out of them."

Estelle Cliff was twelve in 1941, and already in the Guides. "Overnight we changed from being untouchable neutrals to enemy aliens in occupied territory. My parents were missionaries in inland free China as many were, but subject to Japanese bombing and a shifting front line. Our staff were wonderful surrogate parents, and we became one big extended family." The Guides enjoyed midnight parties with candlelit singing. Now that they were interned, there was no chance of posting the socks and scarves they had been knitting for British soldiers, so they unravelled their work and began on cardigans for themselves.

Food was sent in to Temple Hill by Irish, Italian and German friends. A former servant from the school smuggled two piglets and some chicks over the wall for the children to raise. "For the first few nights, we hid the piglets under the veranda and fed them aspirin to keep them quiet. When the Japanese discovered them, they accepted them rather affectionately as our pets." They wrote iambic quatrains about life in an internment camp:

> Augustus was a pig we had,
> Our garbage he did eat.
> At Christmastime we all felt sad;
> He was our Christmas treat.

Major Kosaka, the camp commandant, was a distant figure in his polished black boots, with a sword hanging at his side. He had a small moustache and round wire spectacles, and had learned English at a Christian mission school in Japan. His guards' Alsatian dogs were trained to kill, and the girls knew it. Miss Marjory Broomhall, one of the teachers, had smuggled a kitten called Victoria Frisky Snowball into the camp. The girls adored it. "She would purr and suck on my finger as if it were a nipple," remembered Mary Taylor. "I wondered whether mothers felt warm and soft like that. Along with the signatures and the fingerprints of all my dorm mates, I had Victoria's paw print." One night, Mary was tucked under her mosquito net when she heard the familiar crunch of gravel outside, the boots of the Japanese guard on night patrol. "Suddenly," she wrote, "below our window, a terrified, yowling shriek ripped the stillness, clashing in a hideous duet with a guttural barking, muffled by the tiny ball of fur between those bloody teeth. My little body froze, and my throat retched on a voiceless scream. I buried my head in terror and stuffed the pillow around my ears. They cleaned the mess by morning — perhaps our teachers, perhaps our older brothers. But we knew. Miss Broomhall, always sensible and very proper, walked a little slower after that."

For the Chefoo school children, Temple Hill internment camp was not much different from pre-war life. They were still living in a compound, protected from China beyond its walls and separated from their parents. They started boarding at seven years old, and most expected to see their families only once a year, either when their parents came to Chefoo for the summer holidays, or when they went to stay with them for Christmas — rarely both. Even when their parents went back to America or Britain, they would leave their children in China so that they did not miss out on school. The teachers were used to looking after them during the holidays, but even so, the children now knew they would not see their parents until the war was over; many of them had no idea if they were even alive. The only way to survive was to develop independence and self-containment, and to learn not to show any feelings.

There had never been Scouts for the boys at Chefoo, but Inez Phare had been a Scoutmaster during World War I. When the boys visited their sisters under escort each week, she secretly trained six of them till they passed the Second Class Scouting tests, which required proficiency in Morse code, nature study, knots, making a fire, covering a mile "at Scout's pace", first-aid and using a telephone. One of the teachers, Stanley Houghton, who had been a Scout twenty years before, organised a Cub pack.

The 1st Chefoo Rangers had been going since 1932, and continued in Temple Hill camp. Their optimism knew no bounds, and they filled an exercise book with uplifting songs to celebrate their tenth anniversary.

> Flowers, flowers, uprising after showers,
> Blossoming fresh and fair — everywhere
> Ah. God has explained why it rained.

And,

> Life ain't all you want,
> But it's all yer 'ave;
> So 'ave it;
> Stick a geranim in yer 'at
> An' be 'appy."

★   ★   ★

"Smile girls, that's the style!" they shouted. But the experiences of the Chefoo schoolchildren in the following years would test even the bravest Brownies' courage, and the high spirits of the jolliest Guides.

CHAPTER
TEN

Thrift and Gift

As soon as hostilities began, British Guides started planning how they could help with the war effort. Older Guides remembered that during World War I, household supplies were very limited, so before the government had even set up its own drive, the Girl Guides launched the "Save All Supplies" scheme in December 1939. Baden-Powell had been careful to explain that being "thrifty" was not the same as being a miser: "A *thrifty* person uses everything to the best advantage and wastes nothing so as to help other people." The Guides' scheme was founded on this belief, and soon Guides everywhere realised that by making *and* saving they could make a difference for their country.

In December's *The Guider* "Save All Supplies" was laid out in great detail, a prime example of the Guide motto, "Be Prepared". The aims of the scheme were to increase supplies by not wasting anything useful, to maximise food supplies by growing more, and to raise money for the fighting forces by collecting and selling things including jam jars, rags, old iron, used postage stamps, broken gramophone records and tins.

During 1939, Lanarkshire Guides collected over £1,000 to pay for a motor ambulance and a mobile field kitchen for Finland. Guiding had been established in Finland since 1912, and Finnish Guides had done their best to defend their country against German invasion by watching from the roofs for air raids or keeping people in air-raid shelters occupied with books, sewing machines and typewriters. Days after the new vehicles arrived, Finland was forced to ally with Germany. For the first time since the First World War, there were Guides on opposite sides in a conflict. "But we knew, and they knew, that Guiding went deeper than politics," wrote Catherine Christian. "They were duty bound to stand by their government's decision but as the curtain dropped between us, we knew it was only a passing separation."

In Hull, Guides knitted 732 garments in three months, and collected 420 pounds of tin foil, plus razor blades, bottles, foreign coins and waste paper. They sent the proceeds — £10.5s — to the Polish and Finnish Guides Fund. They also found three men who they supported with small gifts and cards: a British sailor on HMS *Ganges*, a friendless Polish airman in Wales, and a wounded Belgian soldier they met in Hull hospital.

Paper was in particularly short supply: if a housewife wanted her shopping wrapped, she took paper bags with her, otherwise everything was tipped into her shopping bag, muddy potatoes and all. Collecting paper was a dirty, dusty job; it had to be baled and then sent off to mills. The Ambleside Guides in north-west

England collected fourteen tons of paper in less than four months. In Oxford, a Guide reported: "Daddy worked on the *Oxford Mail*, I thought it a certainty that our patrol would collect the most newspapers. I thought he would bring us newspapers home every day. He refused. I was stunned! He explained that it would be wrong to bring me extra newspapers from the office because the *Oxford Mail* had to buy recycled newsprint. It would be stealing and immoral as the firm sold the leftover papers itself. It was my introduction to moral values."

In Kent, Guides collected 1,400 medicine bottles from homes for the local doctors and chemists; in the Lake District, Kendal Guides gathered several hundredweight of acorns to feed to local pigs, wool from fences and hedgerows with which to stuff cushions for army canteens, and old mackintoshes which they sent to Guides in Grasmere, who made them into gloves for men on minesweepers in the Atlantic.

As well as collecting, Guides tried to find replacements for supplies that the nation was short of. A boot-polish substitute made from lemon juice was recommended: "Rub a few drops briskly on black or brown leather boots and they will have a brilliant polish." Unfortunately, lemons were soon unobtainable. Guides also found ways of making the supplies that they had last longer: stirring one pound of washing soda into a large pail of water and sprinkling it over coal apparently made fires burn longer and brighter.

Every Patrol Leader in the country was expected to encourage her Guides. In some towns, empty shops were taken over as collection points. Guides became the embodiment of the Home Front spirit, digging shelters, collecting waste paper and, even if they only had a back yard, taking up the flagstones to grow vegetables. The 1st Kennington Girl Guides, near Oxford, used their trek cart to collect jam jars, old batteries and newspapers. "We pushed it the four miles to Oxford to a scrap dealer," said Sylvia Rivers. "We had great fun giving each other rides on the way home. With petrol rationing, there was hardly any traffic. The money we got went towards our Uniform fund."

All over the country, in cities, towns, villages and hamlets, Guides caught "collecting fever". One village company unearthed and transported a whole disused kitchen range from a farmhouse. The 3rd North Oxford company collected 4,000 books for the Merchant Navy. Newbridge Guides in Scotland collected 1,450 books for the forces, and the North-West Cheshire Guides knitted two hundred garments. The Guides of Birmingham made a thousand garments for air-raid victims, and a Suffolk company collected 9,000 stamps for a hospital. The Brownies of Hull sent 123 toys to local hospitals. Not everything went to plan. A Croydon Guide patrol was pushing their heavy load of paper across Purley Corner on a busy Saturday afternoon when, just as they crossed the tramlines, the linchpin of their trek cart fell out. In the middle of the busy crossroads with buses, army vehicles, trams and cars coming from five different directions, the unflurried

Patrol Leader repaired the damage while her patrol ran in all directions to retrieve the blowing paper. "There y'are — there's another piece!" one army driver called as the youngest Guide dived under his wheels to save a blowing carton. "Don't you miss any now, Missy, will yer!"

Companies without trek carts used old prams, go-karts, wheel-barrows, boxes on wheels and even two bicycles slung together. On a sunny afternoon collecting could be great fun, but as the weather grew colder and the days shorter it became much more challenging. The public were always impressed when they saw Guides braving poor conditions, and tended to give even more supplies than they would have usually. The Guides never refused an offer; they found a market for most things, or a use for anything. Old rags could be washed and made into clothes or toys. Old toys could be mended and painted as Christmas presents for evacuee children. Even bones were collected from butchers and restaurants, and sold to make bone-meal for cattle feed, glue for shoe factories, and glycerine for explosives. Oxford Guides went around pubs and cafés singing, "It's quite well known, the cutlet bone, will make an aeroplane."

Jam jars were washed and stored for hedgerow jam — blackberries, elderberries, rowanberries, hawthorn and crab-apples. The Shropshire Guides made eighty-six pounds of jam and bottled 357 pounds of fruit. In Droitwich, Guides collected 120 pounds of horse chestnuts for "protein porridge" and three hundredweight of acorns to feed zoo animals. The

198

Guides' Law of thrift made them determined not to let anyone stand in their way. One afternoon, a thirteen-year-old Patrol Leader from Westminster found herself arguing with the policeman on duty in Victoria Station Yard.

"You can't go in, Missy," the policeman explained. "There's seven time bombs sitting in the station, just waiting to tick over. They may go off any minute."

"But," said the Guide patiently, "this is our day to collect the waste paper. Can't we just pop in and get it quickly?"

Miss Dorothy Bubbers, an evacuee teacher from East Ham Grammar School in London, started the 1st Kidlington Guide Company in Oxfordshire in September 1939. The Guides chose to call the patrols Searchlight, Victory, Spitfire and Primrose. They combed the village with prams, collecting newspapers, jam jars and rags. They collected books for the forces, which awarded Guide companies army ranks according to the number of books donated. Most remained Sergeants, but a few amassed enough to become Field Marshals.

At Christmas, the 1st Kidlington held a Good Turn party at which the Guides handed out toys to sick children at the Radcliffe Infirmary. Another good turn was helping at Kidlington Post Office so that Christmas mail would be delivered on time. Some Guides even delivered telegrams on Christmas Day. When Captain Bubbers left to join the Women's Land Army, they carried on on their own. "Our Brownie pack soon began to undertake collections of all kinds," said Mary Yates, a Guide in Oxfordshire. "Silver paper, old razor blades, empty jars. We had boxes in all sixteen large shops in town and each Tuesday we collected them up and then sorted and packed up our spoils."

At the start of 1940, when the "Phoney War" had been dragging on for four months, the Girl Guide Association designated the last week of May as "Gift Week". Immediately, Guides and Brownies all over Britain threw themselves into serious fundraising for the war effort. At the time there were no special planes to carry wounded men, so the girls aimed to raise enough money to buy the very first two RAF flying ambulances. These could fly straight to a wounded pilot or gunner who could be picked up almost at the site of a crash and flown to a hospital. The twin-engined Oxford Airspeeds cost £15,000 each.

The Chief Commissioner, Mrs St John Atkinson, wrote to all Guides asking if they would give half a day to their country: "Let us make this gesture at no small cost to ourselves in a spirit of service, self-sacrifice, and humble thanks that so many of life's blessings are still ours. I am setting you a big task — £20,000 is still needed. Please share this letter with your companies and packs and gather together your donations. Can we do it . . . Of course we can!"

One Guide earned a shilling by calling at the police station each morning and cleaning the Sergeant's boots. Another gave three young men skating lessons. A Guide in Scotland taught an African student English phrases. One company used the £3.5s it raised from its paper collection to buy enough material to make a dozen pairs of pyjamas for the Red Cross. Brownies were eager to help too: one Brownie earned sixpence by having her tooth out without crying. A Brownie pack saved £5 from their bus fares by walking to school. Betty Walker, an Extension Brownie from Sunderland, started work as soon as Britain declared war. She was spotted by a friend of her Brown Owl in Woolworths before Christmas 1939, busy buying toys. Brown Owl asked Betty's mother about it, as Betty had both legs in callipers and could not walk easily. She had saved up her pocket money until she had half a crown, and had spent it on toys for the children of a British prisoner of war in Germany. "I am sending you a few toys as your daddy won't be able to buy you any this year," wrote Betty.

One Brownie pack made enough marmalade to buy an ancient ambulance for the Female Army Nursing Yeomanry, or FANYs. Unfortunately, it had started life as a fish van, and the smell inside caused many of its wounded patients to pass out. It wasn't much fun for the drivers either, as FANY Verily Anderson remembered: "I once had the honour of driving the fish-van ambulance. It had no self-starter so had to be cranked, with the left-hand forefinger held in the loop of the choke wire and the right thumb around the crank handle to avoid a fracture when the engine kicked in. Luckily for the patient lying on a stretcher in the back, he was already unconscious."

The Brownies of Cheltenham made washing kits and sent them to soldiers in the Middle East. "They lined them with jaconet [fine cotton]," wrote *The Guide*, "and bought soap, toothbrushes, razor blades and washing flannels to fill them. These same Brownies have also distinguished themselves by taking a prize in the village Thrift competition. They collected wool from hedges, washed and teased it, and made it into a small quilt. They have also knitted babies' vests for welfare centres, garments for children in shelters and a blanket for a Finnish refugee."

"We had a concert," said Iris O'Dell, "with skirts made out of crepe paper, refreshments being a stick of rhubarb dipped in sugar. We spent ages planning the programme, which mainly consisted of hit songs, one called 'Zoom, Zoom, Here we go, Is there a sound of music in the air' as we twirled in the paper skirts and thought it great." They made rugs by cutting up strips of old clothes. "The rugs looked fine on the kitchen floor."

When a Spitfire squadron was stationed not far from the 1st Rudston Company near Bridlington in Yorkshire, the Guides celebrated their company's birthday in 1940 by giving a concert and donating £7 to the local Spitfire Fund. The total cost of a Spitfire was £9,848, and their contribution would have paid for the compass, plus a clock or four spark plugs. The 23rd Ealing Company raised £6.10s for the Ministry of Aircraft Spitfire Fund, then framed the letter of thanks, and charged a further penny to look at the letter!

At the end of Guide Gift Week, Guides had raised not £20,000, but a staggering £46,216.19s.10d. By moving furniture in trek carts, weeding gardens, cutting lawns, minding babies and running errands they had proved that they could rise to any challenge. Enough money came in not just from the British Isles, but from the entire British Empire, the dominions and the colonies, to buy the two air ambulances, twenty motor ambulances, four mobile canteens, ten rest rooms and a hostel for British seamen in Reykjavik. It was an extraordinary achievement. Queen Elizabeth, herself a Guide Commissioner and now Patron of the Association, wrote, "The result of the Guide Gift scheme is simply wonderful, and no praise is too great for those responsible for launching it and for the spirit of those Guides who were quite sure they were going to get the amount needed." The Princess Royal presented the twenty ambulances that Brownies and Guides had bought to the Royal Navy. They were well-sprung, comfortable and roomy, with the Guides' trefoil painted on the side. For many years they plied between the docks and naval bases and London hospitals.

Plans had been made for a grand flight of the air ambulances around Britain to give everyone who had raised money a chance to see them in action. But the start of the Battle of Britain meant that every plane was needed, and there was no time for exhibition flights. However, a few lucky Guides and Brownies were invited to watch "their" air ambulances take off. The ceremony was filmed for Pathé News and shown in cinemas all over the Empire. A small Brownie summed up the spirit of the day when she said to the tall Guide standing next to her: "You must take off your hat and cheer, too! Your money bought them as well as ours!"

Around the British coast, motorised lifeboats were also in desperately short supply. Drifting mines, enemy bombers and lurking submarines meant that shipping had become extremely hazardous. Strong lifeboats were needed which could speed to men in trouble, whatever the weather; they cost £5,000 each. The Guides raised money for such a boat during Gift Week, and it was used before it was even launched. In May 1940 it was almost finished in Rowhedge yard on the River Colne in Essex when word came through that every seaworthy boat was needed to get to France and save the men of the British Expeditionary Force, cut off by the enemy on the beaches of Dunkirk. The boat-makers knew what they had to do, and that the Guides would approve. They took the lifeboat to Dover and handed her over to a crew of naval ratings, who crossed the Channel in her. Backwards and forwards she went, ferrying exhausted men between Dunkirk beach and the larger ships. Her new paint was blistered by the burning oil, her engine was damaged, a rope was tangled around her propeller, her wood was splintered by shrapnel and her foresail ripped. But she came back. Renamed *The Guide of Dunkirk*, she began her real life in a fishing village on the coast of Cornwall. When she retired as a lifeboat in 1963, she became a fishing boat for holidaymakers until the Dunkirk Veterans Association bought her in 1983.

Fundraising and collecting did not stop once Gift Week was over. Sylvia Rivers was a member of the Islip Rangers in Oxfordshire. "Every week we met in the village hall to pack small items to send to prisoners of war."

At Whitsun weekend in 1941 the RAF rang Guide headquarters with an urgent request. Could the Brownies collect 5,000 used wooden cotton reels? They were told only that they had to "act as quickly as possible for a secret job". Within a few months they had gathered together a total of 15,000 cotton reels, which they sent off to the RAF in pillowcases. They were never informed what they were for. Declassified files show that they were used by MI9, the secret War Office department set up to help prisoners of war escape. Tightly rolled silk maps of Europe, microfilm of contacts and German paper money were carefully inserted inside them, after which MI9 arranged for firms in the cotton industry to refill the reels with thread and to attach fresh paper labels to them. MI9 set up a number of bogus welfare associations which despatched games and sewing equipment to officers in prisoner-of-war camps. They did this so that if any of these aids to escape were intercepted, no suspicion would fall on the Red Cross, as the withdrawal of Red Cross parcels by the Germans would have caused hardship for all prisoners of war. How many of these cotton reels helped PoWs escape, we shall never know.

Girl Guides did not just provide practical aid, but helped boost the nation's morale with snappy slogans. Ann Gee of Congleton Guides in Cheshire came up with "Lend to the Nation, Defeat Domination", which her company painted onto a banner and carried around town. Guides also played prominent roles in War Weapons Week in 1941, Warship Week in 1942, Wings for Victory Week in 1943 and Salute the Soldier Week in

1944. At each, firemen, Air-Raid Wardens, any uniformed forces billeted nearby, Scouts, Guides and Brownies, marched through the local town with flags and banners flying. "There was a lot of drill practice, not to mention polishing of badges and shoes to look smart," said Alma Camps. "A particular hazard," wrote a Guide from the 1st Grimsbury Company, Banbury, "was having the heel of your shoe stepped on by the Guide directly behind you and then having to keep hopping in time with the march until the shoe was back on again." Sometimes there were more people in the march than watching it. If there was a fire engine, a tank, or better still a shot-down German fighter plane available, that went in the procession too.

The war effort included more than collecting salvage and raising money: Guides also gave their time in agricultural work. By May 1940, with so many men called up and less food imported, there was a shortage of 100,000 farm labourers. Carthorses were more common than tractors, and most farm work, such as hoeing, was done by hand. Brownies, Guides and Rangers spent their holidays digging potatoes, pulling beetroots or hoeing lettuces, often for no payment except their food.

Farmers applied to the Ministry of Agriculture for labourers, and at first they were disappointed when girls and young women turned up. But it did not take long for their doubts to be conquered. "Bring more girls who are not afraid of hard work," they said, "who are cheerful and persevering, and who clean their tools when they have used them and always put them back in the right place."

In August 1942, Ranger Joan Wright and her friends set off by train from West Hartlepool, County Durham to Pickering, Yorkshire. For two weeks, she and over fifty Guides and Rangers from all over Britain camped in a forest. "We are brashing," she wrote to her friend Teddy, "i.e. cutting all the low branches off the fir trees with a brasher. It is very hard work," Each patrol brashed up to a hundred trees a day, even in the pouring rain: "Every time we started on a tree we got a shower of water." They were fed well, with plenty of bread and cakes, and most nights had campfire singing. "The Twins make us laugh and they taught us many good new songs. Fairy, a big girl from London, also added to the noise of the camp." They took it in turns to cook and then washed in the river. "When I got home it felt so small and stuffy after the great open spaces, and a very enjoyable week at camp." Joan was awarded her War Service Badge for her forest work, and then became a Brown Owl. She returned to Pickering a year later for another brashing holiday. This time there was less food, more turnips, more Spam sandwiches, and even more rain.

In 1938 Lord and Lady Baden-Powell had gone to live in Kenya. Olave set about learning Swahili, as she felt it only polite to be able to speak to people in their own language. She had already succeeded in persuading the Guides of Kenya to be multi-racial, "Despite," as she wrote, "strong anti-Indian feeling in the colony generally."

Although Lord Baden-Powell's heart was beginning to fail, he never lost interest in the Guide and Scout movements he had founded. In 1940, when the British government started to plan a National Youth Training Movement, he wrote a long memorandum, based on his interview with Mussolini, outlining why, compared to Scouts and Guides, compulsory state movements were repressive, lacking spiritual heart and designed to create mass cohesion, rather than encourage individual character. Whether his letter had any effect we do not know, but a British Youth Training Movement was never established.

The following year, Baden-Powell's Christmas card to his friends in England depicted a self-drawn cartoon of himself saying, "We owe a statue to Hitler. He has done more than any man ever to consolidate our nation, at Home and Overseas and has given us friends in America and ALL the countries he has ravaged." Lady Baden-Powell wrote, "I feel like a mother with a very large family of children, and I care for you all very much."

Less than a month later, the Chief Scout died, aged eighty-three. His funeral was attended by hundreds of African, Asian and European Guides and Scouts. "The Chief's Last Message" was published for all to read:

If you have ever seen the play "Peter Pan" you will remember how the pirate chief was always making his dying speech because he was afraid that

208

possibly when the time came for him to die, he might not have time to get it off his chest.

I have had a most happy life and I want each one of you to have as happy a life too. God put us in this jolly world to be happy and enjoy life. Happiness doesn't come from being rich, nor merely from being successful in your career, nor by self-indulgence. One step towards happiness is to make yourself healthy and strong. But the real way to happiness is by giving out happiness to other people. Try and leave this world a little better than you found it, and when your turn comes to die, you can die happy in feeling that at any rate you have not wasted your time, but have done your best. "Be Prepared" in this way, to live happy and to die happy — stick to your Promise always.

Your friend, Baden Powell of Gilwell

Olave received a telegram of condolence from Poland: "In Madam Małkowska's absence, her school sends deepest sympathy." The Polish Guides knew perfectly well that she was actually in Britain, and "her school" was code for the entire Guide movement.

The humourist and politician A.P. Herbert wrote a poem, "On the Death of Baden-Powell", for the *Sunday Graphic*.

If any seek your monument — let them look
    oversea
And up and down the earth, where boys are fine
    and free

Where boys and girls fear nothing but keep a few
    good rules,
Can sing and smile, salute and serve — but not
    for brutes and fools.

Few pioneers live long enough to see what they
    have done;
Most men are glad if they can leave the world a
    single son.
Did ever man, before you died, see such a dream
    come true?
Did any leave so many living monuments as you?

Olave, Lady Baden-Powell, could easily have stayed at her beautiful Kenyan home, Pax-Tu, but in 1942 she returned to England, because "I want to be with my Guides." She undertook the long and dangerous voyage by sea, and en route she had her first experience of real war, when a Nazi bomber attacked her ship. "I stood there and watched that great black brute," she said, "and I thought — at last I am in danger with the others. It was lovely. And then, of course, one of our planes showed him out and by then I knew that was lovely, too!"

As the army had commandeered her house, Pax Hill in Hampshire, she slept on a camp bed in the Scout office in Buckingham Palace Road, before being offered an apartment in Hampton Court Palace. She toured the country, encouraging and inspiring Guides everywhere. Even she was surprised to find Brownies learning about incendiary bombs and how to put them out if no adults were about.

Guides, Brownies, Scouts and Cubs all over the world wanted to raise money for a suitable memorial to their founder. However, while the war was still in progress it was decided that any money collected would be lent to the government as National Savings Funds "until such time as it shall be deemed suitable for it to be spent on a memorial to Our Founder". The Baden-Powell Memorial Fund, which would extend the worldwide Guide movement's contribution to the war effort, was launched in January 1941 with a concert at Windsor Castle. The ten-year-old Princess Margaret of the 1st Buckingham Palace Guide Company had the lead role, while fourteen-year-old Princess Elizabeth led the HMS President III Sea Rangers, singing rounds, sea shanties and Negro spirituals. Just outside Oxford, fourteen Guide companies camping in Wytham Woods collected 140 pounds of rose-hips for vitamin-C syrup which they sold to the Ministry of Food for tuppence a pound. The Balendoch Brownies and Guides in Scotland raised a guinea by running competitions for a week: "The Brownies lit a campfire and made dampers and cocoa which they sold for one penny. The Guides invited everybody to bomb Germany for a shilling each." They then held a garden party at the local parsonage, where everything was a penny. They raised £22, enough to buy a collapsible rubber boat for the army. The Guides of Norfolk Island in the Pacific Ocean, home to just 1,000 inhabitants, sent £59.14s to the Relief Fund for the people of Sheffield.

The Guides of Victoria in Australia held a "walkabout" and raised enough money to buy 9,540 yards of flannel, 1,537 pounds of knitting wool and seventeen pounds of elastic, and they sewed and knitted for Europe. "Everything is most beautifully finished and lined," wrote an Australian Guide. "There is every variety of garment, from socks to overcoats and there are sets of kilts and jerseys for every size of girl up to fourteen; there are boys' suits of trousers and jerseys; there are vests, pyjamas, shirts, everything to keep a cold child warm."

Guides from Gold Coast (now Ghana) knitted blankets and rolled bandages. Guides living in a leper colony at Itu in Nigeria, all suffering from the terrible and incurable illness, gave up almost the only thing they had — one of their three meals a day. Guides in Jamaica taught new recruits to knit with pieces of wire and string until supplies of wool and needles were available.

Carrier pigeons played a special role in the commemoration of Baden-Powell. These winged messengers carried vital messages for the services, when radio silence was essential to avoid the enemy's intelligence system. They flew huge distances through storms and shellfire, and their messages saved many lives. For fifteen shillings, a loft of thirty pigeons could be fed for a day. Excitement grew as Guide companies competed to see which could raise the most money for this cause. To show their gratitude the Army Pigeon Service arranged for pigeons to fly from all the different

212

counties carrying special messages to the Chief Guide in London on "Thinking Day", Saturday, 20 February 1943. Princess Elizabeth and Princess Margaret supervised the fixing of a message to a pigeon and let him fly. The Princess Royal released a pigeon to carry the message from Yorkshire.

On the headquarters rooftop in the heart of London, the Chief Guide and Lady Cochrane, Army Pigeon Service representative, scanned the skies eagerly for any sign of a homing pigeon. "There it comes! No!" said Lady Cochrane.

Yes! Yes it is — our first messenger! Everyone is in a marvellous state of excitement. The pigeon plays us up — it won't come in! For ten minutes it circles round, till we begin to feel quite dizzy. We are told to hide among the chimney pots while the pigeoneers call it and rattle tins of corn. It alights on a rooftop and plays peep boo with deliberate intent, before it finally goes hoppity hop through its little trap door. The first message has arrived and is handed in to the Chief. It is from Derbyshire and reads: "These messengers, flying from your birthplace — Chesterfield — take Derbyshire's thoughts and prayers to all Guides to form a strong link in the chain of Guiding round the world." The Chief Guide is thrilled beyond words that the first pigeon to arrive should come from her birthplace.

The 1st Grimsbury Company near Banbury met in the small back room of the Old Bluebird Hotel. "We went to feed the carrier pigeons used by the Home Guard," remembered one of them. The Grimsbury Rangers had entire charge of the pigeon loft, and sent and received messages as part of their war effort. On "Thinking Day" a pigeon was sent by them from Banbury to the Chief Guide. The message read: "Oxfordshire sends greetings to Guides, throughout the world, and looks forward to the time when we shall all be united in the cause of peace."

CHAPTER
ELEVEN

Princesses and Paupers

In 1907, after Baden-Powell had taken his group of boys camping on Brownsea Island, he wrote: "One wants to bring all classes more in touch with each other, to break down existing barriers, which are only artificial after all, and to teach them to give and take in the common cause, instead of being at snarls of class against class, which is snobbery all around and a danger to the State."

From the start, the Guides were open to everyone, regardless of "class, creed or colour": fourteen-year-old parlourmaids were encouraged to join up alongside the daughters of doctors, dukes and even kings. Although the Guides and Brownies of each company or pack tended to be predominantly from a similar socio-economic group because of where they lived, they met on equal terms at rallies, camps and campfire gatherings.

Badge requirements were designed for girls from all backgrounds. For the Domestic Service Badge, a Guide had to demonstrate not only that she could "clean boots and black the stove" but also "look up train connections, answer a telephone and wait on two persons, quietly and neatly, at a dinner". The Poor Law School in Cowley ran the 1st Cowley Guides and a Brownie pack. All the girls were expected to become domestic servants, and their Guide badges were the only qualifications they were likely to gain. While Guides already in work needed both employment skills and qualifications, Guide companies in girls' boarding schools reflected their members' class and future lives. At Normanhurst School for Girls in Sussex, the headmistress, the Honourable Daisy Batteen, appointed herself the Chief Guider. She encouraged her young ladies to achieve the Horsewoman Badge, even if they had their own grooms. "Child Care, Cookery and Cyclist Badges are useful for when my girls have their own nanny, cook and chauffeur," she said, assuming they would never actually need the skills themselves.

The Normanhurst senior science mistress, known as "Miss Funny Bunny" after her Bunsen burner, was Guide Captain. She led the girls in singing the Guide Marching Song as they marched up and down the rhododendron-lined school drive.

We're the Girl Guides marching on the King's
  Highway
With a heart that it is light and a step that is gay
  (pirouette turn)
There's room for me (hit chest) and there's room
  for you (spread arms)
And there's work in the world (circle arm on turn)
For the Guides to do. (Abrupt turn. Keep
  marching)

So Up Girls! (high kick) Wake Girls! (high kick)
(reel drunkenly on turn and next line)
'Tis no time for sleeping (stand)
(passionately) Set the windows of your heart
   (hold heart)
As wide, yes as wh-y-y-y-y-y-y-y-y-y-y-y-yde
(high register with variations)
As they can beeeeeeeeeeeeee
(hold onto be)
(drop register and march forward)
Left right, left right, left right
HALT (stamp to halt and salute).

Normanhurst School had such spacious grounds that during the holidays they were used by visiting Guide camps. Verily Anderson was a pupil, and returned as a Guide. "At the end of term, I was collected by car by my mother with my school trunk. As soon as we reached home I exchanged my school uniform for my Guide camp tunic and my mother drove me back again. The Guide camp was held on the tennis lawns. We dug latrine trenches behind one hockey goal and grease pits for the washing-up water in the nearby rhododendrons. The other Guides looked up in great awe at the great Victorian-Gothic house with its turrets and spires, and said how creepy it must be for the schoolgirls. I never let on that I was one of them."

Early on, Baden-Powell realised that to help the Guiding movement gain respectability, he had to involve the upper echelons of society. In 1917 the

Mayor of Richmond was proud to present his local Brownie pack to Queen Amélie, the former Queen of Portugal. An immensely tall woman, famous for her charitable work, she was now in exile in London. The Brownies, in gym tunics with wide belts and sailor hats, stood in a row with big grins as she inspected them. A Guide in thick black stockings and her hair in a big bow curtseyed to the Queen, who presented her with a badge. A small boy in a sailor suit gave her a huge bouquet, and she swept him up in her long arms and kissed him.

The British royal family began their close connection with Guiding when the Princess Royal became President of the Girl Guide Association in 1920. At the Guides' conference in Cambridge in 1922 the representatives from over forty countries included Princess Sophie Koudacheff of Russia and Latvia's Chief Guide, Princess Wilhelmine Wilks. Princess Alice, granddaughter of Queen Victoria, was a hard-working President of the Imperial Committee of Guides. When the Prince of Wales (later Edward VIII) toured Australia in 1924, as Chief Scout of Wales he asked that Guides meet him wherever he went. At a rally in Guildford in 1925, huge crowds thronged the streets to welcome Princess Mary and the Surrey County Commissioner, the Duchess of Sutherland, as they inspected 6,000 Girl Guides. The highlight of the afternoon was a demonstration by a patrol of Guides who built a wooden house, before the next patrol set it on fire and rescued a pretend baby from inside.

Verily Anderson had a brush with Guiding royalty in Norfolk in 1927.

When I was twelve, my aunt told me she was going to Norwich to form a guard of honour for Princess Mary. I watched Aunt Richenda being dressed in her District Commissioner's uniform by Harriet, her ancient lady's maid. Aunt Richenda had still never put on her own stockings so I wondered how she managed in camp. Some willing Guide must have done her day's Good Deed by heaving them up the elegant legs that supported her robin-breasted torso. Once she was dangling with lanyards and whistles she turned to old Harriet and said, "We'll put Miss Verily into my old uniform and make her into a Guider for the day. It's a great chance for her to get a glimpse of royalty."

"Don't you be forgetting, Miss Verily," said Harriet, "that you made your Guide promise to the King, when you meet his sister."

Into Norwich we went, Aunt Richenda driving at break-neck speed in her round-nosed Morris with a couple of Guides balanced in the Dickey seat behind us. All Norwich was gathered outside the cathedral and I was placed in charge of a company of Guides, all older than me. My hat was too big but I managed to peep out of one eye as Her Royal Highness Princess Mary marched by, very neat in her beautifully cut uniform. Not even

Aunt Richenda was entitled to follow her into the cathedral.

But Aunt Richenda was very satisfied with the proceedings, particularly when she spotted us next day on the front page of the *Eastern Daily Press*. I was merely relieved that the hat had rendered me unrecognisable by finally falling over both eyes.

Not everyone was so satisfied. When eighteen Oxfordshire Guides and six Guiders went to see Princess Mary, the road was lined for a mile on both sides with Guides. "We were so disappointed," they wrote, "that the Princess drove past in a closed motor, so we did not get a very good view."

Marion Crawford, the royal nanny, was determined that her charges, Princesses Elizabeth and Margaret, should have normal lives, and their parents, King George VI and Queen Elizabeth, wanted their daughters to be members of the community. "Just how difficult this is to achieve, if you live in a palace, is hard to explain," wrote "Crawfie" in *The Little Princesses: The Story of the Queen's Childhood*. "A glass curtain seems to come down between you and the outer world, and however hard a struggle is made to avoid it, escape is not entirely possible. I myself had never ceased striving to keep this miasma of unreality from the children, and thanks to their parents' open-mind-edness in these matters, I often succeeded."

The young Princess Elizabeth was already learning subjects such as constitutional law. In 1937 Miss Crawford suggested that she and her sister should become Girl Guides. "Besides keeping them in touch with what children of their own ages were doing, I knew it would bring them into contact with other children of all kinds and conditions. Both the King and Queen were extremely helpful and encouraging." So Buckingham Palace phoned across the road to the formidable Miss Violet Synge, later Guide Commissioner for England. She was a little appalled at the idea of princesses becoming Guides. "How could it ever work?" she asked. "Guides must all treat one another like sisters." Miss Crawford tried to persuade her that there was nothing Lilibet and Margaret would like better than to be treated like ordinary girls. "Come and meet them and talk it over," she suggested. So Miss Synge went to tea at the palace and found two polite, enthusiastic little girls.

Princess Elizabeth's main concern was that at only seven, Margaret was too young to be a Guide. "You don't think we couldn't get her in somehow?" she asked. "She is very strong, you know. Pull up your skirts, Margaret, and show Miss Synge. You can't say those aren't a very fine pair of hiking legs, Miss Synge. And she loves getting dirty, don't you, Margaret? And how she would love to cook sausages on sticks."

These arguments were so persuasive that it was decided that Princess Margaret could be a Brownie, attached to the 1st Buckingham Palace Guide Company of twenty Guides — made up of the daughters of court officials and palace employees. Later, the 1st Buckingham Palace Brownie Pack was started, with fourteen Brownies. They met in King

George's summerhouse in the palace garden. The King made one stipulation. "I'll stand anything," he said, "but I won't have them wear those hideous long black stockings. Reminds me too much of my youth." So the palace Guides wore knee-length beige socks instead, and soon this innovation was adopted by Guides everywhere.

The Princess Royal, magnificent in the uniform of the President of the Girl Guide Association, came to enrol her nieces and the daughters of her brother's court. The King stood in the doorway looking on, making *sotto voce* teasing brotherly remarks. Princess Elizabeth was in the Kingfisher patrol, Princess Margaret was a Leprechaun.

Not everyone understood the point about Guides and the reason for uniform, and at first some of the new Guides arrived at the palace in party frocks, with white gloves, accompanied by their nannies or governesses who wanted to stay and watch. "We soon put a stop to all that," said Miss Crawford, now the royal nanny, governess and Guiding expert.

In 1940, when Princess Elizabeth was fourteen, she put on her Guide uniform and went to Broadcasting House to address the children of Britain on the wireless. She said she sympathised with those who had been evacuated, as she too was often separated from her parents (though the King and Queen made it back to Windsor Castle on most nights). Princess Margaret, in her Brownie uniform, added her voice to the farewells at the end.

When the Blitz began in September 1940, the 1st Buckingham Palace Company moved to Windsor, where it remained until the end of the war. In 1942 the Princesses were filmed at a Girl Guide camp in Windsor Great Park. Princess Margaret, now Patrol Leader of the Bullfinches, made a speech and handed out certificates to her fellow Guides. She then helped them to cook beans over a campfire, and after their meal Princess Elizabeth washed up in a metal bowl. When they heard the air-raid siren, the Princesses and their fellow Guides leapt into slit trenches. Their mother the Queen, herself a former Guide District Commissioner, and some other ladies sat on velvet chairs and watched. They seemed oblivious to the possibility of an air raid.

That same year, Princess Elizabeth wore her Guide uniform to register at the Ministry of Labour as part of the Youth Registration Scheme. She had by then attained Cook, Child Nurse and Needlewoman Badges. Her Interpreter Badge had tested her ability to recognise over fifty flags, including the Royal Standard, and to tell foreigners where to find the main ports of Britain, the value of British money, and advise about local hotels, buses and the best food in local cafés. A year later she became a Sea Ranger and Boatswain of SRS President III Sea Ranger Company. In August 1943 nineteen members of the company, and the 1st Buckingham Palace Guides, of which Princess Margaret was now Patrol Leader, held a four-day camp. Wartime censorship rules forbade any mention of the weather — in case the enemy used the information to its advantage

— or the whereabouts of the camp. No clues were given to the location except that there was a lake nearby. As the Princesses were within cycling distance of Windsor Castle — for security reasons, they had to sleep in their beds at home — the camp was probably in Windsor Great Park, with rowing on Virginia Water. The Princesses put up their own tent, though it was used for stores.

"Slit trenches had been dug for the camp by the Grenadier Guards and air raid drill was taken by Company Sergeant Major of the grenadiers," reported *The Guider*. "Shortly afterwards, the alert sounded and the Guides and Sea Rangers dashed to the trenches." Five Sea Rangers, including Princess Elizabeth, passed the Boating Permit Test by throwing lifelines and sculling well.

Their good work received a reward beyond all wildest dreams when her Majesty the Queen had tea in the camp and was taken out in *President III*, with Princess Elizabeth coxing a crew of four. They cast off, and clear and crisp came the cox's orders. The crew responded briskly and away they went, followed by the canoe and punt completing the convoy.

During the alert in the middle of dinner on Saturday, plates and pudding dishes were seized and rushed to the trenches where the meal was resumed. During rest-hour yards and yards of string appeared and was transformed into lanyards. For entertainment, the Guides produced a Company effort called *Mein Kampf*.

There was also tent-pitching, gadget-making, boating, rope-work and splicing. The Guides practised for the rounders match against the Sea Rangers. [The Sea Rangers won.] As the Royal car drew in with the Queen, a small Guide said: "Captain — there's a wasps' nest here!" There was a moment's consternation but the trouble was quickly dealt with. At the campfire Shantyman Princess Elizabeth sang the solo parts.

After the last supper came the rag — and what a rag! All went wild ... the excitement spread through the camp. Every Guider, including County Commissioner, had to be taken for a ride in the trek cart and bumped off at the lake's edge. And then the two Princesses jumped on their bicycles and rode off, to the strains of Speed Bonny Boat, with a specially big cheer as they turned the last corner and were out of sight.

For her eighteenth birthday, in April 1944, the Girl Guide Association gave Princess Elizabeth a camping set which included an "Alaskan" tent with ground sheet and sleeping bag, and a rucksack containing a looking glass, clothes bags, "oil-silk sponge-bag" and an aluminium egg cup.

Sea Rangers in London became part of the River Emergency Service on the Thames. River steamers that had formerly been used as pleasure craft were converted into ambulance ships to rescue casualties from bombed ships at anchor. In the overcrowded dockland areas they could take the wounded to hospitals near the riverbank. Each craft carried a doctor and a crew, and two Sea Rangers to help with cooking and first-aid. The authorities were amazed at the girls' usefulness. "Their cheerfulness through the cold grim winter days and long winter nights on the river was a never ending surprise to the men who worked with them," said one report, "and their enthusiasm did much to keep up the spirits of the crews through the long waiting times."

Pamela McGeorge, known as "Chips", had trained as a Sea Ranger on the *Old Implacable*, a French warship built in 1797 and captured at the Battle of Trafalgar. In 1941 Chips joined the WRNS at Royal Naval Base Devonport in Plymouth. During a very heavy raid on a stormy night in April that year she was carrying despatches to the base's Commander-in-Chief when a bomb exploded, blowing her off her motorcycle and wrecking it beyond repair. Although badly shaken, she climbed over a pile of debris and ran for half a mile to Admiralty House, with bombs falling and large fires blazing all around her. Once she had delivered her despatches, she volunteered to go out with more. The next day she sent a postcard home to her mother: "Could you send along my old coat? I seem to have torn my good one." Her mother would have known no more about the raid if the King had not later pinned the British Empire Medal onto Chips's second-best coat. Chips was somewhat embarrassed, as she did not consider she deserved a medal for simply doing her job.

By June 1945, a month after the end of the war in Europe, censorship of the whereabouts of the royal family had been lifted, and *The Guider* revealed that Princess Elizabeth, now the Commodore of Sea Rangers, turned up in Cardiff at the first post-war rally for the Guide Council of Wales. The six Sea Rangers who served the princess dinner were heard to say, "We are the most envied girls in Cardiff." The next morning over 5,000 cheering and waving Guides lined the Princess's route into Cardiff, where she made her first public speech in Wales. That evening Guides from Wales and liberated Europe sat on the grass with the Princess in a giant trefoil shape and joined in the camp-fire singing. The censorship rules about weather had also been relaxed, and *The Guider* could reveal, "Later, rain poured down without ceasing, but nothing dampened the spirits of the two hundred and twenty campers."

Guides and Brownies influenced the lives of girls from all walks of life. Rosalie Brown was one of seven children of an Oxford college chef. She was born slightly deaf in 1912, and when she became a Brownie her Brown Owl explained everything clearly and slowly to her. Rosalie used to rollerskate down Oxford High Street to Brownie meetings. "I was a daft one on roller-skates," she said. "One day I couldn't stop when a coal cart pulled across the road in front of me. I just skated underneath the horse. Unfortunately, somebody saw me and told my mother and I got into trouble." By the time she left Oxford School of Art she had started her own Brownie pack in Headington, with an emphasis on handicrafts. During the war she was in the Land Army. She started by milking cows near Banbury, and then ran a home for evacuee children, where she started another Brownie pack. Her own deafness helped her teach Brownies at a special school where she started a Brownie Extension pack. She went on to write about and illustrate handicrafts for *The Guide* and *The Brownie* and over twenty Brownie craft books. After illuminating the roll of honour for the 4th Prince of Wales Own Gurkha Rifles, a job that took a whole year, she was made an honorary member of the regiment. "I've enjoyed the blether," she said as she approached the end of her life. "Ma eyes are bad, but there's nae wrong with ma tongue!"

CHAPTER
TWELVE

Baedeker Bombing

In March 1942, Hitler was enraged by the RAF's bombing of the ancient German cathedral city of Lübeck. In retaliation, he launched a series of raids on some of England's most beautiful, but strategically unimportant, towns. On 23 April, Exeter was the first cathedral city to be hit, followed by Bath, Norwich and York; on 1 June it was Canterbury's turn. These attacks, which killed nearly 2,000 civilians and destroyed over 50,000 houses, were dubbed the "Baedeker Blitz", because Hitler apparently used Karl Baedeker's German tourist guide to Great Britain to select his targets. In Canterbury, the Guides set up canteens to feed the demolition workers brought in to make bombed houses safe. In one street the gas was cut off but the girls could not light a fire because of the risk of explosion. One Guide cooked an egg successfully on an upturned electric iron.

For fun, Guide Violet Habbard wrote a letter in Morse to *The Guide*. The editor decoded her letter into English, but censorship rules meant that the magazine could not publish where Violet lived. She had been evacuated to an unidentified place which turned out to be on the route of the German bombers, so it may have been in Kent. She was acting as a roof spotter as part of the Fire Squad. "The girls all take it in turns each evening," she wrote. "It is very cold up on the roof and the planes often pass over us on their way to — . Sometimes bombs have fallen near us but only when the guns have opened up on them. It has been interesting to watch the tracer bullets, flares and gunfire."

Guide Eileen Wilson, aged fifteen, lived in Canterbury with her family, quite close to the army barracks.

In late summer of 1942 we were home one Saturday afternoon, and a neighbour's daughter, Grace, was on her first leave from the WAAF. I was very, very jealous; she was amongst all the heroes. Father was having a bath, and whilst we were talking to Grace the air-raid warning sounded. But we didn't take any notice of them any more, and it wasn't until the first aeroplanes were swooping over the city and bombs were falling that Grace decided to go home. Mother shepherded my sister and me into the air-raid shelter, calling my father to hurry out of the bath. Grace went across the paling fence and caught her knickers on the top of a spike. She's screaming out, "Oh my drawers, oh my drawers." Mother's shouting for Father, bombs were really coming down quite fast, and aeroplanes were swooping low and machine gunning.

Eventually Father came out of the bath clad in just a towel. We could hear Grace's predicament, so Father rushed across the garden to help her. It needed two hands, so he let go of the towel and lifted her off her so she could run home. When he got into the shelter my mother looked at him and said, "Look at your feet, they're filthy! You might at least have put a pair of slippers on." He was completely naked, helping Grace over the fence, and all Mother worried about was his dirty feet!

On the night of 31 May 1942, Eileen was woken by the sound of the air-raid siren.

We had an extra danger signal, which was a tug boat horn. We called it Tug Boat Annie, but it had gone so many times when German bombers were actually on their way to or from London. Mother decided that there were a lot of aeroplanes, so she came downstairs with a candle and looked out the back door. The planes were dropping flares. We had a routine: we came downstairs and went under the living room table. Then we went to the air-raid shelter one at a time. One of us carried the basket with sandwiches and a flask, the other took a bag of books and pencils plus a large bottle of sherry, and the third one carried a glass with Mother's false teeth.

Father used to sit by the shelter door, holding the door handle shut. This raid was so bad that when it quietened down, all he was holding was the handle — the door had gone. When it was light we went back into the house. There were no windows left, most of the ceilings were down and the stairs were blocked with plaster. The chicken shed roof had blown off and one chicken was in the kitchen. There was no gas, water or electricity. Mother's best china had shaken itself to the edge of the dresser. In the midst of all this turmoil, she pushed them back onto the shelf to keep them safe. There were unexploded bombs in the street, so we had to go to the Old Hospital. I put a coat over my nightdress. Above all the damage, the cathedral was still there.

The girls' school Violet attended had been destroyed, but not the nearby boys' school, so after a few days the girls moved into it. "It was quite exciting — we used to get messages from the boys left in the desks. In the playground was a barrage balloon which we called Simon. The crew of the balloon were our heroes; to us they were real airmen."

Another Canterbury Guide called Mary and her father were on Home Guard duty on a water tower on the night of 31 May, overlooking the city. "Just before dawn we heard this terrible noise," she remembered, "a whooshing sound. It was from some way off but gradually got closer and closer. Was it Germans coming down in parachutes? Were they now invading? We were more and more frightened." As the dawn appeared, the source of the sound was revealed. "Over the brow of the hill appeared a large black Labrador, followed by thousands of dogs from all over Canterbury, escaping the Blitz. The sound was their panting as they ran past in a river of dogs."

Between July 1940 and September 1944 over 2,000 shells fired by the Germans across the Channel landed on Dover. They fell without any warning. "Only the long, horrible whine of the thing coming at you," recalled Joyce Fagge, a Ranger in Dover. "The crunch of its landing, then the roar of the explosion." "Be Prepared" meant something very real and immediate to Rangers like Joyce, living under the shadow of the enemy guns, night after night. One evening, as she was sitting down to her tea, the shelling started. There was a great explosion close by, followed by the sound of a man screaming. Joyce snatched up her first-aid bag and ran out into the street. A nearby house had been hit, and the screams came from the top floor — but the staircase had been blown away, and a fire had started. Calling to a passing soldier for help, Joyce climbed up to the broken floor above and told the soldier to leave her there and run for help. She found another soldier terribly wounded, the arteries in both legs severed. Joyce wasted no time, and wrapped her scarf tightly round one leg to stop the bleeding. The other leg was wounded too high for a tourniquet, so she applied digital pressure on the femoral artery — a tricky technique that requires considerable strength. The man was conscious, and was frightened by the smoke. Joyce talked to him calmly, asking, "Would I stay with you if the house was on fire?" After twenty endless minutes, help arrived. The man was taken away to hospital, and

Joyce went quietly home. She told no one of her adventure, but after a time the soldier was well enough to ask for the girl whose skill and courage had saved him. Joyce was awarded the Silver Cross, "for gallantry where considerable risk has been faced".

In nearby Maidstone, Guides worked every Saturday morning at the Blood Transfusion Centre. Margaret Collins fitted together bungs, tubes and the bottles which received the blood.

Nan Wheeler was in the Guides and then the Rangers in Dover. "There weren't many youngsters left in Dover by 1942," she said. "But we had a Guide cottage where we met up once or twice a week. We had a good old feed with whatever food we could scrounge and a good night's sleep without the noise of shelling and bombing." The cottage was in the village of Barham, and had been bought by the American English Speaking Union for the Guides and other clubs. After Nan's first visit, she wrote to the English Speaking Union in the United States.

Dear Friends over the Water,
It is Saturday afternoon and although it is raining cats and dogs there is a party setting off on bicycles for the 11 mile trip [to the cottage]. Now may I introduce you to us? There are 10: Cathy our Guide Captain, Edith a Brown Owl, Hettie who will shortly be going overseas, Jean whose husband is fighting in Italy, Mue who has just become engaged to a flying officer newly decorated with the DSE, Binda, Evelyn, Edith, the

other Nan and myself. Will you come along with me in the rear party? We'll leave the balloon barrage of Dover behind us and head along the road to Canterbury, up and up the hill from the valley of the River Dour, through Liden onto the high hills. Woods are rather few as we puff against the strong wind and heavy rain and pssst, calamity! Nan's got a puncture. Off goes the tyre, on goes the patch and we're off again. But Oh dear, the tyre's flat again, but we struggle on, leaving the main road. Hurrah, there is Barham church, past cottages with blazes of flowers, over the bridge, we turn into our road. We just passed a school when we see a house with some well known faces. What a cheer goes up, we are there! Willing hands help us unpack, but what's this singing we hear? Is it a Ranger singing as softly and sweetly as that? There's a wireless, such luxury. Roomy gas cooker, and electric light.

Tired? Mind the low beams up the staircase! This bedroom with five low beds and beautiful patchwork quilts, makes you feel cheerful. From the window we look across the fields and villages and across the slope of the hill, the church spire stands up like a sentinel, daring anyone to come and bomb it. The bathroom, with three washbasins, so no need for tiresome queues, and the bath, show us just how much you have thought of us. We sit in the living room, with the blacked out windows, and sit on the floor by the fire and join in our favourite songs. We are especially fond of the Negro Spirituals. We close with a few prayers.

Upstairs we sit on our beds while the less lazy apply hair curlers, and then we are cooked to a restful sleep, while sirens sound in the night but we are far enough away to just say Phewee and ignore it. Some of us are Air-Raid Wardens and Fire Brigade workers, and to know that we need not leap out of bed, drag on sweaters and slacks and rush to our posts, for goodness knows how long, is just paradise.

Sunday morning sees Edith waking us with cups of tea and we go to church. Afterwards we eat eggs sent by Edith's mother from the country.

Then we walk up a hill into a wood and have a beautiful ceremony at which Phoebe and Nan are enrolled as Rangers, around us we find wild strawberries and wood violets. Over in the distance we can see the majestic towers of Canterbury Cathedral, shining through the clouds.

Oh how we wish we could stay for at least a week, but we have to get back to Dover. Those visits to White Cliff gave us such relief from strain and able to forget for a while that there is nothing to prevent the "Man from Over the Way" from planting a shell just where you are, or hurling death from the skies on those you love so much.

Our eyes had become accustomed to noticing a flash over the channel, and we start counting. When 80 has been reached, we dodge into a shelter. Our ears have become attuned to the

Bur-bur-bur of bombers engines, the pop-pop-pop of machine guns and the Swishsh-sh of a bomb and we know it is Tin Hat time. By now, we see more of Your Airforce. We listen to ascertain whether they have gone just to the French coast, when we shall hear rumbles and our windows and doors will rattle as the Germans and their accomplices suffer for their pig-headedness. Everyone of our party has known the horror of finding their homes and precious belongings gone or our places of work mauled about. Or worst of all, the absence of work-mates to whom we were talking the day before. Then we pause and wonder, where does all this lead to? Is it all worthwhile?

A sneak raider dropped a bomb which sent shoppers hurrying into doorways. When they crept out, the road way was covered in pamphlets. Hurrah! A leaflet raid! Everyone swooped for a trophy, only to discover they were bills blown from a nearby shop.

When the siren sounded Phoebe ran to the fire station to report for duty for the first time. She rang the bell outside for admittance and alarmed the whole neighbourhood as a fire engine came rushing out and enquired from our frightened friend where the fire was. She didn't know she had sounded the main alarm!

A gentleman sold fish from a barrow in Dover market square. When an aircraft dive bombed overhead, he popped under his barrow. When he emerged, his eyes widened when he saw on his barrow in place of fish, two stuffed ducks blown from the museum.

Our best wishes to you all,
from the Rangers of the Dover Patrol

June Mackenzie was a fourteen-year-old Guide living in Herne Bay, Kent. In October 1942 she was travelling home from Canterbury on the top of a double-decker bus when a daylight air raid began.

Because the surrounding land was lower than the road, we could see the aircraft at eye level. It was machine-gunning us, which we thought not very sporting as we were in a civilian vehicle.

When the first bomb dropped, the bus drew into the kerb and stopped. Then several more were dropped which blew in some glass. This caused minor cuts on my face. Although many people were screaming and some ran down the steps of the bus, no one was seriously hurt. We saw the bombers flying very low. Then as they turned and swept down on us again I saw an explosion higher up the road. People were struggling to get out but a man shouted, "Sit still. It will be alright." Many took his advice and some lay on the floor. I stayed in my seat, wrapping my arms around my head, and crouched against the back of the seat.

The nearest bomb landed. I saw a blinding orange flash and the glass silhouetted in a thousand tiny pieces. Then it came in, and we heard a terrific crash and smelt fumes of burnt cordite and dust. I felt my hair singe.

June heard people screaming. She saw others lying dead, covered in blood and wounds, and wrecked buildings everywhere. Her uniform was torn to ribbons, her arm badly wounded and her face bleeding. Because she was in her Guide uniform she felt that despite the horrors she must remain cheerful and help the people around her.

I tried to help a very fat lady with minor scratches. A man came up to us. I was glad, because we were alone except for three people who were dead, two on the floor. The woman asked piteously how she could get past, so I said as cheerfully as I could, that she would find it quite easy to step over or round them. We got her downstairs. On the path lay the conductress. She was unrecognisable. I covered her face with her cap. I thought of the women who would see it and wished to spare their feelings — it was not pleasant. Someone had got some sheeting, and with it I tied up several wounds. I suppose I first-aided at least four, possibly more. I noticed a nurse, and then an ambulance and I saw a young man stride up with a haversack and a tin hat. He was a Scout. After a bit the nurse came and asked if I was hurt. Knowing I could not do much more, unless something was done to my arm, I showed her where I was hurt and asked her to cut the uniform at the seam. I did not realise my uniform was already a total wreck, and I thought I might not be able to get another one.

June was taken to the army barracks nearby. "We were kept in a corridor, where my arm was treated." While waiting her turn in the outpatients, she was still thinking of other people. She and another Guide casualty she met there gave water to a wounded man on a stretcher, and wiped the blood off his face so he might not realise how severe his injuries were. "Eventually I was taken home and my father arranged admission to the local hospital. A doctor was called who stitched up the wound. No anaesthetic was available, so Matron held my hands very firmly!" June MacKenzie was awarded the Silver Cross for her courage under fire.

There were hundreds of Guides who were equally staunch and plucky, but died without anyone knowing it. The ones who lived to receive honours knew that any Guide who went through the war and was decorated for bravery could never feel proud: "She knows how lucky she is to be alive and how many other Guides like the soldiers in the field, 'gave their tomorrow that we might have our today'."

With so many women being called up, the Guide authorities turned their attention to pacifist Guides. After much deliberation, headquarters sent a directive to every district:

A girl on becoming a member of The Girl Guide Movement promises to do her duty to God and the King. It is obvious that her conception of what her duty to her country is, must be subject to and governed by her conception of her duty to God. So long as her view of her duty to God allows her to remain loyal to the laws of her country, she can remain a member. But when her views on her duty to God are such as to bring her in conflict with the laws of her country, then there can be no alternative but for her to resign. The Guide movement recognises that certain of their members conscientiously object to taking life, as for example those who belong to The Society of Friends (Quakers) but they are prepared to help their country in other ways, such as ambulance work. When a Guide's conscientious opinions make it impossible for her to help her country in wartime, in any form of national service such as first-aid or civil defence, it is clear she cannot keep her first promise or the second one to help other people at all times.

In June 1944, only days after the Allied invasion of mainland Europe, Hitler launched V-1 flying bombs, known as "doodlebugs", at England. "You could hear the Doodlebug chugging towards you overhead, even in the dead of night," remembered Verily Anderson. "If it continued on its way you started breathing again — though knowing that soon it would stop over someone else. If the chugging stopped overhead, you jumped under the table as quickly as possible." Those whose tables were not strong enough are not here to tell the tale. Of the 10,000 doodlebugs fired at England, 2,000 fell on London and the rest were brought down by RAF pilots over the Channel, Sussex and Kent. Even so, more than 6,000 Londoners were killed, about a tenth of the total of those killed by the Blitz.

Dorothy Eagleton was a Ranger in the 7th North Lewisham Company in Surrey. In August 1944 she wrote in the company log book: "During the night we first heard what were thought to be aeroplanes exploding. In the morning it was confirmed that pilot-less planes were being aimed at London. London soon learned to duck as the engine ceased prior to explosion. Guides have had to stop all evening meetings. The Doodlebugs have caused a deal of damage but we will win through."

One summer night in 1944, a group of Sea Rangers were on a weekend hike not far from London. Before going to sleep in a field they lay admiring the stars, trying to identify them. One of them said, "There's a planet over there, I'm not sure what it is. Gosh, it's moving. I believe it's a doodlebug." Seconds later they felt the earth tremors following the explosion. "That's the advantage of sleeping *right* out," said Captain. "There's nothing to fall on you except the sky!"

Every morning at Guide headquarters in Buckingham Palace Road began with a sense of triumph that the offices were still there, even if everything was covered in a fine layer of dust.

To enable their London colleagues to have a break from the doodlebugs, two young civil service secretaries from Oxford who were also Guide Lieutenants —

assistants to company Captains — volunteered to swap places with them for two weeks. "We had only ever once set foot in the capital before," said one of them. "This was the height of doodlebugs, the blackout, barrage balloons and beds in the tube stations. Much against our parents' wishes off we went to stay in the Guide hostel off Buckingham Palace Road called Our Ark." The evening they arrived, they found that there was much polishing going on, and the contents of cupboards were being carefully washed. The reason became clear when Olave, Lady Baden-Powell, appeared for supper. "Very shortly after eating the special meal with the Chief Guide, the air raid siren sounded against a background of explosions and we hastened to the basement shelter. Most sat on the floor, while Lady Baden-Powell had the armchair. To my horror she asked me to sit on one of the arms. I would rather have sat on the floor. I felt I had no choice! She of course regaled us with yarns, while I sat with ever increasing embarrassment, much too close to this, to me, illustrious person."

The poet Virginia Graham recognised the strength of the Guides when she wrote in early 1941:

We of England, who are in the battle front
Whose treasured things are menaced from the
    skies,
Whose mind and bodies bear the savage brunt
Of war, have turned with hopeful eyes

To you, our sister Guides, who also fight

On distant hill and shire and veldt and plain,
To keep our fire of freedom burning bright
We turn to you, and do not turn in vain.

Across the world, across the seven seas
Your help comes sailing in with every tide,
Swarms of proverbially busy bees
Must flap their wings and shamefully seek to hide.

Their heroes, when from their hives of honey
They see the harvest of your eager aid;
The ever-mounting gifts of cheerful money,
The heaps of clothes so beautifully made.

Compact parcels neatly tagged and tied —
The coat, the dress, the muffler, and the glove,
Each in its turn proving with woolly pride
The patriotic labour of your love.

When, as is sometimes so, our spirit doubts,
We touch your comforts here beneath our hands,
And something rises up in us and shouts
"Such is the strength by which the Empire
    stands!"

CHAPTER
THIRTEEN

Jersey Island Guides

When war was declared between Germany and Britain, life initially carried on much as before for the inhabitants of the Channel Islands, though everyone was on alert. At the islands' Guides' Whitsun camp in 1940, "Main activities were listening for news, and camouflaging tents. All tents must now be painted in two colours and must be pitched under trees." On 15 June the War Cabinet in London decided that in the event of invasion, Britain could not defend the islands, and advised the local government to surrender if the Germans came. The following week troops, military equipment and islanders of military age were evacuated.

Once France surrendered on 22 June, everything changed. Grace Le Roux, a teacher in St Helier on Jersey, remembers hearing the news: "My first intimation of what was about to happen was when my sister, who was a ledger clerk at de Gruchy's department store, came home in a great flutter — all employees had been assembled to be told that Jersey was to be occupied by the enemy within the next few days."

Everyone was evacuated from the small island of Alderney, as were half of Guernsey's population of 43,000, including most of the children. On Jersey, it was up to individual families to decide what to do, and most of those who had little relationship with England decided to stay on the island: their families had lived there for generations, and they had farms and businesses to run. No one thought that the evacuation would last more than a few months, and those of Norman stock, such as one Mr Dorey, maintained that "We, who were always a calm, steady people, have jogged along in our own way loving our lands and our surroundings."

In just a few days 11,000 people were evacuated to England, in whatever boats they could find. Then, on 28 June, German planes flew out of the clear blue sky over the port of St Helier, bombing and machine-gunning the harbour, killing a dozen civilians. For those who now decided that they wanted to evacuate, it was too late — the islands were cut off. The shocked islanders were left feeling abandoned by the British, and fearful of the enemy. A few tried to escape, but this, and other attempts at resistance, was considered counter-productive by many of the islanders. German reprisals were swift and cruel: Marcel Brossier was executed by firing squad for cutting a telephone line, and shortly afterwards Louis Bernier was shot for releasing a carrier pigeon with a message to England.

On 30 June, eight days after the fall of France, Guernsey was occupied by a small contingent of German troops. Jersey, Alderney and Sark surrendered within the next three days. The Channel Islands, which had been in the unbroken possession of the English Crown since 1066, fell without a shot being fired in their defence. Three days later a German plane dropped leaflets from the sky promising that "in case of peaceful surrender, the lives, property and liberty of peaceful inhabitants are solemnly guaranteed". Jersey's parliament, the States Assembly, had no alternative but to acquiesce, and later that day handed over authority to Captain Gussek, the German Commander. This was the first and only time that the German army invaded British soil.

"The Germans arrived in arrogant mood," wrote Victor Coysh in his book *Swastika over Guernsey*. "They believed that the conquest of Britain was imminent (some thought they were on the Isle of Wight!) and they could afford to be truculent." The invasion of the Channel Islands was both a symbolic victory and a strategic one. The islands' position eighty miles from the coast of England and twelve miles from France made them an ideal submarine base. There were also airports, safe harbours and banks containing gold and valuables.

At first, the islanders' relations with the occupying army were almost cordial, but as the years went on, and food and fuel became more scarce, life worsened for everyone. The inhabitants left behind were, to all intents and purposes, prisoners of war in a huge internment camp. Nightly curfew began at 11p.m., but this was soon brought forward to dusk. Shops remained open, but it was not long before they had nothing left to sell, because the Germans bought everything they could. The only radio stations people were allowed to listen to were German ones. The islands' beautiful beaches were out of bounds for swimming and fishing, cameras were confiscated; the hanging of flags strictly prohibited; and all societies and associations banned. Those that wore uniform, such as the Salvation Army, Brownies and Guides, were beyond the pale. But they refused to be rendered cheerless. Grace Le Roux had joined the Guides when they began in Jersey in 1919, and was now Captain of the 5th St Mark's Company, "I talked it over with the vicar, Mr Killer," she remembered. "He advised me to do my best to keep them going. 'Don't let Hitler best you,' he said. We kept going, but out of uniform."

Grace was not going to be frightened by a few thousand German soldiers. She also realised that with night curfews and everything closed down, the girls left behind on the Channel Islands needed a purpose, and to be reminded that they would not always be under German occupation. So she decided that undercover meetings would be held at her home. Their times were varied to suit changing conditions: "Early evenings in the summer, and later, when the gas didn't come on until six o'clock, the girls had to wait to have a meal before coming. In the winter it was Saturday afternoons. Naturally the girls did not wear uniform. But they came to my house for all the meetings. They came a few at a time, and by different routes, some entering by the back door and some by the front. The older girls, the Rangers, were wonderful, and the

248

parents co-operated marvellously. The Germans never had the slightest hint of what was going on." The Guides wore their badges under their coat lapels. They had to be very careful: when an elderly woman was seen wearing a brooch of the RAF, her husband was deported to prison in Germany, and she died soon after. "We soon found out that it was difficult to know who could be trusted," said Grace. "Plain-clothes Germans were always listening to conversations in the street and in the queues or even accosting Jersey folk to try and talk to them, to try and trip them up. So we kept pretty much to ourselves."

One night the Guides thought they had been discovered when they heard banging on the front door and shouting from the street. Grace opened the door to find a tall German soldier standing on the step. He politely explained that in the dark he had mistaken her house for the one next door, which had been reported for showing light around the blackout curtains. They all breathed a sigh of relief.

Heather Neil was fourteen when she joined Grace's company in 1941, and was soon taking her Second-Class Badge. "One clause was lighting a fire with two matches. As I lived in the country, and wood in towns was very hard to come by, Miss Le Roux asked me to bring in the kindling. I set my fire up in the garden, but wasn't allowed to light it. Even so, I passed. When I left school, it was too far to come into town, but my friend told me about the Sea Rangers, who met nearer my home. We met at Skipper's house, Miss May Rive. She was a wonderful lady, so full of fun. She found us badges, hats and ties, and her brother made our woggles. I spent many evenings sewing my top, made out of worn-out sheets, and she found some very scratchy navy blue wool for us to knit our jumpers."

May Rive held meetings for up to twenty Rangers at a time in her home. She also ran the 10th St Aubin Guide Company, and encouraged them to make slippers from old felt hats, and to practise outdoor cooking and fire-lighting. They sometimes went on weekend camps. "One weekend," remembered Heather Neil, "we stayed in a potato shed at my father's farm. Food was rationed but because we were on the farm there was milk, French beans and potatoes. On the Sunday while we were washing outside in the field, we heard the tramping of boots, coming down the road on the other side of the hedge. It was a group of German soldiers going back to their camp. Skipper made us all keep quiet until they had gone. We didn't camp there again, it was too dangerous." After that, despite the risk of deportation, the Sea Rangers camped in an empty cottage at St Brelade's Bay, arriving at different times from different directions. On at least two occasions they were questioned by German soldiers. They explained that they were a group of friends out together, and had not realised they were trespassing in a military zone.

The Germans allowed church services, and even prayers for the King and the royal family. "We decorated the font at St Mark's church with flowers for all the major festivals," said Grace Le Roux. They also took part in church parades, just as they had before the war. "We did not come in uniform or with colours, but we gathered at the church, marched up the aisle and sat in the places we used for normal parades. The Germans had no idea that we were doing it. We were just a group of girls. But we knew we were on parade, carrying invisible flags."

When the Rev. F.W. Killer told his congregation one Sunday that the altar linen was getting very worn, the Guides leapt to the challenge. Despite all the shortages, they managed to get a piece of table linen from De Gruchy's department store, and embroidered a set of purificators.

Within a month of the occupation, food rationing was introduced, with strict rules for farmers, who were not allowed to harvest or sell their own produce without permission from the German authorities. On 30 August, a man who owned a cow was fined £12 for making some butter for his own use. By the end of the year the sugar ration was three ounces per week, and the baking of rolls, cakes and pastry was forbidden. At first each person was allowed twelve ounces of meat per week, but after only a week that was halved. The wild rabbits and birds were soon all eaten. The bread ration started at four pounds per week, and was eventually cut to one pound per week, made with half wheat and half potato flour. Before the war, Jersey's main export had been potatoes but by 1941 there were so few that the public was implored to stop peeling them, and to eat them skin and all. They were also advised to eat stinging nettles, sorrel and dandelions. Eggs soon cost up to four shillings (the equivalent of £5 today) each, and only those with gardens had vegetables to eat.

Grace Le Roux spent much of her time making flour out of boiled potatoes, and sugar syrup from boiled sugar beets — "That was of course if we managed to produce a few potatoes or sugar beets." The beet was chopped up and boiled all night until it became a black pulp. This was then squeezed in a pillowcase under a car-jack, and the resulting juice was boiled again into a black treacle. Guides learned how to make "coffee" from ground acorns or roast parsnips, "tea" from the leaves of blackberries and roses, and "toothpaste" from powdered cuttlefish. Despite the ban on walking on the beaches, and the risk of treading on one of the 76,000 land mines, at night they would creep out and collect limpets, periwinkles and sand-eels. They used carrageen moss, a red seaweed, to thicken soups and jellies, and after the harvest they gleaned the fields for fallen wheat husks.

Women spent most Saturdays queuing — first in the market for the odd cauliflower or swede; then the apple queue; then, at two o'clock, the "skim queue" for the skimmed milk left over from butter-making. "Many times I saw the one in front of me get the last ration," said Grace. Once a fortnight she and her sister received a small piece of meat, "about the size and thickness of your palm, for the two of us". By spring 1941 the heating of public rooms was prohibited, and electric cookers and fires were banned. The coal and wood allowance were sufficient for about three hours' cooking or heating per day. "When fuel began to get short all the Guides had to crowd into one room," said Grace.

"Throughout the weary period of the German occupation the Military Authorities appeared to be constantly seeking means of every description to depress, dishearten and cast down into the lowest depths of despondency the civil population of Jersey," wrote R.C.F. Maugham in *Jersey Under the Jackboot*. "Every possible means was employed to render their cheerless lives if possible a shade more cheerless."

Hundreds of bicycles had been abandoned by evacuees at the ports, but once the fuel ran out, they became so valuable that the Germans confiscated them all. They also introduced driving on the right instead of the left, replaced the pound with the Reichsmark and made all schoolchildren learn German. Two newspapers were published, one in English and one in German, both claiming that Germany was assured of victory in the war and had successfully occupied the Soviet Union, and depicting the happy people of the Channel Islands enjoying life under Nazi rule. One sign of this happiness was a military-band concert in St Helier's Royal Square, largely attended by children. The bandmaster asked them if they liked chocolate. If so, they should raise their right arms on the count of three. They eagerly obeyed. At that moment a waiting photographer snapped, and the next day the *Insel Zeitung* showed the "Jersey Nazi Youth" singing along to German songs.

On Empire Day, 24 May 1942, Grace Le Roux's Guides met in St Aubin church hall, wearing their uniforms hidden under their coats. It was an offence to display a Union flag, but they felt the risk was worth it for special occasions. The company colours were smuggled in, and new Guides were enrolled. Then their uniforms and colours were returned to their hiding places in barns and under floorboards.

Two weeks later, all radio sets on the islands were confiscated. A few were hidden in attics and garden sheds, and news from the BBC was scribbled onto small pieces of paper and handed round in matchboxes. Despite the risk of a Gestapo raid, Catholic priest Father Rey made and distributed crystal sets on Jersey. One old woman known as Auntie Lily had no time to hide her crystal radio set when German soldiers came to search her house. Knowing she risked a fine of £3,000 or a prison sentence, she dropped it into a saucepan of bubbling soup. The soldier searching the kitchen commented on the delicious smell of the soup, and even lifted the lid for a sniff. Had she been sentenced to prison, she would have had to wait for a place to be available. "So many islanders were sent to jail," wrote Victor Coysh, "that they were obliged to wait their turn. They were notified by postcard when it was convenient to receive them."

The Guides carried on with their badge work as best they could. Before the paper completely ran out, they started to use pencils rather than ink, so they could rub out their writing and use the paper again. By 1942 there was no soap, so they used ash or fine sand for washing. When there was no more salt, sea water was sold at a penny a quart for cooking food. Clothing ration cards were useless, as there were no clothes left in the shops to buy. Once growing girls' skirt hems had

254

been lengthened as far as they could go, extra frills were added from curtains or sheets. Bartering became the norm, and advertisements appeared in the local paper offering "boots for flour", "long-sleeved jumper for tea" and even "a sovereign for 25lb of sugar".

Knitting wool went up in price from 4d per ball to 3s.6d, so to knit a jumper cost over £3, or £75 in today's money. One man was prosecuted for stealing sixteen shillings' worth of wool. When the leather soles of shoes wore out, they were replaced with wood. "The public appeared to grow accustomed to the unholy clatter of unyielding soles, and in the end acceptance of this moderately successful remedy came to be general," wrote Maugham.

"Conditions grew worse as time went on," remembered Grace Le Roux. "Who could do the Cook's test with only swedes and potatoes, or the Laundry Badge with no soap? Needlewoman with no needles or cotton thread, or for that matter, material? But we kept the Guide Spirit going, which is the most important thing." She kept the Union flag and the company colours hidden underneath her spare bed.

As far as she could, Grace continued as if life were normal. "I had a communication from Farley's the builders saying that we still owed £36 from work on the headquarters. So we decided to try to raise the money. We collected old Christmas cards, renovated them and resold them. We held Beetle Drives and the Robin Patrol put on a concert." It took eleven months, and then the Guides held three sales of work in secret in the parish hall, and donated the surplus to the Jersey

Society for the Blind and the Merchant Seamen's Benefit Fund. Despite the ban on listening to the BBC, in January 1941 Guides on the islands heard about the death of Baden-Powell, and the Founder's Memorial Fund. Determined to remain part of the world Guide movement, they raised funds for that too. "We ran a library," said Grace, "and lent each other books for a small fee."

In the summer of 1942 a column of barefooted, haggard men and teenage boys hobbled through St Helier town. They were Russian and Ukrainian prisoners of war who had been force-marched across Europe. Soldiers, holding fierce dogs on leads, surrounded the prisoners and drove them along with their whips. Under *Organisation Todt*, the civil and military engineering branch of Nazi Germany, 10,000 men were brought to build an underground hospital, and coastal fortifications on both Jersey and Guernsey.

Technically the slave workers were Allies, but they were desperate and starving, and so posed yet another threat to the islanders. They were let out after curfew to scavenge for food, but were so cold and hungry that they stole anything they could find from gardens and allotments: chickens, potatoes, even clothes on lines. A few kind-hearted families took pity on the prisoners, risking their lives to hide them in their attics.

In September 1942, all 2,000 adults under seventy who had been born in mainland Britain were rounded up and deported to German concentration camps. This was in reprisal for the internment of five hundred Germans in Iran, when the Shah changed sides and joined the Allies. Shortly afterwards, the twenty Jews living on Jersey were also sent to concentration camps. With so many German troops on the islands, there was little resistance. "You couldn't take to the mountains with arms," said Jersey farmer Norman le Broq. "First we've got no mountains, and second we had no arms."

After the fall of the nearby French port of Saint-Malo to American and British troops in August 1944, the Channel Islanders thought that freedom was around the corner. Instead, new shipments of German naval ratings arrived, resulting in even more mouths to feed. In addition to the 60,000 civilians left on the islands, there were now over 30,000 Germans. There were few horses left to eat, and not many carrots with which to make "tea". A farmer was fined £70 plus £20 costs (over £2,000 in today's money) for failing to declare the birth of a litter of pigs within forty-eight hours. Another man was fined £500 (£12,500) for selling fresh horsemeat without permission.

"The future seemed to hold but little worth living for," wrote Maugham. "Yet the people went about their daily concerns with a cheerful, if noticeably emaciated, appearance. It was easy to get a smile from them. They were not down-hearted." Indeed not, for the 5th St Mark's Guide Company celebrated their twenty-fifth anniversary with a special church parade, and by pooling all their rations were able to make a small cake. They concentrated on good turns such as collecting wood for older people, and making layettes for new babies.

In September 1944 all gas for cooking was cut off, and communal ovens opened in bakers' and restaurants. There were no matches, no candles and no cooking fat. Grace Le Roux was thrilled when she found a small quantity of paraffin left in an oil can. "I put it in a Milk of Magnesia bottle, pierced a hole in the top, pulled a piece of string out of a mop, and lo and behold we had a light. It was wonderful." By then there were only enough dried beans, tinned vegetables and fish to last two months, if they were strictly rationed.

By this time the Germans were commandeering "surplus" food from homes, including eggs and home-grown tobacco, neither of which had been rationed before. The Channel Islanders still felt forgotten and abandoned by Great Britain. Even after the Normandy landings, Churchill refused to authorise sending supplies to them, for fear that they would go to the German troops rather than the islanders. "Nothing came," wrote Maugham, "and day-by-day the future grew darker and more menacing. Little by little, hope died away." As the people had less, so the Germans took more. Even the oats for horses and the seed potatoes for spring planting were commandeered. Families were only allowed one dog each; any others had to be killed. Even cats disappeared from homes.

Just before Christmas, a friend of Grace Le Roux mentioned that he had found a branch for a Christmas tree for his little girl, but he had no decorations. "I remembered that we had some left from when our nieces used to come for Christmas. At the back of a drawer was a carrier bag. Not only did it hold some decorations, but better still, to my delight I found that it contained a dozen Christmas tree candles. It's amazing the amount of light a Christmas tree candle gives in the pitch dark."

The Christmas of 1944 was the toughest so far. "At Christmas time we tried to do our usual good turn," remembered Grace. "We dressed up old dolls for poorer children, and knitted bed socks for the elderly." A former St Helier Guide had just given birth to twin babies, and the Guides collected wood so she could bathe them in warm water. During the severe snow and frost of January 1945, nearly a hundred people died of cold and starvation. "The situation in general was deteriorating," wrote Victor Coysh, "despite the inevitable approach of victory and liberation."

The busiest of all the Guiders was Mildred Wadell, who for some years before the war had run *seven* separate Brownie and Guide companies every week. She had also started and ran the first Sea Rangers, and in 1924 had taken a group of Guides to the first World Camp, held at Foxlease in Hampshire. Hilda, one of the Guides, wrote at the time, "Everyone was very jolly, our only regret was that the whole company was not with us to enjoy it all, Good luck Miss Wadell! Long may she remain our Captain!!"

Mildred and her mother lived in a cottage overlooking Portelet Bay, on the west coast of Jersey. In the winter of 1944–45 it was so cold that old people could not be left at home, so Mildred's mother had moved into a nursing home. Mildred was alone at home on Boxing Day evening when she heard a noise outside. She went to investigate and found a young German soldier trying to steal her rabbits. The Germans were now as hungry as the islanders. In his desperation to find food, he shot Mildred. She died two days later in hospital from loss of blood. She was fifty-two years old, a loyal and devoted Guider.

At last, in January 1945, a Swedish Red Cross ship arrived from Portugal with food parcels, but no matches, soap or lamp oil. Each house-hold was allowed to turn on one electric bulb for an hour an evening, but at the end of the month even that was taken away — there was no more coal to run the power station, and even the communal kitchens were closed. Everyone learned to live in the dark. "Guide meetings were held in darkness," said Grace. "My sister and I used to go to bed to keep warm. To keep ourselves clean, I dug a trench fire in the garden, such as we used on Guide camp. We heated water in a camp Dixie on wood which we walked miles to collect, or cuttings from the rose bushes in the garden. This hot water we shared with our neighbours, and many times I've run out calling out, 'Anyone for a good wash tonight?'"

The Guernsey Girls' Intermediate School had been evacuated to Rochdale, Lancashire, so its Guide company continued to meet throughout the war. But there were still Rangers on Guernsey. Once a week they went to "tea" with the Island Commissioner, Miss Winifred Harvey. "When we went to these secret meetings, we entered one by one so as not to draw attention," remembered Nelly Falla. "We took our own carrot tea, the real thing having disappeared from the shops." Among other activities, they knitted squares for blankets, and made a new Island Standard out of old linen tablecloths. When their shoes wore out, they made new soles out of rope. Sixteen Rangers attended the "Thinking Day" parade in church on 22 February 1945.

By that time even the Germans were eating limpets from the rocks, as well as dogs and cats. Even with each islander rationed to just one small loaf of bread per week, there was only enough flour to last ten days. Another Red Cross ship arrived just in time, but by April the potato ration was only one pound per week per person, and farmers were told that *all* milk was to be delivered to the occupying authority. Any infringement would mean that 750 cattle would be slaughtered every month as a punishment.

The German troops now showed "clear signs of malnutrition and depression", wrote Maugham. "Completely devoid of animation, their uniforms patched and dirty, they slouched along, often out of step, with no longer any trace of their former military smartness." Mutiny was in the air, and on 7 March the Palace Hotel was destroyed by a time bomb, killing twenty-four officers in what was explained away as "an accident". General Wolff, newly arrived from the SS, suffered two attempts on his life from his own men. Admiral Heuffmeier of the Kriegsmarine tried to rally his troops by yelling: "Officers and men of the Fortress of Jersey, we stand by the Führer." But the troops had no desire to hold the Fortress of Jersey: they wanted some decent food, and no more horse sausage, nettle soup or stolen turnips.

"News got around somehow that the end was in sight," said Grace. "On Tuesday, 8 May, a great crowd gathered in Royal Square to hear Winston Churchill's famous speech relayed on the wireless. When he got to 'Our dear Channel Islands are to be freed today' such a roar went up that no one knew what he said after!"

At last, the people of the Channel Islands were free. The Guide flags hidden in barns and under floorboards for five long years were brought out, and within an hour every house flew a Union flag. "Happy, laughing crowds thronged the streets," remembered Maugham. "The atmosphere was one of a carefree holiday. We still had very little food, but nobody cared."

The next morning all the Guides put on their uniforms. Many had grown a lot taller since they last wore them in public, and all were thinner. They joined the crowd to watch HMS *Beagle* steam into the bay, and two British officers alight from a tender to accept the German surrender. By six o'clock that evening, all German troops were disarmed and moved to holding centres. By nightfall, no German uniform was seen on the streets. The tables had turned, and the islanders set to work removing the barbed wire and land mines, and dumping 16,000 tons of ammunition in the sea.

Saturday, 12 May was declared a public holiday. "The brilliant weather continued," wrote Maugham. "While British planes of various types roared overhead, an immense concourse of people thronged the port and the roadway running round the bay, watching the arrival of British troops." The landing ships arrived on the beaches and unloaded food and supplies, and then loaded up again with German prisoners of war. A few were kept to remove the land mines and barbed wire. "Where yesterday there was only misery, today there were only smiles. Everything was joyful, from the unbroken May sunshine, to the coloured flags. Electricity and the telephone service were at once restored, potatoes were still scarce but bread became abundant. Everything German disappeared, from their currency to the restrictions."

The next day all the Guides went to church. "We had thirty in full uniform, with Colours — the first time for five years." When Mrs Obbard, the Island Commissioner, returned, St Mark's Company proudly handed her the receipt for £36 from Farley's builders. They also sent £10 to London for the Founder's Memorial Fund. At the first Sea Rangers camp they flew the burgee, or small pennant, they had made from donated scraps of fabric. A year later, Olave Baden-Powell, the World Chief Guide, visited Jersey and presented Patrol Leader Margaret Artus of the St Mark's Company with the brand-new Queen's Award. Lieutenant-Governor Sir Arthur Edward Grasett, now head of state of Jersey, said it was "a Battle Award for gallantry, courage and meritorious service, in the face of the enemy". It poured with rain all day, but that did not stop the Brownies and Guides enjoying a picnic tea. During the five years of occupation, Grace Le Roux had held over two hundred undercover Guide meetings in defiance of the German authorities.

When the Guides of Wimbledon and Mitcham heard the story of the Jersey Guides, they were so impressed that they made a special flag. It took seven months for all 1,500 Guides to add at least one stitch each, and after they had finished their work in June 1946, they took the flag to the islands and handed it over to the Jersey Guides. Then everyone sang the Guides International song:

Our noble standard, the golden trefoil,
We'll proudly raise to heaven above.
We'll face the future with joy and courage,
And build a new world with our love.

Each Jersey company kept the Wimbledon flag for three months, and as it was passed on, the story of the Guides of the Channel Islands under German occupation was told again and again.

CHAPTER
FOURTEEN

Japanese Internment

In September 1943, nearly a year after being interned by the Japanese, the Chefoo school in China moved again. Nearly 250 men, women, and children were packed like sardines into a small steamer and taken around the Shantung peninsula. In addition to the schoolchildren and their teachers, there were also teachers' babies and a few grandparents.

"The journey was terrible," recalled Margaret Vindon, whose missionary parents were living in western China. "We were all put into the dirty cargo hold of a boat full of cockroaches. Fortunately our teachers had brought food for us all." For Margaret it was even worse than her first trip on a coastal steamer in 1935. At the age of eight, she had been returning from her annual holiday visiting her parents, and had travelled to Shanghai by train to board the SS *Tungchow* for the three-day journey north to Chefoo. Soon after leaving port, Chinese pirates took control of the boat, which was carrying seventy Chefoo schoolchildren and their teachers.

There were about a dozen pirates, with a leader who wore a purple checked jacket. They had posed as second-class passengers. They smashed the ship's radio and painted the funnel black. The Captain and his first and second officers were British, the rest of the crew were Chinese. The crew were forced to obey the pirates. Our teachers behaved very calmly. We had to hand over our pocket money that we had been given for the whole year. We had to put up our hands when the pirates came in. My friend Ethel shared a bunk with me; we slept heads to tails. I was very frightened that a pirate would come in the night so I held a rock in my hands. Ethel thought she saw a pirate come in and take some of Miss McNare's pills. There were some White Russian guards, and one was shot dead.

One of the officers was shot in the leg and he lay propped up in the corridor of the boys' and girls' cabins. We had to step over him to our cabins. We were only allowed out for meals, and the rest of the time the portholes were screwed shut, to stop us signalling to any passing ships.

The *Straits Times* reported that officials believed the pirates had captured the schoolchildren with a view to demanding a huge ransom. In fact they had been told that the ship was carrying gold. When they opened the cargo, it was full of oranges, on their way to Peking for the Chinese new year. The SS *Tungchow* was steered towards a pirates' lair in a bay near Hong Kong, a thousand miles south of Shanghai. The news made the headlines across the world. After four days, planes from

HMS *Hermes* located the ship, the pirates fled and she was escorted into Hong Kong. The children sang:

> In nineteen hundred and thirty-five
> The pirates captured us alive
> But British planes scared off the hive
> Chefoo, Chefoo, for ever!

Now, in 1943, it was not pirates but Japanese soldiers who were taking the children by sea. "They stacked us like cords of wood in the hold of a ship," said Mary Taylor. After leaving the ship at Tsingtao they were bundled into overcrowded third-class railway carriages for the three-hour journey west to the city of Weihsien, now Weifang.

Weihsien "Civilian Assembly Centre" held 1,450 prisoners of thirteen nationalities, mainly British, but also including Belgians, Dutch, Norwegians, Palestinian Jews, North and South Americans, and a Cuban jazz band. There were forty-four families with children, each allotted a single room only nine feet by twelve. Single adults and unaccompanied children slept in dormitories. This was fine for the children, but more difficult for adults who had little in common with their fellow internees. White Russian nightclub singers wanted to chat into the night, while female missionaries wanted to pray and sing hymns early in the morning. Teachers, such as Brown Owls Evelyn Davey and Inez Phare, shared dormitories with the schoolchildren. The wealthy head of the largest British mining company had left behind two Rolls-Royces and mansions in Tientsin, and now shared a small room with two other bankers.

Weihsien Civilian Assembly Centre was a social leveller. Before the war, while the Chinese people had coped with starvation, opium addiction and smallpox, European businessmen and their families had lived in large, comfortable houses with servants. They may have seen starving beggars, dead babies in gutters and Chinese men bayoneted by Japanese soldiers, but their lives were pleasant and easy. Now, professors, missionaries and businessmen became bakers, carpenters and hospital orderlies. Monks, a restaurant owner and two aged Iranian bakery owners taught the new cooks how to make a little food go a long way. An American woman welcomed the Chefoo school as she flourished a big carving knife: "Oh folks, it's fun — I'm cutting bread, and it's just like Camp." No Chinese were allowed into the camp, except to carry out sewage in buckets.

"When we arrived in Weihsien camp in September 1943, the existing inmates lined the route," said Estelle Cliff. "Imagine their despair in seeing a bunch of schoolchildren! But we were 'seasoned internees'." "The best-organised and most efficient group of all was the Chefoo School group," wrote William Chilton, a mine manager and internee.

The camp had formerly been an American Presbyterian mission training centre called "The Courtyard of the Happy Way". There was a hospital, a church, three kitchens, a bakery and school buildings, as well as the dormitories and family rooms. The compound was three hundred yards across at its widest point, and two hundred yards long. It was surrounded by a grey brick wall with electrified barbed wire stretched along the top, overlooked at each corner by guard towers with slots for machine guns. The forty-five Japanese Consular Police guards lived in six European-style houses behind a high wall.

There was no machinery, running water or sanitation. There was one working latrine per hundred people, and the smell of sewage pervaded every corner. A Russian woman was heard to wail, "For why I am in this constipation camp?" The boys hand pumped water every day from shallow wells into a main tank, and it was then carried in buckets to the kitchens and the hospital by the girls. In the dormitories, only eighteen inches separated each mattress from the next. Every snore, belch and sound of urine hitting the pot was heard by all. Ailsa Carr, a Chefoo teacher, described the view from the girls' dormitory, while also demonstrating her positive attitude to their situation.

Two large windows of dangerous & uncertain habits owing to broken sash-cords. Red Cross boxes from which protrude tins, paper wrappers, & other erstwhile contents of local garbage boxes. Between windows hang medicine cupboard (medical inspection not invited) overladen bookcase & highly coloured Wolf Cub noticeboard.

South Aspect. Kitchen. Large brick stove, somewhat out of perspective. Stove pipe, an artistic arrangement of Spam tins, invisibly joined.

Remaining wall space taken up by blackboard, over which all school subjects wrangle for right of way, proving truth of saying "the weakest goes to the wall". Shelves holding soap, soda, scrubbing brushes & other paraphernalia of the modern laundry, laundry baskets, & shelves containing entire educational stock in trade; i.e. a few textbooks. A little stationery & lack of everything else.

The Floor. Boards interspersed with holes; air holes, rat holes, & holes which obviate the need of a dustpan. Any of the following activities may add a human touch to this artist's paradise: children sleeping, children washing, children cooking, children eating, children learning & children playing. Finally children praising for "all good gifts around them" & praying that one day they may know the joy of another, "better" home.

The Camp Commandant, Mr Tsukigawa, was nicknamed "King Kong", and the Chief of Police, Mr Nagamatzu, was known as "P'u-Shing-T'i", his only phrase in Mandarin, which means "No can do". Although the camp was under the control of the Japanese, they left the prisoners to govern themselves with nine elected committees, run on socialist-Marxist principles: "*From* each according to their ability and *to* each according to their need." Even the most capitalist businessmen agreed that with so little to go round, and nothing to spare, it was the only way.

The young helped the old with physical tasks; the old helped the young with intellectual ones. "The prisoners did everything — cooked, baked, swabbed latrines," wrote Mary Taylor. "My older sister, Kathleen, scrubbed clothes while my brother Jamie pumped long shifts at the water tower and carried garbage. Before and after school, I mopped my square of floor, mended clothes, stoked the fire. Awash in a cesspool of every kind of misery, Weihsien was, nonetheless, for us, a series of daily triumphs — earthy victories over bedbugs, rats and flies. The Battle of the Bedbugs was launched each Saturday. With knife or thumbnail, you attack each seam of your blanket or pillow, killing all the bugs and eggs in your path." "One day I caught fifty-eight bedbugs and squashed them between my fingernails," said Kathleen Strange's younger sister Beryl. "They bit every night." The bedbugs left itchy bites, smears of blood and a terrible stench.

For the summer's plague of flies, schoolchildren were organised into competing teams of fly-killers. Mary Taylor's brother John won the first prize of a tin of liver pâté, with 3,500 flies in his bottle. "If you shudder at the rats scampering over you at night," wrote Mary, "you set up a Rat Catching Competition, with concentration-camp Pied Pipers clubbing rats, trapping rats, drowning them in basins, throwing them into the bakery fire, Our Chefoo School won that contest, too, with Norman Cliff and his team bringing in sixty-eight dead rats — thirty on the last day. Oh, glorious victory! The nearest competitor had only fifty-six."

The Japanese allowed complete religious freedom, and church services were held every Sunday for Anglicans, the Salvation Army and Catholics, or all together. Meetings, plays, concerts, piano recitals, orchestral concerts and exhibitions provided an escape from the barbed wire, stinking latrines and hunger. One Good Friday the choral society of eighty were singing Stainer's *Crucifixion* when the electric lighting was cut off. Without stopping, each singer produced a home-made peanut-oil lamp, and the programme continued without a hitch. The twenty-two-piece orchestra combined the brass of the Salvation Army band, woodwinds from the Tientsin Dance Band, and violins and cellos of assorted internees.

According to Witte Kant, a German reporter on the propaganda newspaper the *Peking Chronicle*, "Life is comparatively comfortable, although they are interned; and this is evidence of the greatness of the magnanimous spirit of Japan. They may visit their friends, hold tea parties, read, write and exercise, but they have to do their duties. The guards on the Japanese Consulate have become well acquainted with the school children and they often send them some dolls, toys and small birds as presents."

By the time the Chefoo school arrived, the six doctors and dozen nurses in the camp had the hospital of twenty-six beds up and running, with dental and eye clinics, an operating theatre, laboratories and a psychiatric ward. Before internment, the medical staff had filled their trunks with equipment and drugs, and had given every person they met some medicine to bring in their luggage.

Constance Mann, matron of the Chefoo hospital, had brought linen, surgical instruments and drugs. Mary Layton, a midwife from Yorkshire who had worked in China for ten years, brought her tool kit, her violin, her folding deckchair and a broom. They set to work in the hospital, which had no running water or central heating, but was clean and efficient: considering the overcrowded conditions of the camp, the death rate was quite low, with more babies born than people dying. A new baby always cheered everyone up, and gifts of a few ounces of sugar or extra flour were collected for the christening cake. Kathleen Nordmo had been born with a heart defect, although her parents had not known this when they left her at Chefoo school. Once interned, she spent much time in the hospital. "As a Brownie, I tried to do a good deed every day. I mended underwear and the ladders in the teachers' stockings with a special hook. I helped take care of a baby born in camp with a cleft palate. The food came out of her nose." The Weihsien doctors constructed an artificial palate for her out of melted-down toy soldiers. When one of the doctors delivered a baby for the Commandant's wife, her follow-up care of both mother and baby softened the Japanese guards' attitudes to all the internees.

Monsieur Egger, the Swiss Consul in the nearby city of Tsingtao (modern-day Qingdao), visited the camp once a month. A stiff, formal man, he had been an importer before the war whose life had revolved around playing bridge and sipping whisky in his club. Now he found himself the Red Cross representative, smuggling in supplies of aspirin and soap under the seat of his car. After Mr A. Jost, Assistant-Delegate of the International Red Cross, visited the camp in November 1943 he wrote: "Although the Weihsien camp is remote, the locality is a pleasant and healthy one. Inmates looked well and cheerful and expressed their appreciation over the good treatment accorded to them and the kindness of the Camp Commandant." This strangely positive account remained classified until 1996.

Twice a day, all internees had to assemble at their allotted places for roll call with their prisoner numbers pinned to their chests. The guards counted them and then tallied the totals from all six roll-call assembly points. The numbers rarely added up. "Delays to the all-clear bell often dragged on and on," wrote Mary Taylor. "In summer we wilted in the insufferable heat; in winter we froze in the snow. While the Japanese tallied the prisoner count, we played marbles, or practised semaphore and Morse code for our Brownie and Guide badges. We never had to take the Thrift Badge, we all got it immediately."

When no one was looking, some of the Brownies befriended the Japanese guards, who talked about their own children at home and sometimes gave the girls sweets. The Chefoo children helped the guards with families to overcome their homesickness, and the Commandant was proud of his charges. "When visiting Japanese officials monitored the camp," wrote Mary Taylor, "our roll call was the highlight of the show —

little foreign devils with prep-school manners, standing with eyes front, spines stiff at attention, numbering off in Japanese: *Ichi . . . nee . . . san . . . she . . . go . . .* "

After a few months, everyone's clothes were worn out, and no one wasted shoe leather in the summer. "We wore only hand-me-downs and swaps," said Kathleen Strange. "In the summer we only wore shoes on Sundays. The rest of the week we hopped from shadow to shadow to avoid the scorching ground." But standards were not allowed to slip: "We could roll up our sleeves for Guides, provided we did it tidily."

The children were hungry most of the time. Breakfast was rough sorghum or bean porridge, sometimes flavoured with orange peel. "Lunch was always stew, stew, stew," wrote Mary Taylor. "S.O.S., we called it: Same Old Stew. Supper was more leftover stew — watered down to soup, and bread." Meat came in unrefrigerated trains, and was often too rotten or maggot-ridden to eat. There was no fruit, but the Brownies made peanut butter by grinding peanuts between two flat stones. Vegetables were rare, but occasionally included sweet potatoes, field cucumbers, coarse winter radishes, water reeds or weeds such as clover. Adults worked twelve-hour shifts in the three kitchens, besides cleaning out latrines and carrying water. Guides helped to prepare food while Scouts washed up.

People were generous to each other in many ways, such as making stoves out of old tins, but when it came to food, with so little to go around, there was frequent rudeness, anger and accusations of unfairness. "Having been taught self-control," said Mary Taylor, "we Chefoo children watched the cat fights with righteous fascination. Shrieking women in the dishwashing queue hurled basins of greasy dishwater at each other. Fights were common. But not among the Chefoo contingent. The teachers insisted on good manners. 'There is no such thing,' they said, 'as one set of manners for the outside world and another set for a concentration camp.' You could be eating the most awful-looking glop out of a tin can or a soap dish, but we had to be as refined as the two princesses in Buckingham Palace. 'Sit up straight. Don't stuff food in your mouth. Don't talk with your mouth full. Don't lick your knife. Spoon your soup toward the back of the bowl, not toward the front. Keep your voice down. Don't complain.'"

The black market provided eggs for the youngest children and hospital patients. Chinese farmers were eager to sell, so while the children distracted the guards with wild-goose chases, the goods were slipped over the wall. This continued until two farmers were caught, and were executed by firing squad within earshot of the camp.

By the end of 1944, supplies of flour, oil and meat had been halved, and were often rotten when they arrived. An American vet in the camp inspected all meat to determine whether it should be eaten immediately or buried. Soup was described as "Consommé Royale — with 47 eggs": greasy water with white flakes floating in it, and one egg for every thirty people. The guards too were running out of food,

276

and their increasingly erratic behaviour showed they were worried.

Despite the difficult conditions of the camp, the Chefoo teachers were determined to continue educating the children. "All of our teachers were remarkable," said Guide Audrey Nordmo, the sister of Kathleen. "They gave us a normal existence. They had to teach, be involved with camp chores — and do all the things that in Chefoo they had Chinese servants to do."

"Our teachers fashioned a protective womb around our psyches, insulating and cushioning us with familiar routines, daily school and work details," said Mary Taylor. "Structure. Structure. Structure. Our teachers taught us exactly what to expect. They marched us off to breakfast for a splash of steaming *gaoliang* — sorghum gruel (animal feed, even by Chinese standards). They trooped us back to our dormitory, mug and spoon in hand, to scrub the floor. We grouped for morning prayers, and sang the psalms and hymns taught us by our parents. We lined up for inspection. Were we clean? Were we neat? Did we have our mending done? We settled down on our steamer-trunk beds for school: English, Latin, French, history, Bible. School must go on. Structure was our security blanket."

In the very crowded conditions, with no classrooms and very few materials, teachers and children managed the best they could. The children did their lessons sitting on their beds, which were their trunks pushed together, with a thin mattress on top. "There were six female teachers and we did lessons round the trunks," remembers Beryl Strange. When they ran out of exercise books, they rubbed out their work and used them again and again, until the paper disintegrated. With no idea how long the war would last, the children were kept in the same classes throughout their four years of internment.

Chefoo school had been known as the best English-speaking school east of the Suez, and the teachers had no intention of letting standards drop now. The sixth formers studied each year for their Oxford matriculation exams, which were required for entrance to universities in England. "Nothing will change," said the teachers, who had taken old exam papers into the camp with them. "You will go to school each day. You will study. You will take your Oxfords. You will pass."

Sitting on mattresses in their dormitory, the children conjugated Latin verbs with Mr Martin; they studied Virgil and Bible history and French under the trees. Between roll calls, scrubbing laundry, scouring latrines, hauling garbage and stoking kitchen fires, the sixth formers crammed for their exams, and then took them in the hope that one day they would be able to have their papers marked in Britain. It wasn't only the children who had the opportunity to learn. The internees organised adult education classes on everything from bookkeeping to history. They attended discussions on science and religion, with agnostics, Catholics and Protestants debating creation and the Resurrection.

Even though they were now prisoners in an internment camp, the Chefoo Brownies continued to meet every Tuesday from 4.20 to 5.35p.m. As Brown Owl of the 2nd Chefoo Pack, Evelyn Davey was always upbeat, cheering up even the adults. Her Tawny Owl was Isobel Harris, whose parents were teachers in the school. Inez Phare was Brown Owl of the 1st Chefoo Brownies, and her Tawny Owl was Ruth Greening, another Chefoo teacher, aged twenty-nine, who had been in China for seven years.

In October 1943, a few weeks after arriving at the camp, Inez Phare wrote in the log book: "*Weihsien*. Well, I guess there's a good deal of fun to be got out of this. Just the place to earn some badges. Practise semaphore this week, and make a sketch using string, of a well-known person." A week later she wrote: "Make a sketch of a familiar part of our camp." She pasted some of these into the log book — they show wooden huts and a few trees, but no people. She wrote nothing in the book that might annoy the Japanese. A newspaper cutting of Queen Elizabeth in her Guider uniform is labelled only "Who is this?"

"At Weihsien we kept on teaching, and we kept on with the Brownies," said Evelyn Davey. "We had to think of things we could do in a small space, and we didn't have many materials — there was no paper for craft projects. I sent out little notes to the girls, to tell them what we would do at the next Brownie meeting. I think being a Brownie was very important to the girls. It was a change of routine, something to look forward to every week. The worst part was getting homesick. Otherwise, if you were young, it was like a big adventure — a permanent camp. The best part about being a Brown Owl was the adventure. It was different. Most of my friends were at home teaching."

There were forty-one Chefoo girls who had no parents with them. "The Brownie pack kept everyone alive and alert, not just the girls. It stopped us all sitting around feeling sorry for ourselves. The children helped, and vice versa." The Brown Owls protected their Brownies from fear by creating an insulating and comforting daily routine of school, work and Brownies. "Brown Owl kept the children away from the prostitutes, alcoholics, bored adolescents, and scroungers and thieves who filched extra food from the kitchens and stole coal balls left to bake in the sun," remembers Mary Taylor. "Brown Owl, Evelyn Davey, really put everything she had into it," recalled Beryl Strange, the younger sister of Kathleen. "She wrote notices every week for us in exciting ways, such as doors in toadstools. She taught us country dancing and took us through our badges, which were all hand-made. We had proper uniforms. I gained a Craft Badge, Sewing and Knitting, Observer, Toy Making, Signalling, Sport, Jester and First-aid. We also had a special competition with points which I won. Miss Davey had a friend carve an octagonal trophy with a toadstool on it. I still treasure this and my badges."

"Good work is being done in the Concentration Camp," wrote Brown Owl of the Brownies' garden. They made notes of progress for their Gardener Badge. "But in our horribly crowded quarters," Mary Taylor remembers, "someone stepped on my tiny garden."

"Brownies took over our lives," said Jenny Bevan. "We met once a week but we lived being Brownies all the time. We worked for our tests and badges in every spare moment. During meetings we heard all about Baden-Powell, and the stories of Mowgli and *The Jungle Book*. We learnt to light a fire using only two matches. They were genuinely scarce and we were proud if we could manage with only one! Our meetings always drew to a close with campfire songs and ended with Taps. The words, 'All is well, safely rest, God is nigh' were greatly comforting to an eight-year-old girl. We were given a purpose to our lives and were taught independence."

Despite the Japanese guards, tracking and observing remained an important Brownie activity. "It is a disgrace to a Brownie if she is not the first to see or hear anything unusual," Agnes Baden-Powell had written. "So that coming along the road she may say, 'Halloh! That is the same man with the big nose and the old boots whom I saw in the village yesterday.'"

As if they were at home, the Brownies were reminded to clean their teeth, blow their noses and do Good Deeds. They were expected to make their beds with perfect "hospital corners", which was difficult in the crowded dormitories where everyone slept squashed together like sardines.

Like the Brownies, the Guides interned in Weihsien were determined to rise above their situation. Brown Owl Inez Phare was also Captain of the Chefoo Guides, assisted by Constance Mann SRN as Lieutenant, and Miss Monica Priestman, a Chefoo teacher. Marian Bevan kept a log book for the Kingfisher Patrol from October 1943 to December 1944. The first entry reads: "Dear Kingfishers. Here we are in Weihsien! But still carrying on Guides. Let's ask God to help us make this Guide year a success. We are going to do our very bestest to win this year aren't we? To begin with we are going to revise the 2nd class — Fires, tracking, and most important — Posture!"

Margaret Vindon became a Guide in 1936, when she was eleven, and later a Ranger. "We continued with Girl Guides as best we could, learning and earning some badges. We couldn't get badges from England so we embroidered our own. On one occasion we were all sitting on the floor facing our Captain. She spotted the Japanese guard coming and ordered us to take off our ties and sit on them. We dared not appear like a military organisation." In fact the Japanese did not mind uniformed organisations, and the Guides soon wore their uniforms openly.

Margaret remembered, "I did my good turn for the day as a Ranger by caring for an old couple who were limited in what they could do for themselves. I learned how to teach three-year-old children in preschool classes. I had become a Christian a year before I was interned and I had plenty of opportunity to practise and develop my trust in God in camp. My brother learned to cut boys' hair and be a baker."

Six weeks after arriving at Weihsien, in October 1943, the Guides prepared their dormitory for a wedding reception for internees Albert Rouse, a widower, and Rita Dobson, a Chefoo teacher aged forty-two. The Guides made a wedding cake out of bread they had saved, stuck together with the last of their jam. "We got it all ready, also the church," wrote Kathleen in one of the three Red Cross letters her mother, who was living on her own in Szechwan after her husband had died of typhus, received in as many years. "Weather cool. Skirts and jerseys. Went and saw the wedding presents. They were all very nice. I gave her a pincushion with R A embroidered on it. We have lessons now 3 hours a day. Mrs Houghton sends love."

In addition to the Chefoo Guides, the 1st Weihsien Guide Company was formed for girls who had come to the camp from Peking and Tientsin. Their Captain was Mrs Louise Lawless, a fifty-one-year-old Swiss woman who had married an Irishman. Before the war she had been running a Guide company in Tientsin for girls from Britain, Holland and Belgium.

At the end of April 1944, Sue Grice, the thirteen-year-old daughter of the surgeon at Weihsien, and Joyce Cooke, the fifteen-year-old daughter of a British accountant, went to Guide camp held in the school playground. "There was great excitement as we took bedding and slept on the ground in a tent." Gay Talbot Stratford, aged twelve, was interned with her parents at Weihsien. Her father had worked in a British — Belgian coalmining company. "I was proud to be a Girl Guide with the 1st Weihsien Company. It was a novel experience as my family had always lived in mining districts where I had only one or two playmates. We sang a round in English and French: 'La haut sur la montagne il est un vieux chalet.' A round which was not particularly appropriate in the circumstances. Still, we sang it with gusto." "Captain Lawless threw herself heart and soul into making our time in concentration camp days we would never forget," said Margaret Vindon. "It gave us a glorious spirit of adventurous living and service. Our education was very academic, so the Guides filled in the practical aspects. I took my Child Nurse Badge by helping to bath the little ones."

Guide Beryl Welch was awarded the "Weihsien Star", made from a Spam tin, for reading and talking to patients in the hospital. "We were surrounded by electrified barbed wire, a wall and trenches," she remembered. "But we could always look up, as high as you like. Mr Harris came one dark and starry night to teach us the constellations. My best friend was Winnie, and my surname was Welch. Soon after we arrived in the camp Winnie was repatriated to the USA. On our last evening together we looked up at the night sky and vowed that every time we saw Cassiopeia, the W in the sky, we would think of each other. It was many years before we met, but we had shared the same stars."

There were plenty of obstacles to passing Guide proficiency badges, including the need to embroider the badges themselves, but they could usually be overcome. Cook's Badge could only be done in theory — with little food, practical cooking was impossible. "For my daily good turn I made the bed of an elderly couple every day," said Marian Bevan. "Mrs Warren, wife of the school's Business Manager, taught us household skills." When Marian and Mary took the Hiker's Badge they were supposed to hike at least two miles, light a campfire, cook a meal and return home. "Captain told us how many times we had to go around the camp to resemble walking two miles, which brought us back to the hospital building in which we lived. We collected some sticks and laid the fire but — we forgot to bring the matches! So we dashed upstairs and knocked on her door — she gave us a severe look and said, 'Did you run all the way back?' Of course she knew we hadn't. She gave us the matches and we ran downstairs, completed our lunch and hiked the two-mile circuit back."

"We worked hard at earning badges," said Gay Talbot Stratford. "For 'Invalid Care', we had to draw the ideal sickroom, with attention given to the placement of windows, purely an academic exercise." Gay embroidered a sampler on a handkerchief for her Needlewoman's Badge, which other Guides passed by making pyjamas for the hospital. They then helped patch and repair in the sewing room, run by Dorothy Potter, the wife of a British customs official. "One of the best British cutters in North China cut out shorts, trousers and overalls from chair covers, curtains and bedspreads," wrote Dorothy.

The 2nd Chefoo Guides Patrol Leaders met once a month to discuss the programme. Three troublesome girls, whose behaviour was not up to scratch, were not allowed to be enrolled until they could face up to the responsibility of being a Guide. "Dorothy and Joyce must both pull up on carriage and general neatness & cleanliness," noted the minute book. "Captain advises use of mirrors though not with a view to inculcating vanity!" Talking after "lights-out" was a test of a Guide's sense of honour and obedience: "Joy has improved a bit but not enough for her All-round cords."

In September 1944 the Japanese forbade both campfires and the drawing of maps, even of the compound, but Captain Phare decided it was more important for her Guides to pass the First-Class Test, so ignored this new rule. "A rough sketch map does not mean rough, but simple and clear," she told the girls.

"We had to draw maps of places like the children's library and the clinic," said Marion Bevan. "They had to be folded into very small pieces and hidden in our socks in case the Japanese guards saw them." Six months later, the Japanese changed their minds: "It is now alright to draw neighbourhood maps from memory, but we must not walk around the Camp drawing them." A new patrol called Thrushes was formed, and "Captain expects good singing from them. The Singing at the meeting needs to be improved, we should sing as though we enjoy it."

CHAPTER
FIFTEEN

The Warsaw Uprising

In the summer of 1944 the Polish "Home Army" resistance movement in the Warsaw ghetto decided it was time to rise up against the Nazis. Over 4,000 female doctors and nurses, many of them Guides or Rangers, set up eighty-four first-aid posts, and allocated 560 medical patrols to combat units. They knew their neighbourhoods well, and so were able to lead the partisans, while carrying documents, weapons and medical supplies. More than three hundred Guides joined the Home Army as liaison officers; known as the "Messengers of Joy", they crawled through the sewers, carrying messages and laying telephone wires. The Uprising was only planned to last a few days, until the Soviet army arrived. But it turned into a bloodbath that lasted two months.

From the start, on 1 August 1944, there was chaos as Germans obliterated one district after another. Some first-aid posts and hospitals lasted just a couple of days before they were destroyed. Of the eight Guides running the medical unit in Moniuszki Street on 5 August, three were wounded and one was killed.

One Guide company worked in a hospital in the basement of the PKO Bank. "It took us a couple of days to organise the medicine, medical equipment and dressing materials in the bank's archive department," wrote their Captain, "Iza" Zofia Schuch. Between shifts, they sewed clothes for children, delivered post or sang with the wounded.

A field hospital in Trzech Krzyzy Square was staffed by thirty Guides from the Wybrzeze Kościuszkowskie Company. One of them, Zofia Zawadzka, wrote in her diary:

At night Celina comes: "Get up." I crawl from my bunk, wake up Kasia, take my bag, a torch and we are off. "This passage," I hear the voices. "Come through this hole." I see a tiny hole in the wall, just made. I can hardly squeeze through. They pull me inside. I am in the basement. It is almost dark because of the dust. Some people are working in the weak light of a torch. They are digging out people from the rubble. A horrible view. A woman is lying, her legs still under the rubble. Under her body her 8-year-old child is already dead. She is dying. How to help her? I send Kasia to bring some camphor. Meanwhile I put a wet hanky to her mouth. Finally I have a syringe, out of spite the needle is blocked. Kasia runs to get a second needle. You could suffocate from the dust here. Some more superhuman efforts and the woman is pulled out. Now we take her through the hole in the wall and finally she gets some fresh air. We put her on the stretcher. I try to give her an injection but the needle bends. What bad luck. In a rush we carry her to the ward. Unfortunately we brought a corpse.

Guide Karina Kujawska was working in the same district of Warsaw.

It is night. We have to join the rescue at Zurawia St. The Germans have started systematically bombing relatively calm streets. It is quite dark. Suddenly the illuminating red light of a rocket. It is lighter, so light that this lightness reaches all my body cells. I feel as if I am naked and there is nowhere to hide. There is a moment of horrifying fright, and then nothing, a kind of motionless composure. The sound of an approaching aeroplane, a whistle, rumble, shake, rush of air that makes everything collapse, a fog of dust and a terror of what might be left.

We are running with the stretcher. I can see people, rubble and flames from the other side. A man in a burning jacket is carrying somebody out of a collapsed house.

Crying out of wounded people. My hair is burning. Somebody puts it out. The Guides have taken out some wounded people already. Then we realise that there was a bomb shelter under the collapsed house. The exit is full of rubble.

I don't know where I get it from but I begin to command loudly. My voice has changed, strange, not mine. After a few moments the people become subordinate, the tension has eased up.

I am terribly tired tonight but there is no possibility of rest — all the time we have to run somewhere and save someone.

The first-aid post commanded by Guide Captain Irena Zychowska was in an air-raid shelter, but it did not protect those inside: "There are Germans everywhere. They have found vodka somewhere, they are drunk. They attack women, shoot the sculptures of saints. They have shot a mentally ill person in the corridor. One of the soldiers took out a grenade. He was shouting that he had enough and wants to die, but everybody else will die with him. Recently a young woman joined us, her codename is Ewa. She speaks German very well. She went to the German, stroked his cheek and led him outside. We were all saved." Later that night a group of drunk Germans wandered into the shelter, demanding girls. Irena and Ewa hid the young Guides at the back of the shelter until they had gone.

"The Germans were ordered to conquer the Old Town at any price," continued Irena a week later. "They boast that they have many planes. But really they are frightened. More and more troops are sent to the Old Town but nobody returns. They drink or look for something to save them. They want to swap canned food for pictures of saints to sew into the lining of their jackets. 'Black Madonna' has the highest value. Ewa

290

arrived with a big tin of horse meat. The wounded are hungry and the Guides can hardly stand on their feet."

Guide Wieslawa Kamper was working as a nurse in the "Umbrella" battalion of the resistance army. "The Germans invaded the Old Town hospital and ordered all patients to leave the building; they left the badly wounded in bed. They put us in rows by the wall. From that moment our ordeal began. We were 15 Guides aged 15–18 years. All the Girl Guides have shown a true Guide's attitude. The Germans started shooting. First they killed the doctors, in front of us, shot in the back of the head. Then it was our turn. They told us to step forward and started shooting in groups." Wieslawa stepped forward and started singing "*Jeszcze Polska nie zginela*", the national anthem, "Poland is not yet lost". "I fell when I heard the sound of the first shots. Beside me lay the girls with their heads smashed. I lay still and heard the whole tragedy. At the end they took out the ten nuns." They were praying "*Pod Twoja obrone*", "In your defence, Holy Mother of God", a third-century prayer.

"The Germans shot them one by one. Until the last one, I could hear their prayers." The hospital was then set on fire, from the basement up. Any patients still in bed had no hope. "The Germans started leaving the hospital, which was now full of corpses. Very slowly I began to move, when I saw a soldier robbing the bodies of the dead people. I must have attracted his attention by my different position. He approached me and began to kick me. Then he took off my bracelet and a ring. Then he sat by me. He checked our bags and wallets.

Then he stood up, he must have realised that I was alive." The soldier stood above her and shot twice at her head. "I felt the bullets touching my hair. The dust covered my eyes but I was alive. The German went, unaware that he had left a witness to his crime. I don't know how long I lay there. The smoke from the burning hospital was hurting my eyes. I decided to escape. And then I saw my Guide Captain, Wanda. I ran towards her. One of the patients joined us. A pregnant woman and a ten-year-old boy survived too. All five, we climbed through the hospital wall. Then we split up. It was midnight."

Just over two weeks later, Wieslawa was living in a basement shelter. "There are tins but there is nothing to open them with. I have stomach problems. There is a kitchen in the Baryczkos' building. I helped to make *kasha* porridge but there was not enough water and it burned. We take water from a bomb crater on the street corner. Initially we used it to put out the fires but now we need drinking water. Fortunately there is some water dripping from the broken pipes. Infernal scenes are taking place in the shelters: hungry & thirsty children, their mothers cannot forgive the neighbours, who are eating, for not sharing their food. They look at us angrily — completely different from the beginning when they were throwing flowers at the soldiers."

Dr Alina Morawska was Captain of a Guide company in Zielna Street which organised a refuge for mothers with babies. "Guides collected food and medical equipment from generous neighbours," she wrote. "Malnourished mothers did not have enough milk to feed their hungry babies. Giving medical advice was not enough. How to provide the little ones with just a little milk?" Alina looked everywhere for baby milk, until she heard through the underground network that there was some on the other side of the city. "Our youngest Guides went to help. They went across Al Jerozolimskie in a very shallow trench, and brought the life-giving milk powder. It was only a small amount but it saved the most vulnerable babies from starvation."

On 2 September 1944 the Old Town fell. "We are crying," wrote Irena Zychowska. "People, black, bearded, in rags are appearing from the ruins. A few children have survived. I am looking for Ewa. I ask everyone about the house where I left her. They say that it has been bombed."

As it became clear that the Germans had finally overcome the Warsaw Uprising, the network of underground sewers was used to evacuate districts that could not be defended any longer. Entering the sewers involved first running the gauntlet of German planes firing on anyone in the streets, and then finding a manhole to squeeze down. One night Guide Krystyna Sroczynska was sent into the sewers to learn the route. "We gathered in a house in Franciszkanska Street. The square in front was on fire. It looked like a decoration in a theatre." German planes fired on them as they huddled around the manhole. Once they were inside they could not carry torches, and everyone had to walk in silence in case the Germans saw or heard them when they opened manholes at random. The sewer was terrifying — dark, deep, cold, smelly. "We were about thirty people — wounded, a few doctors, a Lieutenant with his wife and children, 'Maks' the guide, and myself. One of the doctors was persuading the others to take some pills so we would not fall asleep during the march. He gave sleeping pills to the Lieutenant's children. A wide canal, water up to our knees or higher, a big echo. We are walking under Mickiewicza Street, under Wilson Square, turn to Krasinski, exit near Zmarchwywstanek Convent. Strong order — complete silence and discipline." Sometimes the sewer floor was slippery mud; in other places the stinking, cold sewage was up to their chests. Barricades of logs, rubbish and bodies got in the way. Those without shoes found themselves walking on stones and broken glass. There was only the muffled sound of explosions from above. They knew German soldiers were guarding the manhole by Gdanska Railway Station.

Not very far from this dangerous point a child begins to cry. At Gdanska Station "Maks" lets them through one by one. You have to hold a rope attached under the manhole and jump up; the strong current makes it exhausting. The rope has broken. I go first. I have to go as far as possible along the higher, dry sewer and wait for everyone, with "Maks" at the end. A difficult passage, although I am a healthy person. I help them to climb a steep step. Suddenly the darkness is illuminated. A youth whom I am holding by his hand falls backwards in the water, I can see his face. The remains of a grenade is burning a metre away from me. Am I alive? Yes, a taste of blood, a zooming sound in my ears. We have to continue before they drop more grenades. I warn the others and get up in the light of some torches. I wash my bleeding head in the water, somebody gives out some sugar. The Lieutenant is very nervous, he is giving orders — a soldier who was carrying his child must stay with a wounded person. I object — we must all go. The wounded youth should stay on his own until we send him help. They ask if I know the route. I don't. But I have to lie because otherwise we don't have any chance. We have to get to our people. I know that the route is marked. With all my effort, I say that I know the route. I lead. We are nine people. We walk, the wounded one is setting off too.

The tunnels constantly forked, and in the pitch dark it was impossible to know which way to go. If someone put their head out of a manhole to check their progress, they risked being shot at. It was impossible to judge time or distance, and the journey seemed to last forever.

We are all holding onto a rope. I realise that a manhole ahead is being opened and soon the Germans will drop more grenades. I do not speed up in order to prevent any panic. I hope that we will pass in time. The grenade explodes behind us, just after the last person. Suddenly a child slips out of somebody's arms — shouting, he is drowning — saved. A few minutes later the wounded man falls down unconscious, without any will to live. It is the doctor who was giving out pills. He is drifting in the fast current of the water. I swim with him, we are tied to a rope. I tell him to stand up, that help is just around the corner. I swear at him. He does not answer. The rope between us is getting longer and longer. I try to hang on, I call again. Silence. I let the rope go. I know what it means.

Suddenly I hear a splashing in the water behind us — the Germans. "Who is there?" It is Maks, our guide. He is shouting at me that I was not at the end of the dry sewer as I should have been, that I should not have been wounded, that there were 14 grenades.

The two groups joined up, with Maks leading.

I am holding on to his belt, somebody is holding mine and so on. We are approaching the most difficult place where we turn into a storm sewer. I did not know the route. I would never have been able to choose the right one on my own. Then very high steps, we trip over some bodies. Then the exit, fresh air, medical help.

Emerging into the city centre was bewildering: there was glass in the windows and people were clean and well dressed. Best of all, those who survived the sewers could wash, eat, put on clean clothes, and sleep.

On 31 August the order arrived from the Home Army that all the walking wounded who remained in the ghetto should attempt to leave by the sewers: the Old Town had fallen. Three days later, the Germans flooded the sewers with petrol and set fire to them. Many people inside died, and manholes collapsed, making further evacuation through the sewers impossible. Krystyna Sroczynska never made it back through them to help anyone else.

The Uprising was over; it was a last-ditch attempt at fighting back, and nobody had predicted that it would last as long as the sixty-three days that it did. On 3 October 1944, a cold, grey day, over a hundred Guides and Scouts gathered in the remains of Wilcza Street. Many of them had worked in a hospital that was now burned down. A few were Guiders and Scoutmasters from the Home Army, but most were teenagers, some as young as twelve. They had carried messages, manned first-aid posts, looked after homeless children, operated the post office, printed and delivered newspapers, sung to divert terrified civilians hidden in cellars, cooked for the Home Army. That morning they stood in a semi-circle in the ruins of their city, and forty of them were decorated for courage and gallantry by the Chief Commissioner. He made no speech, and they recited the Scout and Guide Promise, then sang the Polish national anthem, telling each other that Poland still lived, and would always do so. "Czuwaj" — Be Prepared — they said. They had learned the motto's importance through bitter days and terrible fighting. The Chief Commissioner called them to attention and gave the command to Dismiss, knowing that they would probably never see each other again. They dispersed among the ruined houses, breathing the smoke-laden air of the burning city. Those in uniform would become prisoners of war, the civilians slave labourers in concentration camps. Few would survive.

CHAPTER
SIXTEEN

Three Aunties

During the summer of 1940, for many councils all over rural Britain, the prospect of being invaded by hordes of evacuees was not one they relished. The small town of Alyth in Perthshire, seventeen miles from Dundee, was no exception. A year earlier there had been plenty of homes in Alyth willing to take in children evacuated from cities. But after most of these children had been sent back as "unsuitable", their generosity dried up. Billeting officers were now the enemies of social cohesion. As Evelyn Waugh described it in his novel *Put Out More Flags* in 1942, "The billeting officer had been transformed in four months, from one of the most popular women in the countryside into a figure of terror. When her car was seen approaching people fell through side doors and stable yards, into the snow, anywhere to avoid her persuasive, 'But surely you could manage one more.'"

Alyth council decided that the town had enough to worry about during the war without having to accommodate evacuee children as well. Besides their men being conscripted, conditions were already difficult for local women. "We can't sleep for rats," wrote one mother of seven to the council. "Even now they are running about the room ... this last two nights we have all been in the kitchen sitting on the bed and chairs trying to sleep. In fact if the rats had a brass band one would think it was the Poles coming. I don't want to be a bother to anybody but the Baby will not lie in bed now after the fright she got."

In April 1940 the council unanimously adopted a motion "That this Council believes that the billeting of evacuee children upon householders in Perthshire imposes unnecessary hardship." They decided that all they could offer was "the establishment of hostels" in unoccupied mansion houses within the county for children "unsuitable for ordinary billeting" or for whom billets could not be found. The council proposed to ask the head teachers of evacuated schools "to arrange for Nuns and other personnel to staff the hostels. Any kitchen and house maids required might be obtained locally at the usual rates of wages, if not obtained from Glasgow." The children, "preferably not Roman Catholic", could be educated at the local schools, which were "predominantly Protestant". The council agreed to accommodate forty evacuee children in Balendoch Hall, just outside the town.

No one in the Perth area or Glasgow could be found to run Balendoch, so Perth Education Authority put an advertisement in *The Guider*. Three Guiders who had been running a summer hostel for Guides and Brownies in Broadstairs, Kent, which was no longer considered safe after Dunkirk, applied. At the end of June 1940 they set off on the 550-mile journey in a van with their dog Jockie. The oldest and most senior of the Guiders was Esther Reiss, a tall, portly woman aged about thirty-five, known as "Auntie Esther". "Miss Reiss was great fun," remembers Moira Findlay, a Brownie in Alyth. "She was a plump lady with golden-coloured hair tied back in a bun." Thirty-year-old Ada Edith Ashby, known as "Auntie Ash", was the cook, and Jean Rutherford, "Auntie Jean", was the housekeeper.

"We came with all our equipment from our Guide and Brownie House in Broadstairs," wrote Auntie Esther in her log book, "to a dirty, empty house. However, with the help of three volunteers the house was scrubbed and polished from top to toe and the rooms attractively rearranged. We have a charwoman for scrubbing on five mornings a week. On July 3 the first children arrived — seven including baby Doris, aged 8 months."

Within a few days there were twenty-four in total. Some would be there until the war was over, while others only came for holidays so their foster parents could have a break during the long vacation.

Among the first children were the Ritchie sisters, Jessie and Joan, aged six and seven. They had been living in a tenement in the east end of Glasgow, sharing a narrow mattress on the floor with their younger sister. When their mother abandoned the family, their father had pushed his three daughters in a handcart around his relations. His parents took the youngest, and Jessie and Joan were left with a childless aunt. As soon as evacuation became possible, they were sent to

Balendoch. Their father went off to fight in the war, and was not seen again.

"We walked into the basement kitchen at Balendoch," remembered Jessie. "Miss Esther greeted us from the big black cooking range. It was the first time in my life I had seen an adult smile." Up to now they had known only fear, and they were malnourished and miserable. But all that was about to change.

The number of children soon increased to forty, aged between five and fifteen. Once they were settled in, Esther Reiss set up a Guide company. "As far as possible we run everything on Guide lines," she wrote. "The results certainly seem to prove that these lines are the best. We give gold, silver and bronze stars for work well done and run a monthly competition with a prize at the end of the month." The children were divided into patrols, and allotted work such as table laying, chopping vegetables, washing up, cleaning and sweeping. Everyone made their own beds. The children all went to the local school, carrying their packed lunches with them — cheese, corned beef or Spam sandwiches.

All billets, including Balendoch, were paid 10s.6d a week for the first child in each home and 8s.6d for each further one. This hardly covered the cost of food when butter was 1s.7d a pound and milk was fourpence a pint. The Red Cross sent hampers of food to Balendoch, which included dried egg. On Sundays, after their porridge, the children were fed "French bread". "It was wonderful to be allowed to stir the dried egg into the milk and then dip the bread into it before it was fried," said Jessie. "French bread was a great treat."

The hampers were locked in the pantry. One day someone broke in and opened a precious tin of peaches. "The Aunties were fair, but firm," remembered Jessie. "They lined us all up according to age and we had to hold out our hands to be strapped with a leather belt. 'I hope that someone will own up soon,' Auntie Esther said. When she got to me, one of the younger ones, she apologised. Before she got much further, one of the older boys owned up to eating the peaches. I never saw her use the strap again."

The hostel had a strict timetable, with a typical day as follows:

7 a.m.: Up. Wash, dress, make beds
7.45 a.m.: Breakfast in silence on schooldays owing to lack of time. Children go off to school with their packed lunch and come home at 4.30p.m. At five o'clock they have a meal — a mixture of tea and dinner.
6 p.m.: Those with no homework have activities — country dancing, organised games, campfire, singing etc.

During the winter, prayers were at 6.45p.m. and the children went to bed according to their age. Everyone was in bed by 8.30p.m., even the fifteen-year-olds. Brown Owl, Auntie Ash, made Brownie uniforms of brown cotton romper suits. Few of the girls had shoes. "Most of the children come from the slums of Glasgow and have had no real training," wrote Auntie Esther. "They come dirty and underfed, and with practically no clothing. It is amazing to see how quickly they become part of the machinery here. Their baths are a source of great joy. If one child has to have his temperature taken, so does everyone in that bedroom. Even if he has a 'dirty' head [nits], everyone else manages to have 'an awful itchy head too, Miss'. Toothpaste is such a novelty that most people eat theirs — so much was eaten that we now have to keep it hidden and put a little on everyone's brush for them."

The Brownies grew flowers in the kitchen garden, and arranged them around the house in jam jars. The Guides learned stalking, woodcraft and campfire singing, and cooked dampers over an open fire. They all learned to swim in the nearby River Islar. When the local woods caught fire, they practised their fire drill with two stirrup pumps. Once the fire was out, a water fight ensued. "One pump team against another and soon everyone was dressed in a mackintosh back to front and by tea-time a group of soaking, cheery children were ready for tea," wrote Esther.

In August 1940 Balendoch held an Open Day for the local people, including the members of Alyth Town Council. The *Perthshire Advertiser* reported that "The Alyth District Hostel Brownies and Guides organised teas, dancing and songs. The day raised enough money for medical supplies, and games for the winter."

At the end of September, school stopped for a week while the children earned 9d an hour potato lifting. For Halloween, the Guides organised a surprise party for the younger children with apple-bobbing and treacle buns. To raise money for Christmas, the Brownies and Guides had a sale of work; they made purses, comb cases, handkerchief sachets and sang carols. "The practising of carols was hard work with no piano to help. The tableaux and carols were very reverently done," wrote Esther. "The costumes were all made from bedding and clothing from the house, yet everyone was in a definite Eastern Garb." They raised £10.5s. The three Broadstairs Guiders then set off to buy presents, crackers and oranges for all the children.

Three days before Christmas, a further fifteen children arrived from Glasgow, and "What scrimmage this meant, making the money stretch sufficiently. However, by midnight on Christmas eve all the stockings were filled and ready to be taken round to be hung up." The Guiders finally got to bed at 1 a.m. — but an hour later they were up again. "One bedroom discovered that Father Christmas had arrived and all its inmates were sitting up in bed unpacking. 3 a.m. music from the first floor. 4 a.m. more music. — At 5 a.m. we gave up and let the children have their way." After church and "a Royal Spread" of sardines in pastry, followed by prunes, each child received a present from under the tree. Then they all went to Alyth Town Hall where they were entertained by Polish soldiers who gave each child sweets and oranges. During Lent they gave up sweets and gave the money saved to a local orphanage. Every Sunday morning they all walked the three miles to church in the village of Meigle. When two bicycles were donated to the Guides, those who had been awarded the most gold stars that week were allowed to ride them to church.

While Balendoch's girls could join the hostel's Brownie and Guide companies, there was little for the boys. "We have a Brownie pack and a Guide company but we cannot find a Scouter," wrote Esther. While they were looking for one, the would-be Scouts went to the Guide meetings. The problem was solved when eleven-year-old George Pollock wrote to King George asking if he could help set up a company of Air Scouts, which had just been started for boys living near aerodromes. His letter was passed from Buckingham Palace to the Scouts in Scotland, who decided that the local Scout troop would meet at Balendoch instead of in the Alyth village hall.

Out in the country, miles from anywhere and busy with their various activities, Balendoch's residents felt removed from the war and the devastation that was being inflicted on Britain's cities: "Of the war we hear nothing — no guns, no sirens, no soldiers, and only a few passing aeroplanes," wrote Auntie Esther. But they were reminded of what was going on around them when a bomb was dropped in a nearby field in 1941. "Auntie Esther took us to see the hole," said Jessie Ritchie. "She reassured us that the Germans didn't intend to hit us. They had dropped it to empty the bomb hold before returning across the North Sea. There was a huge crater in the field. We all stood around it, like watching a volcano." In June 1941, Balendoch's residents took part in the War Weapons Week march. "After much scrubbing of uniforms, ironing of ties and polishing of sandals," wrote Esther, "the Guides and Brownies emerged looking very spick and span for the Grand March through Alyth."

The Balendoch children were also kept busy in the holidays. The market for soft fruit had not diminished — the army needed huge quantities with which to make jam. But Alyth Town Council need not have worried about a lack of labour to pick the local cash crop: the Balendoch children were only too keen to spend their August holidays earning money by picking raspberries. "Towards the end of the month the berry picking was in full swing," wrote Auntie Esther. "Every morning a little army set off in their oldest clothes for the raspberry field. They were provided with a large pail and a small one, which was fastened round the waist. When the big pail was filled, it was weighed and the pickers were paid ¾d per lb." Some of the Guides spent their earnings on War Savings Certificates. The Countess of Elgin, wife of the 10th Earl, visited from her mansion in Fife and wrote that she was "greatly struck by the splendidly healthy look of the children. I noticed how particularly helpful they seem and how happily they perform their various duties."

After a year, one of the Guides, Sheila Gray, won a bursary to the local grammar school. Another, Helen Luke, was employed as an under-maid at the local big house, owned by a Conservative MP. His wife was very impressed by the hostel, and had arranged for it to receive free milk from the government.

At Christmas 1941, the stockings were distributed at 4a.m. "But by 4.40a.m. the entire house was up," wrote Auntie Esther, "trumpets sounding, bells ringing, and crackers being pulled. No more sleep." She was thrilled to find a steel sterilising drum from the children under the tree.

Milk, bread, and meat were delivered to the local railway halt and collected once a week by the Guides with a trek cart. When the snow fell so heavily that nothing with wheels could get through, the girls set off with shovels, cut their way through six-foot drifts, and dragged the supplies home on a sledge.

During Alyth's Warship Week in 1942 the Guides dressed as Red Cross nurses, made an effigy of Hitler and carried him around Alyth on a stretcher with a banner reading "Your pennies will help to pay for his funeral." A total of £10.6s.7d in pennies was thrown onto the stretcher. This helped to pay for the latest radar equipment to be fitted on the destroyer HMS *Highlander*, which was soon escorting convoys across the Atlantic again.

That summer, Balendoch's Guiders took their thirty-six charges camping for a fortnight to Duchally near Gleneagles, fifteen miles to the south-west, where it rained every day. "It was great fun though, and the local Guides proved friendly," wrote Auntie Esther. Jessie Ritchie remembers the holiday as the highlight of her entire childhood. "We learned how to cook outside on proper campfires. We went trekking. One morning we made a large bowl of custard for our tea. Then we all went off for a walk. When we returned, a herd of cows had got into the field, and eaten every drop of the custard. We were so upset — all that delicious custard gone." On the one fine afternoon Sir Ruthven and Lady Monteath, who owned the Duchally estate, came to tea in the camp. "But we were invaded by flying ants and each guest had to be provided with a serving maid to fan them whilst they ate."

At the "Wings for Victory" fund-raising party in the Alyth parsonage garden in May 1943, everyone wore fancy dress. "I was a Dutch girl in clogs and had to sing 'I'm a little Dutch girl'," recalled Jessie. "Other Brownies dressed up as Hitler and Goebbels. None of us had any idea who these men were." Prizes were awarded to all, in the form of War Savings Stamps, and they raised £18 for carrier pigeons for the RAF. "Alas," wrote Esther, "this party succeeded in spreading a chicken pox germ as by Sunday fourteen spotty Balendochers had to be isolated from the others." The hostel was divided into "chicken poxers" and "non-poxers" until eventually all the children had had it.

That year Ruth Balfour, the chair of the Women's Voluntary Service, who had visited Balendoch, wrote to Esther Reiss: "There never were more splendid examples of the Guides principles in action than your children, but I also realise that to breathe life into those principles does require very special qualities. Those children will owe you a debt of gratitude all their lives. You have made them healthy in body and fearless in mind. I noted with delight their independence combined with their sense of discipline; their robust attitude to life and yet their kindliness to each other; and above all their trust and love for you. They all took pride in doing every patrol duty really well, and were benefiting from the spirit of competition without showing the slightest jealousy."

By now the Balendoch Guide Company was so well established that Guiders came from all over Perthshire to train with them. The Captain of the Alyth Guides and the Alyth Brown Owl regularly walked their pack and company the four miles to Balendoch to be "guided" by the Guiders there.

In the middle of the October "potato holiday" in 1943 the Brownies and Guides of Balendoch set off to Perth to see the Chief Guide, Olave Baden-Powell. "No easy matter to get rid of all traces of potato dirt and for thirty-three people to arrive bright and shining, clean and polished, but we did it and what a reward was ours," wrote Auntie Esther. "Not only did we get a front seat where we could see the Chief and smile at her, but we were privileged to stay behind for a few extra private words with her." Jessie Ritchie was now a nine-year-old Brownie Sixer. "Going to see the Chief Guide was like a visit to the Queen," she recalled. One Guide, Margaret, even shook hands with Olave. "She won't be able to wash her left hand ever again, we understand," wrote Auntie Esther. "After this thrilling experience we all went out to an excellent high tea." The local farmer was so pleased with the Balendoch evacuees' potato-picking skills that each of the thirty-six children was paid ten shillings a day. All the girls bought new frocks, and then gave £10 to the Guide International Service Fund.

The following "Thinking Day", in 1944, the Balendoch Guides organised a treasure hunt around the house, and saved up all their rations to make a birthday cake for the Chief Guide in the shape of a trefoil. They sent her one leaf and shared the rest with the Chief Commissioner for Scotland, Mrs Elliot Carnegie of Lour.

Auntie Esther showed the Guides of Alyth how to put on a Christmas show. "This went down well in churches and in our Guide Hut," remembered Moira Findlay, then a Brownie, who played an angel. "The Christmas Story was read by a Guide, to two Brownies who sat in the corner of the front stage. As the story page was turned over, a tableau formed by opening the stage curtains and portraying Nativity Scenes with the choir of angels singing." Christmas 1944 was the last the evacuees spent at Balendoch. This time the Aunties attempted to get more sleep by hanging the forty-four stockings up on a line in the playroom. "Next morning, when the gong rang, there was a noise like thunder as everyone tore down to the playroom at the double and found their stocking packed as full as it would go."

The Ritchie sisters had been christened in late November, and had their first communion on Christmas Day with their Guiders. The vicar, who was now also the Scoutmaster, knew that Joan and Jessie had no parents, and always gave them his sweet ration. Jessie was thrilled that Auntie Esther became her official godmother. "I was proud to have that special relationship with her, that no other child at the hostel had."

Just a few days later, on 3 January 1945, the hostel was closed down: Guide Captain Esther Reiss's last log book entry reads: "It took a good deal of careful manipulation to get everything and everyone packed in but eventually we were all waving goodbye and once more Balendoch was left in the sole possession of the three Broadstairs Guiders who had left the Sunny South in 1940."

When Joan and Jessie Ritchie, now aged twelve and eleven, returned to their grandparents in Glasgow, they found the city "very busy and noisy" after their five years in the countryside. Glasgow was teeming with rain and people, and going back to a rigid, unloving upbringing, with one toilet for eight families, was tough. On their first night they cried themselves to sleep.

In 1998 Jessie Ritchie visited Auntie Ash in Wolverhampton, and read the Balendoch Hostel log book. She wrote in it: "I am crying as I read this because we all cried and cried at leaving Balendoch. It was years before we realised just what these three wonderful ladies had done for us, and what a life-giving example they had set for all of us under-privileged children. I was beside myself when we left Balendoch, those spinsters gave us forty-five children so much love. With Brownies and Guides we learned all the social skills — knitting, sharing, country dancing, singing. They made Christmas so special. We were always encouraged to think of others first."

In the five years from the arrival of the evacuee children at Balendoch Hall, the attitude of Alyth Town

Council to outsiders had changed. A Thanksgiving service was held in the parish church not only for peace in Europe, but also for the good relations between the townspeople, the Polish troops, the Italian prisoners of war who had been interned near the town and the Balendoch evacuees. The children had shown them something new, thanks to the three Guiders, Auntie Jean, Auntie Esther and Auntie Ash.

For Jessie Ritchie, "Those exceptional ladies should have received medals for what they did. They were the parents I never had. They were saints who gave stability and love to over forty children, and after the war they went their separate ways, but continued to be beacons of goodness." Jean Rutherford went to Edinburgh, where she ran a Cub pack; Esther Reiss returned to Broadstairs in Kent, where she continued to run the Brownies, was the General Secretary of the local YWCA and chair of the Samaritans; and Ada Ashby became a social worker in Wolverhampton. In 1977 she received a Silver Jubilee medal from the Queen. She died in 2004, aged ninety-four, and left the Balendoch log book to Jessie Ritchie, who passed it on to the Imperial War Museum.

Jessie wanted to train as a teacher, but her grandfather, who was a horse dealer, made her leave school at fifteen. She joined the WAAF, had six children and later succeeded in her ambition to become a teacher. When she moved to Dorset she named her home "Balendoch". She became a politician, and aged sixty-six she cycled around Weymouth wearing the ceremonial gold chain of the town's Mayor.

CHAPTER
SEVENTEEN

Guides in Auschwitz

China was not the only place where Guides were interned during the war. Back in Europe, Guides were active both inside and outside concentration camps and prisons. They risked their lives to help those threatened by the Nazis, using all the skills they could muster. Under the command of Guide Captain Janina Chojnacka, twenty-five Guides of Krakow and Silesia helped prisoners in seven prisons and three labour camps, including Auschwitz, with medication, food and clothing. Wanda Górecka-Wierzbowska, the Captain of the 4th Katowice Company, organised help for the prisoners of Auschwitz. Bundles of jerseys, food and medication were left in eleven agreed places. "We took them to prisoners who were working outside the camp," said Wanda. "In places such as clearings in the woods, we would deliver hot soup and bread for noon. Each place was given a name such as 'Gdynia', 'Brazil', 'Hotel Savoy' or 'Canada'. On their way to work one of the prisoners would say the password, such as 'Gdynia', to children playing nearby. The children would tell the Guides where the prisoners were working that day. If the prisoners were quiet, then we knew that the SS guard was new and we should not approach them at all. Before Christmas we left tiny Christmas trees in abandoned barns where the prisoners used to leave their tools every day. The local people were extremely generous and they would share their last slice of bread with the prisoners." One Belgian Ranger managed to save just a single possession before her imprisonment in Auschwitz: her Guide badge. Whenever she was searched, she hid it in her mouth.

Guides were able to help prisoners in many ways. Thanks to their knowledge of the area, acquired while on treks or taking the Pathfinder Badge, they were able to collect information about the prisoners and inform their families, and deliver secret letters to and from them. A number of Guides were imprisoned themselves; when sent to concentration camps, usually Ravensbrück, Auschwitz or Stutt-hof, they were often labelled "Return not required". They suffered in the camps in the same way as other women, but were among the prisoners who managed to preserve their humanity and dignity, believing that it was important "not to die before our death".

Among the prisoners at Auschwitz were four Guiders and two Guides from the Silesian town of Zawiercie. As Guides they had edited, printed and distributed a local underground newspaper called *Płomień* (Flame), which included information gleaned from their own radio monitoring. After their arrest by the Gestapo they were sentenced to hard labour and later taken to Auschwitz, where three of them died.

Another Guide from Silesia who found herself in Auschwitz was Zofia P. She was imprisoned in a cellar three times for helping her fellow prisoners, and then taken to Birkenau to be kept under strict surveillance. Despite this, she managed to send secret letters to the prisoners in Auschwitz. In 1944 she managed to write to her family, and included lists of people sent to the gas chambers, the plans of the crematorium and documents describing medical experiments carried out on the female prisoners.

The Ranger Guides, "*Wilcze Gniazdo*" (Wolf's Nest), of Poland were founded by architect Natalia Hiszpańska, who became a Guide Captain in 1927. At the start of the war she joined the Home Army, helping to produce underground newspapers. In 1943 she was arrested by the Gestapo and tortured in Pawiak prison. She returned from many interrogations with massive bruises all over her body. "She coped with the unspeakable torture with bravery and dignity," wrote A. Czuperska-Śliwicka, who survived Auschwitz. "She was put to 'drowning' when water was forced up her nose as she lay with her mouth gagged. It was clear that she never gave anybody away and never for a moment gave up her spirits." Sentenced to five years in Auschwitz to be followed by execution, in the concentration camp she worked with the local resistance movement. In a secret letter to her family she wrote about how lucky she was to receive words of appreciation from the leader of the Home Army. She also managed to pass on information from documents she saw on the table in the interrogation room. She died in Auschwitz in February 1944, aged forty.

When Urszula Leszczyńska, Guide Captain, teacher and poet from Kielce, was sent to Auschwitz, she kept her Guide Promise, and taught the principle "We must survive in the best form". She exercised every day, and encouraged the other women to eat all the prison food, however disgusting, to keep up their strength. She fought against enforced idleness by organising foreign-language, history and literature lessons in her cell. "Her passion to study and teach others accompanied her through all the adversities of her life. Until the end she stayed cheerful." She died caring for typhoid patients in 1943.

Guides in Warsaw and Mazowsze tried to lower the morale of German soldiers by distributing illegal literature about an approaching Nazi defeat. They slipped the magazines into coat pockets in the cloakrooms of cafés used by Germans and tossed them into train carriages or the German sections of tramcars. Two Guides were arrested as they dropped leaflets into a German car. They were tortured during interrogation and both died in Auschwitz.

In Krakow prison Guides organised food for the ill and the mentally distressed. After eavesdropping on the guards, they passed on political information that they picked up. While working in the laundry and ironing rooms, they were able to keep records of the prisoners, and to collect evidence of torture based on the state of the victims' clothes, stained with blood and cut by whips.

The female prisoners in Brzezinka, not far from Auschwitz, worked in the towns of Brzeszcze, Rajsko and Budy. Wanda Górecka-Wierzbowska and her Guides visited the families of arrested people and delivered letters and secret messages. She helped people meet imprisoned family members, giving them accommodation and directing them to the working place of the prisoners.

From Pawiak prison, Halina Izbanówna wrote in a secret letter to Scoutmaster Trojanowska: "One of the guards said that women are more dangerous than men, that is why they have to sit and suffer until they lose heart. Stupid, they don't know that this has completely the opposite effect on Polish women. Whatever they do, we will be fine, as long as Poland exists — that will be the biggest reward for us. You always accused me of being stubborn. I have heard them say: 'You, Polish women, are very stubborn and tough.' This stubbornness has been very useful."

In Stutthof camp, twelve Guide Captains from Pomerania recognised each other as Guides very quickly. "However," wrote one, "we did not organise ourselves as a group. We did not need it. We were all active as much as we could be according to the Guides' idea of service." First, they organised group praying and singing. Then they arranged celebrations of national anniversaries and religious festivals. They shared food from their parcels, provided prisoners with clean underclothes and warm clothes. In secret they made gloves for the women prisoners who worked outdoors in winter. The men lived in even worse conditions, and the Guiders dropped socks and clothes through the windows of the laundry as they passed by.

Guide Anna Paszkowska used her position as a manager in the Stutthof cobbler workshop to hide illegal activities such as exchanging letters between male and female camps, and sending the best-quality goods to the prisoners and the worst to the German army. When the Guides heard that Stutthof was going to close down, they managed to smuggle a large number of boots to the prisoners to wear for the evacuation.

Stutthof prisoner Agnieszka Recław was not a Guide, but she noticed them. "When they brought me to Stutthof because of my work in the underground, I noticed a very nice occurrence. I was placed in a room with many Guides mainly from Pomerania. I was impressed by their behaviour in the camp's nightmare. They followed the Guide Law every day. They were polite and cheerful. They supported their companions, never showed any doubt or fear, they were full of hope in the victory of our rightness. They always preserved their dignity in contacts with the camp's authorities. They recited poems of the great national poets of Poland. They also, when it was possible, looked after their ill colleagues in secret. They shared their parcels from home with other prisoners and they encouraged others in acts of kindness. Thanks to the Guides many lives have been saved. I spent three years with them — I liked being with them."

Of the 40,000 women in Ravensbrück concentration camp, a quarter were Polish, many of whom were

Guides. Ravensbrück was run by 150 brutal female SS guards. Polish women wore a red triangle, red denoting a political prisoner, with a letter "P", "Fast thinking, organisational skills, smooth operating, strong will and character — these were factors which decided their own or somebody else's fate," wrote Chor Pomorska of Pomerania. "The hard training during summer camps and hiking helped to develop physical strength, resourcefulness and also teamwork and mutual trust."

Z. Grzesik was a Guide who often walked from Łódź to Warsaw — a distance of over 130 kilometres — after dark in the dead of winter to distribute underground newspapers. "In Łódź I was always welcomed as 'resurrected'. Every border crossing would be another history, a separate experience, full of thrill and fear . . . Every trip was very risky because I travelled with a big packet which was difficult to hide. During my journeys I stayed a couple of times with Guide Tola Chrzonowicz, who would be sitting with a group of children with books, covering the primary school curriculum. She kept the underground newspapers in a shed. I would take the packet in order to pass it on immediately." The work was particularly hard because of the harsh winter. After being intercepted by a guard at the border in early 1945, Grzesik was sentenced to one month in prison. "Then, to my surprise, after serving the sentence I was sent to forced labour camp in Lübeck. From there I ended up in Ravensbrück concentration camp." She survived the war, finally making it home in May 1945.

Ravensbrück was notorious for the medical experiments carried out by Nazi doctors on women. Krystyna Czyz, Janina and Krystyna Iwańska and Wanda Wojtasik were Guides from Lublin used as "*króliki*" — literally rabbits, but meaning medical guinea pigs. Between January 1943 and June 1944 they were able to send secret messages to their families, who passed on the information they contained to the British government. This included the names of people operated on, doctors and camp officials; dates of the operations; descriptions of the living conditions and changes in the camp; and the dates, directions and purposes of transports to and from the camp. The first letters were written in ordinary ink in German, and mentioned a popular Polish book by Kornel Makuszyński called *Satan in the Seventh Grade*, in which the main character uses a coded letter when in a difficult situation. The Guides used the same code, and by naming the book they gave a clue how to read their letters. Between the lines they wrote in urine, which only appeared when the paper was warmed up.

In addition to their duties inside the camp, Guides were forced to work in workshops and munitions factories. Some women had to labour in mines, unload soot from wagons or operate vulcanising ovens for curing rubber. Maria Kostrzewska, another Guide, managed to pass on letters about Polish prisoners addressed to the Polish government in London.

Joanna Muszkowska-Penson, Prisoner no. 7804 in Ravensbrück, wrote: "In the camp we found out that the human spirit is not just an ingredient of a body or a function of the nervous system, but it has some kind of independence, which energises and dictates its own superior laws." A whole Girl Guide company was organised in Ravensbrück when twenty-six girls and women arrived on 12 November 1941. Among them were Guide Captain Józefa Kantor and Patrol Leaders Zofia Jenczy, Maria Rydarowska and Aniela Wideł, who had all come from different prisons. Initially inmates were invited to join the Guides individually, through personal contacts and thorough observation. For safety the patrols did not make any contact with each other. Only the Guide Captain knew who they all were. After six months they organised a company meeting. "It was Sunday, 3 May, Constitution Day 1942," wrote K. Czajka-Rytwinska. "We were given instruction to put a small green leaf under the number on our jackets. Walking during our free hour on the camp's street we had to look for other colleagues 'decorated' in the same way — the Guides from the secret Guide company. We were not allowed to talk to them, only just bow our heads slightly, exchange smiles and count how many we were. We were about sixty."

By 1945 there were over a hundred Guides in Ravensbrück, even though many had been executed or had died from disease. The Guides' emblem was "Mury" (Walls), a reference to the symbolic qualities of a wall: cohesion, fellowship, strength and support for the weak. They hoped to develop these qualities and to separate themselves from the atrocities of their daily lives. "We told each other that we are the Girl Guides and we have to follow the Guides' Law and the Promise

322

even in these hell-like conditions," said Anna Burdówna, a Guide Captain from Łódź, who was working as a teacher in Danzig when she was arrested on 1 September 1939. After eight months in prison she was moved to Ravensbrück, where she spent the remainder of the war. The patrols were named after elements which contribute to the building of a wall: Bricks, Cement, Foundations, Stones, Trowels, Water and Gravel. In their secret meetings the Guides worked towards their proficiency badges, and played games using agreed signals. Keeping in touch in the chaos of a concentration camp required a huge effort.

The Guides organised secret lessons, and Józefa Kantor ran courses for teachers. They read German newspapers and listened secretly to the BBC World Service. Helping all 45,000 women prisoners was impossible, but they tried to help as many as they could to survive the hunger. The "*Cegly*" or Brick patrol worked in the kitchen, and were able to get extra food for the "*króliki*" guinea pigs without affecting the other prisoners. On Sundays they organised prayers and singing.

Many new Guides were enrolled in Ravensbrück. They took the oath on a Guide badge which one of them had spotted among a pile of things taken by Nazis from executed inmates. It came from the 13th Warsaw Guide Company, and survived all the searches. The precious badge was eventually taken to Sweden when several thousand Polish women were sent there on 28 April 1945, as the war in Europe drew near to its end. Among them were Guides and over forty teenage girls.

Teresa Bromowiczowa organised a company for them called "*Wędrowne Ptaki*" (Migrating Birds), with four patrols: Storks, Wild Geese, Swallows and Chicks.

The Guides' hardest test was facing death. Maria Walciszewska, a teacher, a Guide Captain in Lublin and an intelligence officer in the Home Army, committed suicide rather than betray her colleagues. Halina Bretsznajder, a Captain from Radom District, was publicly executed. Olga Kamińska-Prokopowa, aged twenty-one, was arrested in Belgrade for helping British officers escape from a PoW camp. She gave birth to her son in prison, and was then taken to Vienna, where the baby was taken away from her. In Berlin she was sentenced to death. She was beheaded three months later, but somehow her family managed to get the baby back. Maria Jasińska also helped PoWs escape, and after arrest was tortured and then executed. She was posthumously honoured by the RAF "in appreciation for the help given to the Sailors, Soldiers and Airmen of the British Commonwealth".

In a secret letter from prison, Aniela Zalęska, "Dorota", a twenty-year-old history student in the secret university of Warsaw and a liaison officer for the Home Army, wrote, "Life is beautiful and interesting. It is worth experiencing it in all its forms and kinds. I do not regret the past at all. I would not give back the last year, for five years of a quiet life. But it is not enough for me, that is why I regret." She was executed in May 1944. Between 1939 and 1945, over 130,000 female prisoners passed through Ravensbrück, of whom 90,000 died. Of the 532 Polish Girl Guides known to

324

have died between 1939 and 1945, over two hundred died in the Warsaw Uprising, and the same number in prisons and concentration camps.

While she was imprisoned in Ravensbrück, Urszula Wińska wrote a poem called "The Prisoner's Prayer":

Our Father, Who art in heaven,
Thou seest the misery of our homeless life
Take Thy children under Thy guardianship
and silence the tears which cloud our souls.
Hallowed be Thy Name, here in the foreign land
where, brutally yanked from family homes
and among enemies, secretly we must pray.
Thy Will be done! In humility we call and believe
that the suffering and the joy come from Thee.
Thou givest us everything, O powerful Lord!
This deep belief sweetens our misery.
Give us this day, our daily bread!
And give us the strength to live and the belief
that not without a purpose is our exile
and the suffering for our previous sins.
And forgive us our trespasses, done by our weak-
    ness,
when doubt, pain and despair embrace our souls
when not just one, O Lord, falls under her cross.
And lead us not into temptation, which spoils the
    soul,
But deliver us from every evil,
Then let us happily return home.

CHAPTER
EIGHTEEN

Giant Pandas and Frozen Alligators

Lucy Pendar was an eleven-year-old girl who longed to be a Guide. Her father, Albert, was the Resident Engineer of Whipsnade Zoo, which occupied five hundred acres in the Chilterns in Bedfordshire. The family lived in a little red-brick house by the main gates, set against pine trees "like a picture in a pop-up nursery rhyme book", she said. "But the village nearby was not big enough to have a Guide company." Nearly fifty men were employed at Whipsnade as gardeners, gatekeepers and cooks, and they all became zoo-keepers simply by donning a grey jacket, riding breeches, leather gaiters and a peaked cap. Although Lucy grew up surrounded by exotic animals, zoo-keepers and thousands of visitors, it was a lonely life for a child.

The outbreak of the war changed everything. London Zoo closed down, and many of its animals were evacuated from Regent's Park to Whipsnade. Two giant pandas arrived to join Ming, the first giant panda ever seen in Europe. Five elephants and their keeper joined Dixie, the retired circus elephant, who was invaluable for stacking logs.

The London Zoo chimpanzees were evacuated too. At Whipsnade the babies and adult females lived on an island surrounded by a moat and a low barrier. One day Lucy was selling postcards to visitors near the chimp island when "To my surprise Tiny Tim, the youngest chimp, executing a beautiful crawl stroke, swam smartly across the moat, and with equal aplomb, climbed over the barrier and made off in the direction of the Giraffe House." Nobody had realised that chimps could swim; and no one had noticed that Tiny Tim was growing up until one of the female chimps produced an unexpected baby. When the black bear from London Zoo escaped for the third time, Lucy's father laid a trail of treacle into the ladies' lavatories. "He lay in wait in bushes close by," remembered Lucy. "At long last he heard snuffling. The bear appeared and started licking the step. He followed the treacle trail into the lavatories and Father triumphantly slammed the door on it."

Best of all for Lucy was the arrival of the children of London Zoo's staff, who moved with their parents into the wooden huts normally occupied by summer waitresses. "Then the evacuee girls arrived too. They asked Mrs Beale, the wife of the Zoo Superintendent, to start a youth club. She said she didn't know how to do that, but she thought she could start a Guide company." So began the 1st Whipsnade Company.

"While Captain Beale tended to his stamp collection, we met in their front room." Among the Guides were

Mary Billet, daughter of the Keeper of the Bird Sanctuary; Beryl Rogers, the daughter of Bert the Giraffe Keeper; and Elizabeth and Esther Schuermier from Austria, who came to England on the Kindertransport and were living with a local family. "Lily Strick and her sister Gertrude were refugees from Vienna," said Lucy. "Lily tried to teach me the piano, but as I was tone deaf she mainly told me about the Danube. She and Gertrude never saw their parents again. After the meetings I would walk home through the zoo in the dark, with my blackout torch shining a pinhole onto the ground. I could hear the elephants putting themselves to bed. There was also the roar of lions, the tigers slinking through their jungle, polar bears splashing in their pond and the barking of sea-lions. I wasn't frightened, I knew them all well." Lucy took the wild animals for granted; they had always been part of her life. The keepers considered her responsible enough to hand-feed the rare Chinese Père David deer fauns with bottles. One day she was asked to revive an ice-bound baby alligator. Her ministrations with warm water for several hours were to no avail, and only afterwards did she wonder what it might have done to her had it recovered.

For the 1st Whipsnade Company, war work included mucking out the Shetland ponies. With no public to exercise them, the Guides were also allowed to ride them. When Lucy graduated to the robust Iceland ponies, she was one of the first to experience their unusual gait: the *tölt* — a running walk — and the *flugskeid* — a flying pace.

328

"Captain Beale had been Chief Veterinary Officer of East Africa, so he taught us how to stalk and track both animals and humans. Then Mrs Beale invited a Cambridge undergraduate to teach us Morse. Meetings were always well attended when Richard Bagshaw came — he was blond and very dishy, and we all wanted to do well for him. We were the best in the district at Morse. The local Home Guard didn't know Morse, so we taught them. They weren't much good at tracking and stalking either. We had to show them how to wriggle through a wheat field on your tummy, so slowly that the wheat made no noise."

As Captain Beale was in command of both the local Home Guard and the Air Raid Defence, he was soon promoted to Major. His headquarters were the estate office of the zoo, from whence air-raid warnings were phoned through to the works yard. The five o'clock closing time hooter, high on the side of the water tower, served as the air-raid siren. "The wind carried its sound for some distance and the howling of the wolves, which always accompanied it, added both to its effectiveness and its eeriness."

Lucy's father refused to join the Home Guard because he considered them "toy soldiers". Instead, he started a rifle club in Whipsnade's refreshment rooms for local Air-Raid Wardens. "The walls were protected with sandbags, filled by us Guides. When the Cloisters was needed for serving refreshments in the summer, the rifle club moved to a large chalk pit on the side of the Downs near Bison Paddock."

"I learnt to use a rifle when I was about twelve," said Lucy. "Father used to arrange competitions against the Home Guard, and the Guides always won. When the RAF camped nearby, he suggested a shooting competition. We beat them too."

The first Christmas of the war was a miserable one for the Whipsnade Guides, especially after the death of the black rhinoceros, an evacuee from London. "Disposing of a dead rhinoceros is not an easy task, weighing nearly four tons." Lucy and the other Guides helped collect firewood to make a huge funeral pyre. Then an African elephant died, and its body was added. "The new year was greeted with the acrid smell of burning flesh and the belching forth of black smoke, which lasted for almost a week, until a smouldering pile of ash was all that remained of the great beasts." That was the last time so much meat was cremated and not fed to other animals or to humans.

The war was tough on the animals. Snow engulfed the park, and one of the giant pandas and a litter of tiger cubs had convulsions. Once petrol rationing began there were fewer visitors, so there was less money to pay for food for the animals. "On one February day in 1940 the takings amounted to sixpence, which meant the solitary visitor was a soldier as they got in for half price. At first, visitors were encouraged to bring lettuce, cabbage and carrots, but soon no one had even those to spare. There wasn't really enough food for all the animals, so the zoologist Julian Huxley made public appeals. But he asked for buns for the bears, which of course was not what bears needed at all."

Whipsnade Park had originally been a farm, and now the parkland and cricket pitch were ploughed up. With no combine harvesters, and most of the keepers called up, the Guides helped gather in the harvest. "With British Double Summer Time we could work even longer hours than normal," said Lucy. "June saw haymaking. The sheep were sheared, then dipped in July. Grass was scythed again in August. My back was aching, and my arms sore from scratches, as we gathered up the sheaves and stacked them in stooks. Five sheaves were propped against each other, heads close together, stalks slightly splayed, so that any rain ran down them and the ears could dry out properly as they stood through the long summer days."

Lucy also spent many hours filling sacks of grain. She felt every minute was worth it for the ride to the storage barn. "The joy," she remembers, "standing like Boadicea, on the back of the truck, leaning on the cab as we sped down Bison Hill with the wind in my face. We brought back rough loaves of oaten bread, which had normally been fed to animals."

So valuable was every crop that a local farmer's wife was furious when her orchard was denuded of apples. A colony of Quaker parakeets, originally from South America, lived in a huge communal nest overhanging the zoo's main gate. "There was a constant screeching as flashes of bright green darted in and out or hovered over the branches. They found their way down the hill and stripped Mrs Hain's orchard. The following year they were caught and kept in a cage until the apples had been harvested. By the next spring they had flown, their fate a mystery."

The Whipsnade Guides practised first-aid on each other, and were also practised on by others. "We had to be casualties for the adults in the village," remembered Lucy. "The WVS, Air-Raid Wardens, and Home Guard all used us Guides. I often had to pretend I had a broken arm, and once they asked me to have an epileptic fit." In the blacksmith's forge at the zoo they practised putting out incendiary bombs with a stirrup pump.

Spicers' Field, where the larger animals lived, would have been ideal for enemy gliders to land on, so sharp posts were driven into the ground. The "Whipsnade Lion", picked out on a chalky Chiltern hill, would have made a perfect landmark for enemy planes to navigate to the armament factories in nearby Luton, so the Guides camouflaged it with brushwood. Despite this, between August and October 1940 over fifty bombs were dropped on the zoo. Most fell in the paddocks, making large holes which were later turned into ponds. The only reported casualties were a spur-winged goose — the zoo's oldest inhabitant — and a baby giraffe which panicked itself to exhaustion and developed pneumonia. After one air raid, Rosie the elephant gave birth to a premature, stillborn calf.

The army took over some of the park for tank practice. "One night I was startled by a crash," said Lucy, "followed by silence, then a great commotion. Slipping out of bed and peering through a crack in the blackout, I could just make out the shape of a tank embedded in our garden fence. There was a great deal of shouting and engine revving, until eventually it was disentangled and the tank went on its way, leaving a much buckled boundary fence."

In December 1940, when the German — Italian — Japanese alliance was called the "Axis", the dainty axis deer from India were renamed "spotted" deer.

During Warship Week in 1942 the 1 st Whipsnade Guides raised money with a concert in the village hall. "We chose a patriotic theme," said Lucy. "I produced the company singing 'Land of Hope and Glory' and got one of the Scouts to carry the Union Jack up the aisle. Afterwards someone said to me, 'Why did you ask Rudi Kiekenheimer to carry the flag?' It never occurred to me that just because he was a Jew from Germany he shouldn't carry the British flag."

"Guide Captain Beal encouraged outdoor activities. She sent us out on Home Guard manoeuvres as signallers and messengers. Sometimes we were on all-night exercises, which meant a few hours' sleep, snatched on the wooden office floor close to the telephone switchboard waiting for instructions." One night Lucy was on duty with the Home Guard. "This man and I stood in a field all night in thick fog. As the dawn began, we saw these figures approaching, very quietly, through the fog. Convinced they were German parachutists, we stood quaking. Suddenly the cloud thinned and they were revealed — as Farmer Bates' cows! My, were we grateful that morning for breakfast of poached eggs and haddock, prepared by the zoo chef."

When the Guides went camping, they slept on straw palliasses. But Lucy's mother wouldn't let her. "To my great embarrassment, I had to take a real mattress camping. But we only managed to spend two nights outdoors." Lucy was already a First-Class Guide, and when she passed an additional seven proficiency badges she was thrilled to be awarded All-Round Cords, a length of cotton cord worn around the upper sleeve. "But because of war shortages, the cord was about six inches long and didn't go round anything!"

After Lucy's sixteenth birthday, Captain Beale asked her to become a Ranger. "I said, 'No, I can't do that, but I don't mind being a Bagheera, under the Akela, for the local Cubs.' I never told her the real reason I couldn't be a Ranger. They wore long-sleeved grey jerseys, knitted by the girls themselves. I had only just finished knitting a striped jumper out of my mother's wool scraps. It had taken me four years, and by the time I finished it, I had grown somewhat! But I wasn't going to tell Captain that, so I spent the last two years at school running the Cubs. As I was under twenty-one, officially Akela was in charge, but she was rarely there."

On 2 July 1945 Sir Peter Chalmers Mitchell, the founder of Whipsnade Zoo, died. A radical thinker, he was cremated, and Lucy's father buried his ashes in his chosen place in the zoo park. Lucy helped to dig the hole and lined it with soft green moss.

Dixie the elephant stayed at Whipsnade until her death in 1963. When Lucy Pendar grew up she became a Guide District Commissioner in West Yorkshire and a Fellow of the Royal Zoological Society.

CHAPTER
NINETEEN

The City of
Polish Children

After the Soviet Union invaded eastern Poland in September 1939, over a million Polish people were deported in freight trains to the Arctic Circle, Siberia and Kazakhstan, where they were put to forced labour logging and roadbuilding. The lucky ones had Guides among them, but they were under constant surveillance, and Guides seen organising support were punished.

Eighteen months later, after Hitler broke his pact with the Soviet Union by launching Operation Barbarossa, the Soviets released all their surviving Polish prisoners. They travelled for months on freight trains in a bid to get out of the Soviet Union. Many of them fetched up in Uzbekistan, where there was a labour shortage and they were forced into cotton farming. They included a thousand Polish girls, who found themselves stranded in the desert near Guzar, in a village called Kharkin-Batash, or "The Valley of Death", because all its inhabitants had died of an epidemic in the early years of Stalin's reign.

Among the hundreds of starving children who arrived by train, truck and mule cart were two orphaned sisters, both Girl Guides, Zosia and Olenka Haciski, who helped look after the children. They lived in wooden huts, the cracks between the rough logs filled with moss infested with bedbugs. In summer the temperature soared to 35°C, and the single well produced only ten buckets of water a day. There were constant outbreaks of dysentery, typhoid and cholera. "The children were sad and quiet," wrote one of the women who survived. "They neither laughed nor cried. They did not complain about anything and nothing cheered them up. Many suffered from scurvy, some had malaria, some diarrhoea. They were too worn out even to play. Most of the time they just sat apathetically, propped up against the walls of the huts." There was no medicine, and half the children died and were buried in mass graves. The remaining four hundred girls were accepted into the new Polish army, which had been formed under General Wladyslaw Anders to fight alongside the Soviets, as "*Junaczki*" — girl cadets — and moved to a camp by the River Kaszka in Darya. Within a few weeks, all of them had malaria. There was only enough quinine for those with the highest fevers.

General Anders did not trust Stalin, and decided to take the Polish army to Iran, by then occupied by the Allies. After six months travelling through the Soviet Union on more freight trains, over 100,000 malnourished refugees — a tenth of those who had originally left Poland in 1939 — were finally allowed to leave the country.

Zosia and Olenka, a few orphans and the surviving *Junaczki* girls were packed into a train going to Krasnovodsk in Turkmenistan, on the Caspian Sea. After a few days the train arrived, and the girls were dumped on a beach half a mile from the sea. There was no shelter, and the contaminated drinking water gave them dysentery. The girls who washed in the sea emerged covered with oil and salt. After a few days they marched to the harbour in their heavy new army uniforms. As they approached the ship to carry them across the Caspian Sea, Zosia was stopped by a Soviet secret police officer. She was terrified he would take away her most precious possessions, which were wrapped in her Guide tie: "A Guide manual, a portrait of Marshal Pilsudski [the Polish president and hero], postcards from my uncle in Hungary, a watercolour of our village painted on the back of wallpaper, a prayer book, the names of all the places through which we passed. These relics were the certificate of our ordeal." Luckily the officer let her through. The ship on which they travelled was the last before the Soviets closed the borders, and was packed so tight there was no room to sit down. There was no water on board. The journey across the Caspian Sea to Pahlevi in Iran took twenty-six hours.

Eventually they arrived in Isfahan. With 2,000 orphans living there, it was soon named "The City of Polish Children". There, children who had suffered so much cold, hunger and loss could at last begin to look to the future. The older girls organised schools and started over a dozen Guide companies and a Brownie pack. Once the children had regained their strength, they were sent on to refugee centres in India, Africa, New Zealand and Mexico, where more Polish Guides welcomed them.

In July 1942 the first Polish refugees arrived from Iran in the East African port of Mombasa. From there they were sent to settlements in the British colonies of Uganda, Kenya, Tanzania, and Northern and Southern Rhodesia (now Zambia and Zimbabwe). They lived far from towns and surrounded by wire fences, not to keep them in but to protect them from wild animals. The weakest refugees had by now died, and those who survived were a motley collection of mothers, children and a few grandparents. The strongest were the teenagers, and as soon as they reached their destinations the Guides among them started companies with the other children. There were now fewer than 20,000 Polish refugees, of whom 8,000 were children and 1,500 adolescent girls.

"Only the strong will to live saved us in these severe conditions," wrote Guide Alina Zbikowska. "It was inhuman work, we were hungry and cold. In 1942 a new journey had begun, but as free people. We aimed for Uzbekistan, and this severe and extremely long route took us finally to Krasnovodsk. And then on a ship, together with the army to Iran. Here we were washed, dressed, cured and fed. Now without men, for they were almost all in the army, via Tehran, Ahvaz, and thence from Karachi we arrived in Mombasa, Kenya." From there they travelled west into Tanzania, to the foothills of Mount Kilimanjaro.

"In November 1942 we reached the beautiful Tengeru at the foot of Mount Meru, among exotic nature, and half-naked natives. Here, after the long wanderings, we had our own house! A round hut made of mud, with a cone-shaped roof covered with banana leaves. There was one door and one window without glass, and it seemed to us a luxury." Immediately lessons were organised, initially under the flowering trees, with each student bringing their own stool. "We had a church where we thanked God for the graces received and to pray for our families and reunion in free Poland." The most popular activity was Guiding, which occupied all the children and teenagers. "This was our pride and the best adventure and entertainment." There were seven Guide companies and four Scout troops in Tengeru, each with sixty or seventy members.

One little girl was so miserable that she never spoke and never smiled: she had seen her father murdered by the Germans, and her mother had gone mad. When she arrived in the settlement, a Guide Patrol Leader tried in vain to coax her to eat. Then the Guide had an idea. "Very slowly and clearly she made the Guides' sign," wrote Catherine Christian. "The little Polish Guide fell into her arms and clung to her, sobbing. She had recognised something out of the almost unremembered past before her horror began. She was with Guides! She was safe! She was able to begin again because she had found her 'family'!"

"Camping was our greatest pastime," wrote Elena Grosicka, a Guide who ran Cub and Brownie packs for the orphans, "even though some people complained that it was dangerous. The most attractive place for the Guide camp was a farm on the other side of Mount Meru, completely in the wild. The journey in an open truck took about six hours, with everyone very excited." They were visited by wild monkeys, antelopes and even elephants. "Despite this, we felt safe. A few Africans employed on the farm also watched over us, particularly for crocodiles and hyenas. At night, lions sometimes came to the camp, so the guards kept the campfires going the whole night and walked around with long sticks."

"One day we heard the screams of the Negros," wrote Alina Zbikowska, another Guide at Mount Meru. "They were running, very scared with all their belongings and cattle. It was difficult to guess what was causing the panic. So Mr Zajer, the only man among us, stopped and held a Negro, who was trying to get away and shouting in Swahili, 'Run away home! Maasai are coming!'" The Guide Captain, Elena Grosicka, immediately ordered all the Guides to go to their tents. She told the Patrol Leaders to fetch a basket and fill it with mirrors, trinkets, beads and coloured ribbons.

There was silence and then we could hear the rhythmic steps of the Maasai. We peered through the cracks of the tents. We soon saw them, armed with huge spears and shields. With these primitive weapons they can kill a lion. The Maasai men were wearing leather slung over their shoulders, like a Roman toga. Their hair was braided into tiny

340

plaits, dyed the colour of brick. They were smeared with grease. The women had shaved heads, their ears cut and decorated with trinkets hanging down to their shoulders. They wore cow's skin and carried their children on their backs. We were frightened but none of us let them out of our sight.

Mr Zajer, armed with a gun and a camera, walked forward to welcome the Maasai chief. Beside him stood our Captain in Guide's uniform, holding a basket with the trinkets collected for the Maasai women. Mirrors were something magical for them and the reflection of their faces delighted them. The Maasai performed a dance and went off in an unknown direction. After their departure there was complete silence in the camp!

North of Tanzania, in the Ruwenzori mountains on the border between Uganda and the Congo, the Guides of the 1st Toro Company had little need for money. Hearing of the troubles in Europe, in 1944 they sold vegetables, made cakes of banana and cassava flour and put on an entertainment. They sent the small sum this earned to the Guide International Service Fund. The Toro Captain organised a training camp for African Guiders: "I saw the Colours glowing in the evening light against the background of the foothills of the Ruwenzori. I thought, 'In this hour of our country's utmost peril, there is nothing more worthwhile to be done than just what we are doing.'" No one knew if the Guides of Britain would survive a German invasion, or if any of the Guides who had remained in Poland had survived. The Guides in Uganda feared that they might have to carry the Guide colours alone.

Further south, some African Guides in Northern Rhodesia were very excited to be chosen to attend a rally five hundred miles across their country. While they ground thirty pounds of millet into flour for the journey, they sang joyously. Beans were collected for soup, and packed in the cook pots; uniforms were washed and ironed, and all their possessions were tied in blankets. Complete with bundles on their heads and holding aloft the Union Jack and company colours, they mounted the mail lorry and set off. It was the Guides' first adventure on their own.

The first night they slept in a tin shanty town. Rather than wait two days for the next mail van, they boarded a smelly petrol lorry which took them a further 110 miles. After walking four miles they arrived at Chitambo, where they scrubbed their bodies, heads and clothes in the river. The next day they mounted an ox wagon to reach the main road, where they joined another mail lorry. For all of that day and most of the night they sat on the back of the lorry until they reached the railway. They then travelled by train to the copper-mining district of Nkana, where they arrived in the early evening. After they had walked four miles to Mindola, the District Guide Commissioner presented them with six loaves and some meat. They had never seen bread before, and weren't sure what to do with it. Captain came to the rescue and cut slices, and they were soon munching the new fare with relish. Their long journey had been worth it for the games, competitions, a march-past, and the campfire singing in the evening.

After the war, the settlements of Polish refugees scattered around southern and eastern Africa gradually diminished, until the last one officially closed in 1948. By then, all of them had found permanent homes in Africa, or had emigrated to Canada or Australia. Few ever returned to Poland.

CHAPTER
TWENTY

The Armored Angel of China

On the other side of the world, at Weihsien in China, conditions for the Brownies, Guides and their fellow prisoners were worsening. In order to get news in and out of the camp, a secret escape committee was formed, and one night in June 1944 two men, Laurie Tipton and Arthur Hummel Jr, climbed over the wall and escaped to a group of Chinese guerrillas. Escape from the camp was relatively easy: the difficult part was blending in with the Chinese. Both Tipton and Hummel were fluent in Mandarin: Tipton had been an executive with British American Tobacco, and Hummel had taught English in Peking. They were not seeking their own freedom: they wanted to communicate to the Allies the whereabouts of and conditions in the camp. They took a typewriter with them, and typed coded messages on fine silk which could be hidden inside a messenger's shoes. They also smuggled news into the camp via the Chinese coolies who carried out the camp's nightsoil, who stuffed the silk messages up their noses and left them in the latrines. Only a few men knew of this dangerous secret.

Tipton and Hummel's escape had repercussions for everyone inside the camp. The Guides were moved from their dormitory to the men's one, above the hospital overlooking the outer wall. They now had a view of farmland, villages and the donkey carts, peddlers and women carrying bundles to Weihsien city. Below them, the patients in the hospital had to contend with the sound of trunks being dragged about, doors banging, feet clattering, loud calls and peals of laughter. Roll calls now occurred more frequently, a deep trench was dug around the outside of the camp, and more electrified wire was put up.

Two months later, inmates who had assembled for roll call were deeply shocked when they witnessed the fatal electrocution of a British boy who touched an overhanging live wire. The adult prisoners had to suppress their anger when their own investigations revealed that the Japanese knew the wire was dangerous; and the children mourned a popular friend.

Brownie meetings continued once a week. "We began by a fairyring round our new toadstool," recorded the log book for the Kelpie Six on 7 September 1944. "Then we had a Union Jack Revision. Presently Brown Owl blew on her whistle and we all ran in. Then we all played Thief and Policeman. Then Brown Owl told us a story about a man called Joseph Damien. He left his home and went to preach to the South Sea islanders. He lived with the lepers and got leprosy himself. She told us the story to illustrate 'I promise my duty to God'." Sixer Elizabeth Hoyte included a hand-drawn map of China and the question "What country do we live in?" Later that month, Beryl Strange sent a message to the Kelpies on a toadstool-shaped piece of brown paper: "Dear Kelpies, Please get on with your First and Second class. Please try hard in your observation test. Please come to every meeting promptly because if you do not we would lose a point. Love Kelpie Second."

Although the Brownies and Guides tried to attend as many meetings as they could, they were often forced to miss them due to ill-health. Despite the fact that drinking water was filtered, boiled and distilled, diarrhoea was very common amongst the prisoners.

Like the Brownies, the Guides in Weihsien kept log books. "For tracking, Lefty was all painted up like some people are all the time," the Kingfisher patrols recorded on 20 October 1944. "At first we didn't recognise her because she had dark glasses on. Captain told us a story about a gardener. There was a storm and all his beautiful flowers were destroyed. He was rather disappointed but plucked up courage when he saw his seedlings all safe and sound. She likened us to the seedlings and the storm to the war. Then we prayed and then dismissed." On 3 November the Kingfishers received a note: "Dear Kingfishers, Are you remembering Kind Deeds? Do your best, not because we want to give in a long list but just because it is helping other people. The more kind deeds done by you, the happier place Weihsien will be. Love from Patrol Leader."

If Brown Owl or Captain feared being raped by the guards, or being forced to dig a trench and then being machine-gunned into it, they never let the girls see it. As the Brownies played their games of stalking among the armed guards, they seemed to know no fear. And, as Christian mission children, they drew hope from the stories about God rescuing His people: Moses leading God's children out of slavery to their Promised Land; the ravens feeding the hungry prophet Elijah in the wilderness; God protecting Daniel in the lions' den. "There was no sense in thinking about the future, for there was nothing we could do about it anyway," wrote the Chefoo teacher Ailsa Carr. "Occasionally, I faced the end — whichever way it went — and prayed that my turn might come near the beginning."

Whatever the fears of their prisoners, the Japanese felt that they should show the world that they cared for them well. They ordered all the Brownies, Cubs, Guides and Scouts to put on their uniforms, and had them photographed in their packs and companies. The only clues to their whereabouts are the electric insulators between the wires, and a guardpost number painted on the wall behind them. Although some of the Brownies tried to hide their feet from the photographer, by 1944 none of them were wearing shoes.

For Christmas 1944, the Guides made presents out of rags. "Mary made a duck, Joan a squirrel, Dorothy a ball, Edith a rabbit, Pooh a doll, Betty a cat and Marion made a teddy," reported the Kingfisher patrol. "Christmas promised little," wrote Norah Busby, an internee. "But there was a wonderful Christmas pudding made from the simplest ingredients. Parties for young folk with a Punch and Judy. Christmas service where small children could be seen hugging their gifts. 'Post early for Christmas,' read the slogan on the pillar-box. 'If I post a card to myself, will I *really* get it?' asked one small girl." For the Christmas concert, the choral society performed Handel's *Messiah*, and the orchestra managed Mozart's piano concerto in D Minor, minus violas and tuba. Brownie Sixer Elizabeth Hoyte was chosen to be Father Christmas, and led the Brownies in a song specially written by Brown Owl.

We might have been shipped to Timbuctoo
We might have been shipped to Kalamazoo
It's not repatriation nor is it yet starvation
It's simply Concentration in Chefoo!

We're the Chefoo Brownies
A cheerful company
We've learnt to tie up parcels
We've learnt to lay the tea
We've learnt to plait our pigtails
We've learnt to tie our laces
We always keep our teeth clean
And scrub our hands and faces.
We're only little Brownies
Great things we cannot do
But we are always happy
And hope that you are too.
Our song is almost ended
And so we'll say adieu

We'll stand up on our heads and
Wave our feet to you!

"We would hit the high note at the end and all giggle," remembered Mary Taylor.

At their Christmas party, the Brownies played the matchbox game. "We had to pass the matchbox on our noses right down the columns," said the log book. "After that game we played the Grand Old Duke of York. Mr McChesney Clark came and made a campfire with red paper and put the bulb underneath. Then we departed after having a very happy time."

The Guides' log book ended the year with: "Looking back at 1944: Marion became Patrol Leader and had badges in Child Nurse, Needlewoman, Cook, and First Class. Edith, Betty and Pooh were enrolled in Second Class. Joan had badges in Child Nurse, Needlewoman, Book Lover and First Class. Looking forward to 1945: Marion and Mary must get their All Round cords and more badges. Edith, Pooh and Betty must win more badges and First Class. Come on Kingfishers! Let's win in 1945."

Winters in Weihsien were freezing, with snow and bitter winds sweeping in from Manchuria, Mongolia and Siberia. "I wore a Chinese gown of thickly padded cotton all the time," recalled Evelyn Davey. "Washing your face with a frozen cloth was painful. The only fuel was coal dust, not lumps of coal. The Brownies mixed the coal dust with water and mud to make coal balls. We left them outside to dry. They were liable to be stolen, and in the winter they didn't dry, they just froze.

The Brownies had chilblains, but I never heard them complain."

"The Brownies invented a game to carry the buckets of coal dust," wrote Mary Taylor. "They stood in a human chain and hauled the coal dust back to their dormitory, singing all the way, 'Many hands make light work.'" "We had a grey line at the wrist," wrote Estelle Cliff, "which came off only on shower day, once a week." Some rooms had a "chatty", a small stove made from a five-gallon oilcan, with a pipe made out of bean cans. At night they were banked down with the wet coal-ball mixture, which burned slowly all night. "In the early morning, the one whose duty it was that day would walk across the dormitory beds, to keep off the icy concrete floor, and put the enamel jug of frozen water on the stove, to warm for washing." "The coal dust symbolised the attitude towards camp living," wrote Mary Taylor. "Some people complained about having only coal dust to burn. Others counted their blessings that on freezing mornings, at least they had a jug of warm water to look forward to." The sight of a large pile of coal tested even the strongest consciences. Guide Captains were aware that under circumstances in which pilfering was such a temptation to the adults, it was even more important than usual to maintain high morals among their young charges.

The daily food ration fell to bread in hot water for breakfast, bread with thin vegetable soup at midday, and two slices of bread with still thinner soup in the evening. The adults and teenagers at Weihsien were consuming approximately 1,200 calories per day — less than half what they required. The teachers shielded the children from debates over which would come first, starvation or liberation. Children's new teeth were appearing without enamel, and Brownies often fainted from hunger. Among the Guides, puberty came late, with irregular periods or none at all, and girls of fourteen looked more like twelve-year-olds. Meat was rare, and when even the sorghum and beans ran out, the cooks invented "bread porridge", mixing wet stale bread with flour, seasoned with cinnamon and saccharin. "Only our hunger made it edible," wrote Mary.

When the teachers decided that eggshells could provide a good calcium supplement for growing bodies, the Guides washed them and ground them into a powder. "They spooned it into our spluttering mouths each day in the dormitory," said Mary. "We gagged and choked and exhaled, hoping the grit would blow away before we had to swallow. But it never did. So we gnashed our teeth on the powdered shells."

In January 1945, donkey carts arrived piled with Red Cross parcels, only the second consignment in three years, but with enough for everyone in the camp. "They contained eatables," wrote Kathleen Strange to her mother. "Tinned goods, milk, meat, chocolate, butter, sugar. I got sewing kit, toothpowder, comb. It snowed on Thursday. We had fancy dress party. I went as 'Little Miss Muffet'. I had a tooth out but recovered an hour afterwards. Lamentations three twenty-six." This reference to a Biblical verse contained a message to her mother: "It is good that man should hope and quietly wait for the salvation of the Lord," indicating that they were waiting patiently for release.

"In our hungry camp," wrote Langdon Gilkey, an interned American lecturer, "Spam, butter, Nescafe and raisins seemed to us the last word in gustatory delight." Each parcel was eked out for months, and although smoking was off limits for Guides and Brownies, no one objected if they exchanged their Red Cross cigarettes for tinned milk or jam. Everyone made an effort for birthdays: cakes were made from dough mixed with a few raisins and sugar. On Mary Taylor's eleventh birthday, her teacher marked the occasion with an apple. "The apple itself wasn't so important as the delicious feeling that I had a 'mother' all to myself in a private celebration — just my teacher and me — behind the hospital. In the cutting of wondrously thin, translucent apple circles, she showed me that I could find the shape of an apple blossom. On a tiny tin-can stove fuelled by twigs, she fried the apple slices for me in a moment of wonder. No birthday cake has ever inspired such joy."

Despite the freezing weather, Guide and Brownie meetings continued. There were no more exercise books to record minutes, and no material left for badges. Patrick Bruce, the Chefoo headmaster, encouraged Guides to carry on as best they could, but nerves were beginning to fray. "Doris was asked to encourage Carol not to lose her head and get discouraged so easily," read the Guide log book.

"When we ran out of knitting needles," said Estelle Cliff, "we used a packet of pick-up-sticks. The British hold the wool in their right hand, and the Americans of Scandinavian origin hold it in their left. So we taught ourselves to knit Fair Isle designs with one colour yarn in each hand! We re-knitted our stockings as ankle socks, and re-knitted jumpers with worn-out elbows into sleeveless ones. We unpicked and wound the wool into skeins, dipped it in hot water to get the kinks out, dried it and wound it again into balls. An American man asked me to re-knit a jumper for him. This I did for the unimagined reward of a tin of condensed milk!" "We knitted bands of different coloured wool onto our jerseys as our arms and bodies grew," said Beryl Strange, who was awarded a Knitter's Badge.

Faith kept many of the internees going. "There was no way of making shoes bigger to fit growing feet," remembered Margaret Vindon, so she prayed for a new pair. "I was overjoyed when the answer came in a completely unexpected way. Someone I knew in camp just walked up to me one day and said: 'I can't help noticing that your shoes are almost worn out. Try this pair and see if they fit you.' They did! This was one of the many direct answers to my prayers."

One of the most popular people in the camp was Eric Liddell, who was born in China to missionary parents, and had been teaching in a mission school at the outbreak of the war. He was famous for winning the gold medal in the four hundred metres at the 1924 Olympic Games in Paris, after refusing to run the hundred-metre heats on a Sunday. In 1932 he married a Canadian missionary, and in 1940 he sent his two daughters and pregnant wife home to Canada, expecting to follow. But he was imprisoned by the Japanese, and would never meet his third daughter. He now devoted himself to the children of Weihsien, cheering them up with his brightly coloured shirts made from curtains.

Eric Liddell did more than any other person for Weihsien's adolescents. "He was absorbed, warm, and interested, pouring all of himself into this effort to capture the minds and imaginations of those penned-up youths," wrote Langdon Gilkey. "Now in his mid-forties, lithe and springy of step, and overflowing with good humour and love of life, Eric's charm and enthusiasm carried the day."

In other Japanese prison camps, doctors advised against games and exercise in order to save prisoners' energy. But Liddell believed that nourishing the spirit was as important as feeding the body. So after school, the children played basketball, rounders, hockey or football. He also organised country-dancing lessons. "Eric used to come and play with the Brownies," said Brown Owl Evelyn Davey. "He organised races and taught them basketball." "Uncle Eric," remembered Margaret Vindon, "taught me chemistry, and he organised hockey matches with makeshift hockey sticks." "Uncle Eric would mend a hockey stick with strips ripped from his sheets," wrote Mary Taylor. "When the teenagers got bored with the deadening monotony of prison life and turned for relief to the temptations of clandestine sex, he organised an evening games room."

354

In February 1945 Liddell collapsed, he thought from exhaustion: it required six people to take over his work. The camp doctors realised that he had a brain tumour, and that there was nothing they could do either to treat him or to relieve the pain. Liddell asked the Salvation Army band to play "Be Still, My Soul" to the theme from *Finlandia* by Sibelius. They gathered outside his window, and the strains of his favourite hymn floated into his room to ease his suffering.

Liddell died on 21 February 1945. "When Eric died the whole camp was in mourning, everybody loved him," remembered Margaret Vindon. "It was bitterly cold," recalled Estelle Cliff. "The temperature was about minus 20°C. We wore our threadbare overcoats over whatever warm clothes we had left." The boys wore trousers made from blankets, but the girls had only skirts and ankle socks.

"The camp was stunned," wrote Mary Taylor. "Through an honour guard of solemn Brownies, Guides, Cubs and Scouts, his friends carried his coffin to the tiny cemetery in the corner of the Japanese quarters. There, a little bit of Scotland was tucked sadly away in Chinese soil." The next day was Thinking Day, and Brown Owl tried to cheer up the Brownies with Sheila Fraser's enrolment. The pack played games involving throwing balls and skipping, and showed Sheila how to salute correctly.

By the end of March it was warm enough to meet outside for the fairy ring and songs around the toadstool. "Tawny asked us some questions on flags — St George's, St Andrew and St Patrick. After which we played Fox and Chickens. Then we played a game of Sardines. Then we sang, 'Every Brownie likes an Irish Stew'."

Looking for signs of spring, the Guides found catkins, budding walnut, Judas and plane trees, bulbs sprouting, a woodpecker's nest in a poplar tree, grass growing, lilac budding, hollyhocks, wild carrots, yellow boys, bamboo and shepherd's purse growing near the hospital. Over the wall they spotted wheat in the fields, a red-tailed thrush, a pomegranate, weeping willow and apricot blossom. They started a garden, and found that radishes and marigolds did well. However, after the effort of carrying water across the compound, they were disappointed when many of their vegetables were stolen.

On the night of VE-Day, 8 May 1945, two young men climbed the Weihsien church tower and rang the bell. They didn't realise the bell was the Japanese guards' code that there was trouble in camp, and that troops should come and help. The Commandant roused the entire camp, demanding an explanation. "It was a beautiful starry cold night," remembered Beryl Strange. "King Kong was right in front of us, shouting angrily and waving his sword about. The interpreter had to dodge about to avoid it." The two culprits gave themselves up, and the discipline committee run by Europeans agreed that they should be beaten. But now everyone knew that the war in Europe was over, and there was hope for Asia too.

On Empire Day, 24 May, the Brownies and Guides held their annual Sports Day. "We began with our knot

356

race. Brownies then had their first-aid race. We went to watch the Scouts lashing, the Cubs skipping and the Guides' obstacles race. The Scouts had a three-legged race. Mr O'Hara then spoke to us about Empire Day and then distributed the pennants. The roll-call bell went so she dismissed us all." The following month the Guides were involved in a production of George Bernard Shaw's *Androcles and the Lion*, with a full-scale lion costume made from old fur coats, and Roman guards' armour made from Red Cross Spam tins.

At the end of June, the Brownies went on camp. "We brought our things out at 10.20 — wood bag, canvas bucket, dishes, curtains. We made tents from rope, poles and curtains. At 11 o'clock we made gadgets — towel rack, basin stand, soap stand, hat stand and mug stand. At 1 o'clock we had our dinner" — a fried egg cooked on a campfire made with bricks. "Between 2 and 3 we rested and Brown Owl read us Edith Nesbit." From 1 to 4p.m. they played games, and then at four o'clock "The Weihsien trophy was presented to the patrol that had won most points." This was to be the last ever meeting of the 2nd Chefoo Brownies.

By the end of July, Elizabeth Hoyte, Sixer of the Kelpies, had passed her First-Class Brownie Test and achieved seventeen proficiency badges including Toymaker, First-Aider, Jester, Signaller, Gardener, Homecraft, Observer, Minstrel, Country Dancer and Athlete. "Brown Owl hand-sewed the badges, but sometimes we had to make do with just a small paper certificate," she remembered. "It was amazing what badges we could try for. This shows how much we longed for something different to break up the boredom; and our leader's dedication to us children to make Weihsien as bearable a possible." There was no "flying up" from Brownies to Guides — everyone stayed in their pack or company however old they were.

The possibility of peace meant greater danger for the prisoners. As the American army closed in on the Japanese in China in the summer of 1945, the adults in Weihsien learned through their "bamboo radio" that Japanese guards had been told that if Japan fell, they were to kill all prisoners, regardless of age. Another rumour claimed that the Chinese Communists planned to kidnap all the children and use them as hostages to bargain with the US Army.

Brown Owl Evelyn Davey was wondering whether her camp romance would survive peace. She had been courting Eugene Heubener, an American missionary accountant and a talented musician. "We'd been going for walks around the camp for about a year," she said. "We used to read *Winnie the Pooh* to each other. One day he gave me a present: he'd made me some book-ends from old tin cans and wood, carved with a Brown Owl."

The Salvation Army band knew that victory would require a special march, so in a small room next to the shoe-repair shop they practised a piece composed for the occasion by Eugene. "He could transpose any piece of music to the instruments in the motley brass band," said Evelyn. "For months they practised a Victory

Medley, made up of all the national anthems of the Allies. During rehearsals they never played the melody, so that the Japanese wouldn't recognise it."

Food was now so low that cases of dysentery and typhoid were increasing. Guide Captain Louise Lawless, among others, was lying in the camp hospital with typhoid. She died on 8 August 1945, aged fifty-three, just two days after the atom bomb was dropped on Hiroshima. "My last view of her was through the window of the morgue," said Gay Talbot Stratford. "It was a great shock."

On Friday, 17 August, Mary Taylor lay suffering from diarrhoea in the second-floor dormitory. "I heard the drone of an airplane far above the camp," she remembered. "Racing to the window, I watched it sweep lower, and then circle again. Beyond the treetops, its silver belly opened, and I gaped in wonder as giant parachutes drifted slowly down. Oh, glorious cure for diarrhoea!"

The plane was an American B-24 named *The Armored Angel*. As it flew slowly over Weihsien camp, the Brownies were having a singing lesson in the church. "I raced for the entry gates and was swept off my feet by the pandemonium," recalled Mary. "Grown men ripped off their shirts and waved them at the sky. Prisoners ran in circles and punched the sky with their fists. They wept, cursed, hugged, danced as the plane circled back, its belly open. Seven parachutes drifted into the fields of tall ripening *gaoliang* grain beyond the Camp. The Americans had come!"

A thousand cheering, weeping, disbelieving prisoners, dressed in rags and emaciated by hunger, surged through the forbidden gates into the open fields. The Japanese guards laid down their guns and retreated to their homes. The American paratroopers were hoisted onto shoulders and carried into the camp in triumph. The Salvation Army band was playing its joyful Victory Medley of national anthems, and an American flag appeared on the tower. "Crowds of child prisoners trailed these gorgeous liberators around," remembered Mary. "We begged for their insignia, begged for buttons, and begged them to sing the songs of America. They were sun-bronzed American gods with meat on their bones. My twelve-year-old heart turned somersaults over every one of them."

These seven-man American rescue teams had been trained to locate camps and evacuate prisoners, and warned that it was unlikely they would return alive. The Japanese-American interpreter, Tad Nagaki, was on only his second jump. One girl cut a lock of his hair as a memento. The Lieutenant, Jimmy Moore, had specially asked for this mission — he had been a pupil at Chefoo school. The team's leader, Major Stanley Staiger, walked over to the commandant, who surrendered his sword. Much to his surprise, Major Staiger ordered the guards to retain their arms so they could defend the camp against Communist forces or starving civilians. The escapees Tipton and Hummel returned on horseback, and one of the sewage-carrying Chinese coolies appeared in a business suit: he had been a spy for the Allies all along.

The next day, leaflets were dropped on the camp: "ALLIED PRISONERS — The Japanese Government has surrendered. You will be evacuated by ALLIED NATIONS as soon as possible. Until that time your supplies will be augmented by air-drop of U.S. food, clothing and medicines."

The sewing-room ladies and Guides sat up all night making giant letters out of the seven parachutes to read "OK TO LAND" for the nearby airfield. They were finished in time for the first B-29 planes dropping canisters containing food, clothing and other comforts. The trousers, shirts, razors, Lucky Strike cigarettes, chocolate and chewing gum had evidently been chosen for soldiers, not children. But no one cared: they could share it all out. "These were unbelievable riches and our joy knew no bounds! Our ordeal was over," said Margaret Vindon.

Some of the containers burst on landing, and the children returned to the camp with their faces smeared with chocolate and sticky with fruit juice. One crate of Del Monte peaches crashed through the kitchen roof, while a few landed in the camp trees. "Our teachers issued orders for us to run for the dormitories whenever we sighted bombers," said Mary. "They were not about to have us survive the war and then be killed by a shower of Spam."

At the church service of thanksgiving, most of the worshippers were barefoot, but everyone who had a uniform of any kind wore it — ex-servicemen, Salvation Army members, Guides and Brownies. "Scouts, Guides, Brownies and Cubs brought home the realisation of how much the Camp owed to youth," wrote Norah Busby. "And what a desolate place it would have been without the laughter and games of children. When the Camp disperses they will go out into the outside world and carry with them impressions of friendship, co-operation and service, formed in an Internment Camp in China."

The sickest prisoners were evacuated by air, and five hundred others left by train, but after one of the American soldiers went down with scarlet fever, the camp was put in quarantine. And when a few weeks later the Communists blew up the railway line, the remaining internees, including many Chefoo schoolchildren, were forced to resume queueing for water and doing the same deadly chores they had done for the past three years.

The Americans were determined to bring them good cheer, and installed loudspeakers to broadcast music. But the internees, weakened by undernourishment and exhausted by years of living in a state of suspense, found the unaccustomed noise more than their nerves could stand. The Americans had forgotten that not only had these people lost five years of cultural history, they were already a decade behind the times when they were first interned. Frank Sinatra singing "Oh What a Beautiful Mornin'" played at full volume at dawn was not their idea of liberation. "We were all horrified by the loud music," remembered Margaret Vindon. "The Americans couldn't understand why even us young ones couldn't cope with it. We hadn't 'missed' Western pop music, because we had never heard it before." "We all put our heads under the blankets and tried to sleep," said Evelyn Davey. "We didn't want to wake up early any more."

Estelle Cliff had just turned sixteen, and was revising for the Oxford Matriculation School Certificate exams. The teachers had brought copies of old examination papers into the camp, and from these had devised new ones. "The Headmaster said we should take our exams straight away, before we left camp," remembered Estelle. "To avoid repeating grades when we got 'home', he gave us a week to swot in the blistering heat." While cicadas buzzed in the trees and US planes dropped food parachutes outside, eleven students, including Estelle, were indoors sitting their School Certificate examinations. Once the headmaster was back in Britain, he presented three years' worth of exam papers to the examining board, and explained the circumstances. The papers were marked in the normal way. Nearly all of the Chefoo students passed the Oxford School Certificate and were admitted into universities.

The new camp administration, run by the US Army and the internee committees, employed pairs of Guides as messengers. "We have chocolates and sweets," Kathleen and Beryl Strange wrote to their mother on 26 August 1945. "Every day now there is a market outside the camp to exchange old clothes for eggs and fresh fruit. Beryl has sixteen Brownie badges, including First and Second-Class. Kathleen has 6 Guide badges. With gallons & gallons of love." The Guides camped outdoors under canvas, at last permitted to cook over a campfire.

Elizabeth Hoyte was eleven years old at the end of the war. By then her mother had died of typhus, and her father, a doctor, spent months travelling across China in search of his six children, all prisoners of war. He finally caught up with them in Hong Kong, where they had been evacuated. Elizabeth didn't know if she would recognise him. "I had been only six when I had last seen him," she wrote. "Then I was in his arms, the strong arms of the half-familiar stranger who was my father, and we began the gentle probing business of getting to know each other again."

Estelle Cliff's mother had moved from inland China to Durban, in South Africa, hoping her children would be repatriated there. "It was years before we met," wrote Estelle. "We left the ship at Port Suez, and travelled by flying boat to Durban, sleeping at Officers' Clubs all down Africa's lakes. We lived out of suitcases, but I took my Guide uniform and the Guide song book. It was a terrible wrench from our camp extended family, and we hardly knew our parents after six years."

The Taylor children — Kathleen, Jamie, Johnny the Scout and Mary the Guide — had not seen their parents for five and a half years. They flew six hundred miles into the Chinese interior, then travelled a hundred miles by train, mule cart and finally on foot. Chinese peasants blinked in amazement at the four foreign children struggling through the mud. "There, through a back window, I could see them — Daddy and Mother — sitting in a meeting," said Mary. "Caked

364

with mud, we burst through the door into their arms — shouting, laughing, hugging — hysterical with joy."

Margaret Vindon didn't know whether her mother and father had remained in China, or had left for England or Canada. "We eventually learned that our parents were still in China." She and her brother were reunited with them over a hundred miles away in Kunming, and they returned together to England on a troop ship. "After the long years of separation the closeness of our family was as precious as it had ever been," said Margaret. "We all thanked God for His loving care of us through everything that had happened."

"On coming to England after the war, my sisters and I found things so strange, and it was difficult to fit in," remembered Jenny Bevan. "However, we found a Guide company in Hereford and were welcomed in, and from then on, all was well. Even now I find myself muttering over a hard job, 'A Brownie smiles and sings under all difficulties'!"

Kathleen and Beryl Strange were among the last to leave Weihsien camp. On the train, Kathleen became very ill with osteomylitis in her hip, caused by malnutrition. At Tsingtao port, a German surgeon operated on her while the teachers prayed. A British frigate arrived with the recently developed drug penicillin, and to everyone's amazement she recovered in weeks rather than months. While she was convalescing in Hong Kong, she lent her woollen swimming costume to Beryl Welch for an outing to the beach with British soldiers. "It had been sitting in a trunk for five years," said Beryl. "Moths had attacked it, and while I was swimming, the bottom half fell away!"

Kathleen and her sister Beryl set off in mid-November 1945 for the six-week journey home via the Suez Canal. "It was great," recalled Kathleen. "We were thoroughly spoilt by the British troops, who hadn't seen a European child for years. At every port there was a band to greet us. In Port Said the Red Cross kitted us out with winter clothes — and we spent Christmas Day in the Mediterranean. The ship felt safe; I wasn't sure I wanted to arrive." The ship docked at Liverpool in thick fog on 30 December. They had not seen their mother for five years. "I wondered what she would look like," said Kathleen. "The last time I had seen her, she was wearing Chinese clothes, with her hair pulled back in a tight bun. When my teacher Mr Welch said, 'This is your mother,' I said, 'No it isn't. She would never wear a brown hat like that.'" The two sisters lived in a London mission home with their mother, and went to Highbury Hill High School. "I stayed being a Brownie when I got home, and I won a trophy for having so many badges," said Beryl. "I could never understand the fuss over school dinners. Compared to camp food, they were great!"

When she was liberated, Evelyn Davey weighed ninety-eight pounds and had not had periods for some time. "We just got used to being thin and hungry. We now know how much better we were treated than most other prisoners of war. I got double food rations for six weeks and recovered fairly quickly. I was riding a bike within three weeks." She and Eugene Heubener married in Cornwall and went back to Shanghai. "I worked in a nursery for Chinese workers' children. Then the Communists came, and we had a baby by that time and we didn't want to be in another prison camp, so we came home." Home was Seattle, where Eugene worked as an accountant.

Many of the adults returned to their pre-war jobs in China, at least until the Communists took over in 1949. Miss Inez Phare returned to Chefoo School — by then moved to Kuling in the mountains — and continued to be Brown Owl until the school closed in 1951. But most of the Chefoo Brownies and Guides had parents far away to find again, and were sent to Britain, South Africa, Canada or Australia.

Their suffering was not over. They had already coped with capture by pirates, internment by the Japanese, and years away from their parents. They now had to endure separation from their friends and teachers, the "family" they had grown up with. It didn't seem to occur to parents or teachers that taking children from the security of a concentration camp halfway across the world to a strange country where they knew no one would mean further emotional pain. But the children had learned not to express their feelings, or to make a fuss.

Few of the Guide or Brownie internees talked about their experiences after the war. "When you are a teenager," said Estelle Cliff, "all you want to be is 'normal'. At a reunion forty years later, we discovered that none of us had talked about it in all that time. We just shut the cupboard, and didn't open it again until we were middle-aged. We had earned a living, raised a family and seen the world before we allowed it all to come flooding back into our lives."

All 1,450 prisoners were rescued from the Weihsien Civilian Assembly Centre, and somehow the Guide and Brownie log books made their way back to Britain.

In August 1945, as the Guides and Brownies of Weihsien were being liberated, back in Britain the 2nd East Oxford Guides were camping in Nuneham Courtenay, Oxfordshire. "We swam in the river but it was very cold. It rained some more, while we were peeling spuds," they wrote in their log book.

It was quite a fine morning. But unfortunately it poured with rain again just after Colours had been erected. During this ceremony, Captain told us that Japan had surrendered to us, at midnight, last night. So Wednesday, August 15 shall be remembered as VJ-Day. After tea, we played a stalking game, and a sort of cricket, which was quite enjoyable. Supper followed and we all agreed it was lovely. Then we had an extra long campfire, to celebrate the Victory. We all made up songs to sing, then we watched fireworks going off over Reading. After cocoa, late at night, we sang Taps and some of us slept under the stars, watching the fireworks.

CHAPTER
TWENTY-ONE

The Army of Goodwill

Even as the Second World War ended, the work of Guides across the world was not over. Back in 1941, Rose Kerr, the International Commissioner of Guides, had written in *The Guider*. "More important even than winning the war is the question of winning the peace. Whatever happens, Europe will be left weak and exhausted and will need an Army of Goodwill composed of women, ready to bind up the wounds of those who have suffered. For this, no training can begin too early." She spelled out the need for training in nursing, catering, languages and politics — all of which proved vital after the war.

Throughout the war, the contact that British Guides had with the *Golondrinas* from France, Holland and Poland reminded them of other Guides who were suffering cold, imprisonment and torture. Stories leaked out about orphaned, homeless children in Greece eating roots and berries, and children in occupied countries rounded up and taken as slave labourers to Germany. It was impossible to send food, clothes or medicines, but the Guides remembered their motto "Be Prepared".

The Guide Emergency Committee first met in London in May 1942, a time described by Prime Minister Churchill as "a stormy lull" in the war: the Nazis were within twenty-two miles of British soil, and bombs were falling on cities all over England day and night. The committee were less concerned with the war raging around them than with its aftermath. They had all done relief work in the 1914–18 war, and knew that after hostilities had ceased Europe would be left in chaos. Miss Rosa Ward, JP, set aside her work running emergency canteens and was assisted by Lady Arthur, the Chief Commissioner Miss Anstice Gibbs, the Countess Rentlow of Denmark and Olga Malkowska, the founder of Polish Guiding. They began planning to raise enough money to train and equip teams of relief workers to leave Britain the moment the war ended, if not before.

The response from Guides and Rangers was immediate, but the task would not be easy. The British government was only interested in winning the war; it didn't have time to think about its aftermath. When the Guides first offered their services to the War Office, they did not even get a reply. Only when the Quakers intervened were they accepted, joining the Red Cross, the Quakers and the Salvation Army in planning for peace. The name "Army of Goodwill" was rejected on the grounds that, like the Salvation Army, its purpose could be misinterpreted, and so the "Guide International Service" (GIS) was formed, using former Guides to offer relief work wherever it was needed after the war.

370

The Quakers recommended that relief workers should be "ready to specialise in the impossible". The Guides added "self-confidence, initiative, dogged determination — yet close co-operation too". Alison Fox, a Quaker who had spent years in relief work, cautioned, "Be prepared to have some trouble from your *good* workers." The GIS committee started looking for former Guides and Rangers over twenty-one who were adaptable to different cultures, and were prepared for unexpected responsibility, long periods of frustration and living in each other's pockets under difficult physical conditions. Anyone seeking adventure or escape from home was to be avoided. "There will be no glamour about the work," the first GIS leaflet declared. "Only those Guides and Rangers who have a sufficient steadfastness of purpose to carry them through the day to day hardship, strain and monotony should volunteer." Twenty times the number of volunteers needed applied; over two hundred were put through a rigorous vetting system, and then fitted the training around their wartime jobs.

The GIS Fund was launched in July 1943 with a target of £100,000, a vast sum of money which had to be raised by Brownies and Guides as quickly as possible. Guides sent in their ration coupons to buy blankets and vacuum flasks. A young mother with several children to feed sent £1 with a note: "This is the most I can afford, so I feel it is the least I can give." One Brownie pack collected "splash money" — every time one of them stained a clean tablecloth, she had to put a coin in the GIS box. Guides fined themselves for getting up late or using bad language. They never begged: they picked mushrooms, re-covered lampshades, put on pageants, made lavender bags, mended hot-water bottles, and dug worms for fishermen. A Sea Ranger found a wallet on a train and returned it to its owner by post with a note: "If you wish to, you could send anything you can afford, even 1d, to the GIS." The owner sent the note and two shillings and sixpence.

Disabled Guides lent their books to each other for a penny. Two bedridden girls made a rag doll and then raffled it. A Captain in an Approved School for Girls sent in fifteen shillings: "Every Guide without exception, and of her own free will, gave up all her pocket money this week."

Guides from thirty-nine countries as far away as the Virgin Islands contributed funds. The Girl Scouts of America paid for two trucks which were filled with baby clothes, blankets and shoes. A Guide in Arctic Canada earned money by keeping a water hole free from ice and continuing to fish through the winter. Any Guide who earned more than one shilling for the GIS fund without assistance from her Captain could join the "Dragon Slayer's League", based on Baden-Powell's maxim that "It is better to *do* good than *be* good."

The Guide magazine launched its "Journey to Europe" scheme in 1944. Brownie packs and Guide companies were invited to buy an imaginary ticket for £2 from Calais to the capital of any country in Europe where there had been Guides before the war. First they had to buy a train ticket to Dover for fifteen shillings. A

Channel crossing cost another fifteen shillings, imaginary customs packages were five shillings, a groundsheet ten shillings, a medicine chest £10 and a trek cart £36. "Working passages" were available at half price if holders of the Knitter's Badge sent in a knitted item of clothing for a refugee child in Europe. (The Knitter's Badge ensured that the garment was worth wearing!) Each participating pack or company received a miniature train, a passport and an illustrated map on which to follow their progress. The Blackbird patrol of the 1st North Oxford Company bought a train ticket to Norway by turning off the heating and dancing "Gathering Peascods" to warm up. One County Division booked an entire imaginary train to Dover, resulting in a donation of £1,000.

By April 1945, in only eighteen months, the total raised was a staggering £120,820. The editor of *The Guide* wrote, "This is something more than cash — it is thousands, perhaps millions, of hours of hard work, done by Guides and Brownies, who if they could, would have put in those hours doing the job over in Europe." They were putting into practice Baden-Powell's belief that they should "Look wide, and even when you think you are looking wide — look wider still!" This was the first time that international relief work had been funded almost entirely by children.

In 1943, no one knew how long the war would last, so even though GIS volunteers had to be over twenty-one, Guides from sixteen years were encouraged to begin training. "Sleep on the floor (indoors and out) for seven consecutive nights, regardless of weather," they were advised. "Be able to put up a bed, and dress in the dark. Practise walking at night over rough ground without using a torch. Light three consecutive fires in the open using one match for each, and cook three good two-course meals in the wet, without artificial shelter. Learn at least one extra language. Obtain practical experience in de-lousing heads. Learn how to treat fear, loss of self-confidence and mental breakdown."

The Guide Patrol system had given good grounding in teamwork. Some Guides visited psychiatric hospitals; others worked in children's hospitals or schools for disabled children. Rose Kerr was not only concerned about their skills. "Above all," she said, "they must train themselves morally and spiritually, so as to be able to stand firm."

In December 1942, 153 women gathered at Guide HQ to learn about feeding, sanitation and crowd control. Quaker Alison Fox emphasised, "There is only one thing certain about relief work: *all things will be uncertain*. You may find yourself struggling with something with which you are unqualified, in a field where you did not expect to serve, or taking responsibility far beyond anything you believed you could carry." She advised that the Guides should be "Good Jacks of all trades, and master of at least one — preferably two; experts will be useful only if they are adaptable; in relief work things are done as they *can* be done, not as they *should* be done." Olga Malkowska added that volunteers should train when they were hungry, or thirsty, or short of sleep, or all three. Only then would the organisers know who could cope under stress. Trek-cart trips were undertaken to find the best people: eight or nine young women were given a trek cart and hauling ropes, a little food, thin blankets and badly drawn maps, and had to practise large-scale feeding, first-aid and making beds from leaves and bracken. Younger Guides helped by acting as refugees, meeting at secret locations wearing their oldest clothes and taking no food with them.

Beatrix Chapple of Bradford was thirty-five when she joined a training trek in Surrey in January 1944.

It was all very matey and informal. We slept in a barn with rats, and lived in the pig-sty. We had to be up at 6 and trek to Dorking — about 5 miles — to do some scrubbing and painting in a welfare clinic. Then we trekked through fields and woods and over bogs and downs to Westcott. It was the dickens of a trek over stiles and tank traps and we kept finding things such as a spectacle case with a name and address in it, which also happened to be our landmark, and we smelt "emergencies" at every turn. That night we slept in a warden's post. The "emergency" came just as we were in bed and in spite of all our preparations we coped incredibly badly! A boy arrived and told us in French (of a sorts) that his father had fallen into a lake. Everybody dashed off except two of us — one went to get a rope off the trek cart for a lifeline and I stayed to pour a stimulant into a flask. We hared around the countryside in our pyjamas and boots and then gave up and got beds ready instead. The others had wonderful tales of what they did, including artificial respiration done on the wrong part of the body.

I've never worked so hard in my life. That night we had a pretend "air-raid", and then Miss Pilkington came in to say we'd got to evacuate in 5 minutes! When we were all packed up she removed one of the wheel pins on the trek cart and after 50 yards it had collapsed! What a party! We finally got to bed at 5 a.m. and the next day we went to a war nursery and scrubbed floors, mended clothes, washed up and took the children for walks and arrived back to our camp to be told to get back to Westcott before the evening meal. Arrived Dorking by 8 a.m.

Not only did this training sort out the chaff from the wheat, it also meant that those who survived it got to know each other well for the real task ahead. Despite her best efforts, Beatrix was not chosen. Critics wondered if this tough training was wise — surely relief workers should be administrators, not labourers? But the women were learning to expect the unexpected, and to replace the question "Can I do that?" with "How shall we start?"

The British Army provided billets, board, transport and uniforms, which resembled a female soldier's with the Guide trefoil badge on the sleeve. All the women had to provide their own tin plate and mug, and they were soon glad that they had passed their Camping, Cooking and Thrift Badges. When the United Nations was formed at the end of the war it paid high salaries to get the best staff; members of the GIS, however, were paid just £1 a week pocket money. Olga Malkowska pointed out that for people who had lost everything, being helped by a paid charity worker would be "a bitter pill to swallow".

The last time that Alison Duke, or "Chick", the Classics lecturer and Guide Captain, had been abroad was for Pax Ting, the international Guide camp in Hungary in August 1939. During the war she had run a Guides' mobile canteen, feeding air-raid workers and the Land Army. She had returned to captain the 1st Cambridge whenever she could, taking them hop-picking in the holidays. Now a member of the GIS, she was about to be called upon to take part in a dangerous but vital operation. In January 1944 the War Office called for a team who spoke Greek "to go somewhere in the Middle East". The GIS ignored the demand for a male leader, and offered a team made up of Alison, eight other Guiders, with a driver and a sanitation officer from the Boy Scouts. They all began Greek lessons by correspondence, devised by Alison.

They were accepted, given the code name "RRU7" — Relief and Rehabilitation Unit 7 — gave up their jobs and said goodbye to their families. But as plans for D-Day mounted in the spring of 1944, no one was allowed to enter or leave Britain. In June, RRU7 was sent to a secret army camp in Sussex, set up to receive refugees from Normandy in case the D-Day landings failed. The camp was easily visible to enemy planes, and soon the marquees were peppered with machine-gun fire. Even so, they managed to keep them up during the gales that swept the Channel that week. On 6 June 1944 planes roared over the camp and the Allied forces landed in Normandy. That night other Guides replaced RRU7 — they had finally received their orders to make their way to Liverpool for embarkation.

On 11 June they were in a convoy of troop ships zigzagging towards the Mediterranean, which was still plagued by mines and enemy ships. The nine women of RRU7 shared a tiny cabin, and were grateful for their training in uncomfortable sleeping conditions. Although no one had told them officially where they were going, Alison continued to teach the team Greek. But Greece, which had first been occupied by the Germans and then the Italians, was now in the throes of a bitter civil war. The ship berthed at Port Said, Egypt, and the team was despatched to an army camp in the desert outside Cairo. One of their drivers, Miss Georgie Hall, had driven an ambulance in North Africa and France. She was reputed to be able to make a serviceable vehicle out of the wrecks of three lorries, and decided that they all needed more truck practice, including "single-handed reversing". This involved reversing the lorry with the door open, then, with the engine in gear, leaping on and off to check the back, until the lorry was in the right place.

RRU7's first task was to run a large camp for Greek refugees on the shores of the Red Sea. Their workload was huge, and the team were grateful for their basic Greek. On 11 January 1945, seven months after leaving

Britain, they arrived in Athens. The armistice between the warring Greek factions and Allied troops had been signed that very morning. Street fighting had been fierce, and now half a million hungry, cold and homeless people wandered among the burnt-out buses, overturned trams and millions of worthless paper drachma. Seeing all this, the GIS team were disconcerted to be billeted in a luxury hotel. But they had no need to feel guilty — all the windows were shattered and there was no heating in the marble-floored rooms. They had one candle between them, and the staff had left. Water had to be carried upstairs, but from their fifth-floor windows they had superb views.

Alison Duke was put in charge of a political prison in Piraeus which held a thousand women who were sleeping with their children on cement floors, twenty to each windowless, unheated cell. None had eaten for days, and many had lost their minds. The price of bread rose 800 per cent in the first month of 1945, and Alison went from one official to another desperately searching for food and medicine for the prisoners. When a young Greek woman in the army canteen noticed her Guide trefoil she flung her arms around her neck. "The Guides from England — the Guides from England — you've come — you've come!" she sobbed. The Guide movement had been banned in Greece for the last eight years, but many had continued their work in secret. "Tell us what we can do to help," she said. "I cannot think how we are going to live up to their expectations," Cambridge-educated Margaret Pilkington wrote home. "It is they who can give to us, not we to them."

Now that peace had been settled in Greece, both sides were anxious to exchange prisoners of war. ELAS — the Greek People's Resistance Army — trusted no one, but agreed that the GIS team were "neutral civilians" and could drive the lorries to transport the PoWs. Before leaving Britain they had been instructed to pack only their uniforms, but now they were warned that if they wore uniform they might be shot at. So Jock Henderson, the Scottish GIS driver, wore his striped pyjamas over his uniform, and Beryl Gibson from Lancashire turned her Guide tunic inside out and adorned it with a bright scarf. The roads were a nightmare of hairpin bends and sheer drops, with only inches between the lorry's wheels and the crumbling precipice. On their first trip they brought back seventy-one British and Indian prisoners and returned with seventy-one ELAS guerrillas. Food was so short that the guerrillas offered "one hostage for one tin of bully beef; seven hostages for six tins".

The mountain people had lost everything when their homes were burnt down by Italians, then Germans, and then rival guerrilla factions. Many of the villages could only be reached by mule — and even these were in short supply, as most had been stolen or eaten. "We went up on mules to villages high in the mountains," Alison recounted later on the BBC World Service, "taking with us all-too-scanty supplies of clothing for distribution. The men and women were in rags, the children looked old, wizened and starved, but nevertheless we received friendly and enthusiastic welcomes." However poor they were, the villagers maintained their traditional good manners, offering the GIS party *retsina* or garlanding their mules with flowers or leaves.

The second-hand clothes donated to Greece included an odd mixture of beachwear, chiffon frocks and worn-out shoes — no use to people who did not even have a needle and thread. It was impossible for the GIS team to allot them fairly, so they were sorted into family-sized bundles, with a roughly equal distribution of useful and useless garments. The team arranged clothes meetings at churches or the nearest crossroads. Usually the whole village would be there to greet "the English Ladies". Alison Duke knew that the ancient Greeks often settled political disputes by lottery, so they told each village that the bundles were a lottery — there was no favoritism, just luck; families could swap among themselves. This broke the ice, and soon everyone was laughing about their allotted polkadot swimsuits or evening tail-coats. The greatest shortage was of black dresses for older women, so it was decided that only widows could have black. One old man was so desperate to clothe his wife appropriately that he said, "I know, but my wife *is* a widow."

In February 1945, three of the Guides — Muriel Lees, Alison Duke and Georgie Hall — drove up a winding pass near Delphi and down into the town of Amphissa to distribute clothing. Dark snowclouds loomed overhead as they crossed the pass, beyond which they would be out of touch with their colleagues and inside ELAS territory. They counted forty-one demolished houses en route, and arrived in Amphissa just as the blizzards started. "The Bishop is away, so we have the use of his parlour," Muriel Lees wrote home. "We started sorting clothes; very soon the snow began, continuing for two days. We are snowed up. It is the worst here since 1892 and the pass is blocked."

No one had told the GIS team that Amphissa was the designated point for ELAS to surrender their arms to the British army. As the snow deepened, a thousand armed guerrillas came down from the mountains. It had been agreed that in exchange for their guns, the British would give them food and transport to Athens. When the men asked for the British, they were told, "The three English ladies are in the warehouse." They marched to the warehouse, where the ladies were certainly British, so surely they must provide? The GIS Guiders were worried — there was no food, the pass was blocked, and the men might soon start to loot the town. The ELAS leader insisted that the women telephone "their army". They were taken to a primitive telephone exchange, where Muriel found an old hand-wound phone. When she eventually got through to a military telephonist, he did not believe her. "British women in Amphissa? They *can't* be — Amphissa is in ELAS territory — there are *no* British there." Once his officer was convinced that this was no joke, he told Muriel to persuade the guerrillas to walk over the pass to meet the British Army on the other side.

The GIS team continued their work, lit in the evenings by rag wicks floating in saucers of oil. Among the clothing was a bundle of blue cotton gym-dresses which they converted into Guide uniforms. When the snow finally melted and the bells rang out to welcome an advance party of a British battalion, the Colonel was very surprised to find three khaki-clad British women and a Guide company already in the village.

In May 1945, Margaret Pilkington, Muriel Lees and Marjorie Jarman were asked to renovate an old orphanage near Athens as an assembly centre for displaced people. The building had no water, lights, fuel, sanitation or furniture. They reckoned that if they worked hard, they could clean it up in about ten days, but that very afternoon 250 Greek soldiers, thirty-six women (six of them pregnant) and ten babies arrived. "The water tanks were empty," wrote Marjorie. "The drains blocked. There was a hundred-gallon boiler, but no fuel. No pots or pans of any sort, and no rations. The Greek soldiers had been fourteen days aboard ship and were *filthy* and starving. All the officers had been repatriated so nobody had any control over them." The GIS women persuaded the British Army to provide two days' rations, twelve small cooking pots and a single hurricane lamp. They had one tin-opener, one knife and one first-aid kit between them. A water cart was found, and Anna, the Greek caretaker, lit a fire under the boiler. They did not ask where she found the wood, but they noticed that the cupboards had no shelves. They obtained four hundred blankets from the Red Cross, and by nightfall everyone was fed and bedded down. Only then did the three British women settle down in the attic and eat a tin of peaches each.

The first, and only, consignment of equipment contained 2,700 blankets, twenty rat traps, fifty fly swatters, four Primus stoves, fifteen padlocks and six shaving brushes. One day five barefoot Turkish orphan boys were spotted playing somewhat furtively in a bush. From around the gardens they had collected live mines, incendiaries and unexploded bombs.

Until Alison Duke arrived, there were language problems, such as a medical report from the Greek doctor which stated: "We have had a case of weasel which was transported to the special hospital for pestilential diseases." The "GIS Ladies" were called at any time of the day or night to powder newcomers with DDT against tick-typhus, and to sort out fights, attempted suicides, a haemorrhage, a snake in the watertank or a child who had swallowed a safety pin.

Gradually the soldiers left, but the families remained, among them stateless people with no identity papers, and women who had married Italian soldiers. To everyone's delight, in July an empty bomber plane landed nearby to collect these women. The GIS team had an hour to get over a hundred women into huge "Mae West" lifejackets, and strap their babies onto the bomb racks to carry them to Italy.

In the winter, driving gales blew through the glass-free windows. Even cardboard to nail over the windows was difficult to find, and nails were very expensive. At Christmas, paper hats made from sugar bags adorned the heads of Polish, Greek, Russian, Italian and Turkish children, and every one of the six hundred residents ate Christmas pudding — steamed in Red Cross slings. In nine months the GIS team became godparents to twenty-five babies, and attended weddings as bridesmaids and even best men.

By the time they left in May 1946, Greek Guides had taken over the relief work and over twenty new Guiders had been trained, their badges made from scraps of bomb shrapnel. Alison Duke moved on to Germany to re-establish Guiding there. She eventually returned to Cambridge as a lecturer in Classics, and remained active in the international Guide movement until she died in 2005, aged ninety.

By August 1944 there were one hundred trained GIS volunteers, and in November a request came for a team to run a fifty-bed mobile hospital with a laboratory "somewhere in Europe". Bulk medical supplies were non-existent, so Guides tramped the streets of London buying up small quantities from individual chemist shops. The GIS teams practised loading and unloading the nine tons of supplies and equipment at speed and in the dark. There was nowhere to store the loaded trucks without risk of their being either stolen or bombed, until the King offered the Royal Mews at Buckingham Palace.

They were finally ordered to move on 22 February 1945 — Thinking Day, an auspicious date for Guides — and the three-ton lorry, two trucks and two ambulances assembled with teams from other relief societies in Hyde Park. All wore khaki uniform, but the GIS women were identifiable by the World Guide badges on their tin hats and painted on their vehicles. They took their knitting, but were not allowed to write letters or keep diaries. At dawn they crossed the Channel in an army landing craft, and arrived in the south of Holland before the north had been liberated. The entire country was mined, and they had to keep the cumbersome fifteen-hundredweight truck's wheels on the narrow, potholed roads. "Our driver could not see her back wheels — sitting in the back we could," wrote one of the team. "Again and again they touched the white tape marking the edge of minefields. We passed through ruined town after ruined town. As the convoys slowed, girls climbed on our vehicles to touch our hands, to touch the golden Trefoils on our sleeves — the emblem which they had been forbidden to wear for six years."

After France and Belgium had been liberated by the Allies in early 1945, the Germans made a determined stand at Arnhem in mid-Holland. There was a fear that epidemics would spread among the refugee population, so the GIS mobile hospital followed close behind the army. Even though the work was heavy, the regulation that each team should include a man had been abandoned. While fighting continued only three miles away, the GIS team fed 3,000 displaced Dutch people who had been taken by the Germans for forced labour and were now trekking back home. The only food available was army biscuits, small tins of evaporated milk and dried peas for soup. A Dutchman brought news of potatoes, coal and wood stored at an abandoned airfield. Over twenty unexploded bombs and undetected mines shared the site, but the team obtained the food and fuel without mishap.

The GIS had strict orders that only refugees could be fed: if they were caught giving food to anyone else, they would be sent home immediately — they had to keep their strength up. But none of them felt hungry when starving local children tapped at their windows, their shrivelled faces peering in. Their ordeal, and that of the local population, was eased when a consignment of sugar beet was tipped into a cellar with an open grating. All through the night small figures with improvised spears pulled up the beets and ran off with their hauls. The Guides could hear them, but they had no orders to investigate noises; what they could not see, they did not choose to know.

Meanwhile, Olave Baden-Powell was doing her bit too. Armed with some intensive French lessons, she set off to greet the Guides of the newly liberated France. She was met by a V-for-victory sign made out of bananas laid out on her train seat. She learned that Guide meetings had continued in forests, and that French Guides in attics had listened to BBC broadcasts and secretly translated them. Uniforms had been hidden in cellars or sewn inside mattresses.

On 23 April 1945 she laid a wreath on the tomb of the Unknown Warrior in Paris, and then watched 40,000 Guides and Scouts march down the Champs-Elysées past the Arc de Triomphe in their white blouses and navy skirts. As they passed the podium draped in tricolour flags, their eyes turned left towards Olave and General Lafont, the French Chief Scout. Just as she stood to salute, she heard someone in the crowd shout,

"It's nearly over! We're in Berlin!" The Allies had reached their destination.

A few days later, thousands of French prisoners of war began to arrive home from concentration camps and slave-labour camps in Germany and Poland. They were all malnourished, tired and confused. Most were still wearing their striped camp uniforms. Olave joined French Guides who were waiting to welcome them at railway stations and airports with cups of tea and sandwiches.

One GIS team was led by Dr Meredith Ross, who had been released from the Australian Air Force, and arrived in Britain on a troop ship via the USA. Her team crossed the Rhine on one of the first prefabricated Bailey bridges in order to identify a mystery epidemic in a mental asylum in northern Holland. She discovered it was highly contagious amoebic dysentery. After that, wherever they went, the water was tested thoroughly. Holland had still not been liberated, and reliable news was hard to come by: the GIS wireless set had broken down, and the Germans had confiscated all local radios. She was told to move her mobile hospital back, then the next day to move it forward, and then to stay put. One day news circulated that Holland was free; the next day this was denied.

Then, one night the noise of guns was replaced by the more cheerful sound of fireworks. The GIS team hurried to the nearest Red Cross base to hear the midnight news: the Germans had surrendered. "The night before VE-Day, Arnhem Scouts invited us to a

388

campfire at which the Hitler Youth book was ceremoniously burnt! We left Arnhem early on VE-Day and drove through cheering crowds wearing orange scarves, dresses, skirts — everything orange. When people saw the Guide Trefoil they cried; 'Now we know the war is really over.' We saw hanging from the overhead tramlines the skeleton of a man, still with a few tatters of clothing drooping limply like half-mast flags. We saw, among the jubilant crowds, men in German uniforms, driving farm carts or plodding soberly along, taking no notice of the people around them and attracting no attention."

Back in Britain, Guides were organising street parties. "We had a piano which was dragged out into the street and Father played it non-stop," said Guide Eileen Wilson in Canterbury. "Everyone brought out their tables in a long line. The party went on for hours and hours, I have never known such happiness or jubilation."

Gisela Eisner, a Kindertransport Guide, was now a student at Nottingham University. "The main square of Nottingham was absolutely packed with people singing and dancing 'Knees up Mother Brown'. I didn't get excited myself; it didn't seem to make any difference to me. I didn't have any family to look forward to." Both her parents and her older brother had just been declared dead.

"Well how do we feel now peace is here?" asked the 1st North Oxford Guides in their log book on 11 May.

"Today we were all feeling very vitrified after our two days' holiday."

In Holland, on the day after Victory in Europe Day the entire GIS team of hospital, teaching and canteen units were told to go to Amers-foort concentration camp. The SS guards and most of the prisoners had disappeared, leaving only patients in the last stages of starvation. The stinking army huts were packed with bunks in tiers up to the ceilings, their filthy blankets infested with ticks and fleas. The team's first job was to clean the camp, and set up kitchens and a delousing unit, ready for the influx of displaced people.

A Guider wrote: "I am typing this inside the barbed wire; behind me are the watch-tower and the searchlight which was trained on the enclosure. The conditions inside the huts are appalling — they are being cleaned by Dutch Guides and Scouts. The prisoners still here are gaunt living skeletons hobbling along with spade handles for crutches. Many of their fellow-prisoners lie in unmarked pits behind the camp. In one block lie the sick — they have been dying for a long time. For them, liberation seems to have come too late." In the wood outside the camp, German soldiers filed past a handful of British soldiers and handed in their weapons. The silence was punctuated by exploding mines, which rattled the windows. "Conversation remained normal. It was too fantastic to be credible."

The GIS team felt ashamed that although they had lived through food and clothing rationing, they had

390

never really gone hungry, and had always had a blanket and enough clothes to keep warm. "It was difficult relating to these people who had suffered so very much. What on earth could one say? I decided that all we could do was to be there, and show that we cared, and carry on as best as possible. There would be time for our nightmares later."

The GIS feeding team was summoned to Rotterdam to care for 1,700 people who had been living on sugar beet, tulip bulbs and potato peelings. Their houses had been bombed, and in the winter they had ripped out the insides of their wooden shelters for fuel. Up to fourteen people were living to a room, without heat, water or furniture. The Guides built an open-air kitchen and distributed clothes and shoes. Dutch Guides and Scouts, themselves weak from hunger, insisted on helping to carry sacks of biscuits, powdered milk and potatoes from the lorries to the stores. They had not eaten for days, but did not ask for anything for themselves. GIS trucks took children and pregnant women to hospital, suspected collaborators for interrogation, and the mentally ill to asylums.

As the Dutch social services began to function again, the GIS team were able to move on to Germany. But then they were urgently summoned to Gorinchen, not far from Rotterdam. Typhoid had broken out in the town, and had to be contained before it spread. Although neither of the team's doctors had dealt with the disease before, within forty-eight hours they had converted a school into a hospital. Barbara Hughes from Devon organised collaborators under armed guard to clean up the building. "Then began a strenuous and unremitting struggle," wrote Doreen Mills from Henley. "Typhoid is one of the most difficult illnesses to deal with, entailing unceasing care and watchfulness. Bed-linen, utensils, and everything that comes into contact with the patients is highly infectious and must be sterilised."

The patients came from over thirty villages, and many spoke only a local dialect. They were debilitated, undernourished, and often suffering from other illnesses too. Laboratory diagnosis of typhoid took days, but in the meantime these people had to be treated, with limited equipment. When blood was urgently required, the GIS drivers had to fetch the equipment from one place, round up donors somewhere else, and then rush the blood back. They drove hundreds of miles every day, collecting food, petrol, patients on stretchers, and vegetables from farms. They took bedding to and from the local laundry, surgical drums to and from the local hospital, and even supplied the local ferry, used for carrying ambulances across the River Waal, with coal.

The GIS nurses admitted patients, cared for people in comas, served meals every two hours, gave mouthwashes every four hours and remembered to wash their hands in disinfectant every time they handled patients. They also had to make sure that no patients left the hospital until they had fully recovered and could not re-infect others. At the end of each day there were no hot baths — only boiled water in a basin — no chance of a swim since the river was contaminated, no fresh milk, salads or fruit, and no other British units to talk to. When a Dutch Guider offered training, over eighty prospective Guide Captains turned up at her house. "They all wanted to know about the hospital and how they could help. We told them the patients had nothing to read, and within a week they collected enough books to fill an army lorry." Two Dutch Guides joined as night cooks, and Brownies came to peel potatoes. When things got really tough, they remembered Baden-Powell's maxim: "Always stand with your face to the sun, and the shadows will fall behind you."

Four months after the outbreak, the typhoid was overcome, and only twelve out of 120 patients had died. The local Burgomaster was so grateful he wrote, "With many thanks for the enormous countenance which has been lended by you in fighting a rather dangerous epidemy. Herewith I forwarded you some cherries." Sadly, the Guides could not risk eating them, but they were pleased that they could now move on. Their orders were to go to Germany, though they had no idea what lay ahead.

By September 1945, four months after the final fall of the Nazi regime, there were thirteen million homeless people in Germany, as well as two million former slaves, now living in camps, caves and tents. The harvest had failed, and starving children scavenged on dumps for rotten food, firewood and half-smoked cigarettes. What lay ahead for the GIS team was going to push them to their limit — but they were absolutely determined to get to work.

After spending their first night sleeping on drying racks in a cigarette factory, the volunteers' next stop was Bergen-Belsen in north-west Germany. After the typhus-infested huts of the concentration camp had been burnt down by the Allies, a nearby site had become a huge transit camp for 14,000 people from twenty-two countries. Known as the "Western Bounders", these refugees all wanted to return home, but many were too ill. "The only reminder of the old horror camp was the lingering scent of death that drifted over the pine woods, and the wired-off sections with 'Typhus Keep Out' notices," wrote Edgar Ainsworth, art editor of *Picture Post* magazine. "But in the hospital, you can still see that 'gone away' look of the absentminded. I mean absent-minded in its true sense."

The GIS nurses oversaw the "human laundry", where men and women were deloused and washed down by German nurses. A stable signposted "Harrods Store" was piled with women's clothes which had been commandeered from Germans. "Women stood in the entrance and gazed glassily," wrote Ainsworth. "When it dawned on them they could have their choice, they rushed in as fast as they could, snatching, and grabbing anything. They left any garment that was black or blue striped."

Stella Cunliffe had joined the Brownies in 1925, and was now a qualified statistician with the GIS team. "When we got to Belsen, the people were cold, hungry and unhoused," she wrote. "They were lying about on the floor with no clothes, just scraps of bone." But gradually their health improved, and they started to work — as hairdressers, teachers and clerks. The GIS set up a shoe-repair shop with a Polish shoemaker who found a box of tools and offered to train others. When it was announced that all workers should be paid at German labour rates, Stella worked out a system of payment, and soon 1,350 employees lined up to receive their first wages for over five years. "The majority of their names seem to include three Z's, or three K's," she wrote. She was assisted by a Polish lawyer who spoke no English, a few clerks of various nationalities, two typewriters and very little stationery.

As the death rate in Belsen dropped, the GIS arranged entertainment. "Soldiers, relief workers and doctors tried to dance with women who were hardly able to walk," observed Edgar Ainsworth. "Every woman had tried to turn her 'Harrods' frock into an evening dress. They wept as they danced, tears running down on the sprays of wild flowers they had pinned to their sagging breasts. As the band played God Save the King, they all stood leaning against the arms of their liberators, the British soldiers."

Once Belsen had been reorganised, the team continued to work with refugees all over Germany. Officially, the host country was responsible for them, but there were not enough resources for the German people, let alone others. "The task is even more appalling than anyone thought," wrote Lorna Hay of *Picture Post*. "Relief work is nobody's baby, nobody quite expected it. It is rather a bore that it should have arrived at all, and should have to be given billets." Although the GIS workers were given the rank of officers, they did not expect comfortable lodgings. They were responsible for feeding 8,000 children every day with insufficient food, whose parents had little employment, who had been through six years of war, and who had little hope for the future. "When it all gets too much, you just keep on keeping on," one GIS observed.

In early 1947 a GIS team was sent to Schleswig-Holstein in northern Germany to deal with sixty refugee camps housing 10,000 Germans who had trekked back from the east. The bare huts erected on bleak, flat, treeless land did nothing to alleviate the state of apathy into which they had sunk. The GIS set up children's feeding schemes, and distributed cod liver oil and medicines, and toys and books sent by Guides in Britain.

"Though we knew we might be working in Germany, we never expected that our work would be for Germans," wrote one GIS leader in her report. "Surprising as it may seem, we do find that we want to help these people, not as Germans, good or bad, but as individual human beings who are suffering severely. It seems at first to be little short of treachery to go from work in Holland to work for Germans, but we have learnt that it is the work which must be done . . . and surely it is fitting that Guiding, part of the greatest Movement for peace in the world, should take its part in this work."

In all the camps, the GIS teams organised sewing rooms, English classes, discussion groups, sport for youth, and playrooms for small children — always working with committees elected from among the refugees themselves. Skills acquired through Guide proficiency badges helped inspire creativity: the debris from wrecked planes became cutlery; embroidered butter-muslin became an altar cloth; old felt hats sent by British Guides were turned into children's shoes; blackout curtains were made into suits. Sandals were made from car tyres, with wooden packing-case soles, sewn with the thread from flour sacks. Parachute silk was saved for first communion or wedding dresses, passed from one girl to the next. Five pairs of boys' shorts were made from one donated man's kilt. An old army dump provided ammunition bags for trousers, and some attractive striped fabric which looked as if it would be ideal for boys' shorts. Luckily a British officer recognised it as the wrapping from paratroopers' maps — designed to explode at the touch of a match. Among the things sent by the GIS from London were vitaminised chocolate, knitting wool and bales of mattress covers (to be filled with straw).

At first the refugees were pathetically grateful for a blanket or a cup of cocoa. As they grew stronger, they were desperate to start their lives afresh, but were frustrated by the bureaucracy of post-war Europe. Some wanted repatriation, others wanted to emigrate, but their destination depended on which countries were prepared to take which refugees. For example, some countries wanted only the fittest and most qualified, while others would suddenly state, "No more single men, families wanted," or "No more grandparents, carpenters only." The GIS had to handle both the applications and the disappointments. Many people were either too old or too ill to be accepted for emigration. Old people had to remain alone in Germany while their children and grandchildren emigrated without them. If one member of a family had tuberculosis, the others had to choose whether to stay together in Germany, or leave the sick person behind. For most of these displaced people, the world had no welcome.

Alicia Wilson had been enrolled as a Guide at boarding school in Switzerland, where she learned French and German. Before the war she had started a Brownie pack in a poor part of Darlington, and had learned to drive a truck when taking them on camp. As a volunteer for the GIS in 1946 she drove a fifteen-hundredweight truck around Germany, accompanied by a German prisoner of war, still in his uniform. "Sometimes we carried blankets, sometimes beer, sometimes refugees to hospital — you never knew." She then drove a post office delivery van fitted with bunks to Austria with an Irish and a French Guider. Their task was to organise Guides among the Polish and Yugoslavian refugee girls. "We had never met before, and it was all rather vague — sometimes we had accommodation, sometimes not much food. One night we stayed in a castle with a very distinguished aristocratic family. They had hosted Germans, then Americans and now British women. Occasionally we could swap some powdered milk for a few eggs. We tried to find girls who had been Guides before, who could help organise games without any equipment."

In Germany, restarting Guiding had to be done carefully, without appearing to be another version of Hitler's *Bund Deutscher Mädel*, who had also camped and learned first-aid. "*Pfadfinderinnen*" (Pathfinders), as the German Guides were known, were soon thriving, and in 1948 British Guides joined them for a summer camp in Schleswig. "Their Guiding is of a very high standard and their tests extremely stiff," wrote a British Patrol Leader, "which is wonderful when one realises that most are refugees who have lived under terrible conditions for years. We hiked fifteen miles to a youth hostel which was being used as a health-holiday home for German children. 'The thin ones are to be made thick,' explained a German Guide. One evening we had a campfire circus, with a menagerie, fortune telling, bare-back riding, a wild Indian show and tightrope walking (on the ground)."

The GIS was the last of Britain's voluntary organisations to be working in West Germany when the German federal government took over responsibility for the 60,000 remaining refugees. Whatever the volunteers were doing at midnight on 30 June 1950, they had to stop helping people leave the country; it was too late for anyone whose papers had not been processed. Guide companies and Brownie packs in Britain "adopted" some of these families who had been left behind, and sent them letters and parcels. Finally, in April 1952, the last three GIS volunteers went home, ten years after the organisation had first been conceived, and eight years since the first teams arrived in Europe.

Nearly two hundred Guiders and sixty Scouters from Britain, Australia, New Zealand, Canada, Eire and Kenya served in GIS teams with refugees and homeless people in Europe, Egypt and Malaya. Their story is one of foresight, imagination, flexibility and steady perseverance in the face of adversity. They not only made a huge difference to the lives of thousands of people, they also paved the way for relief work for the rest of the century.

CHAPTER
TWENTY-TWO

Into the Twenty-First Century

As the Second World War ended, the Guiding movement could take stock of its contribution to the success of the Allies, from the youngest Brownie to the most senior Guider. Former Guides and Guiders had been leaders in many spheres of wartime life, holding half the important executive posts in women's war services. The first head of the ATS (the Auxiliary Territorial Service, the women's branch of the Home Guard), Dame Helen Gwynne Vaughan, was a Guider, as was the head of the WRNS, Dame Vera Laughton Mathews. In November 1945 a brief notice appeared in the awards column of *The Guider*. "Bronze Cross. The Island of Malta." Like those of Poland, the Guides of Malta had qualified *as a whole* for the movement's highest award for courage. Cut off from almost all supplies, with no hope of any help, the island's 270,000 inhabitants remained unbreakable in spirit, under continuous bombardment by the German Luftwaffe and the Italian air force for two years. They never gave in — and the country's Guides were among the most dauntless, tending the wounded, sharing their meagre rations with the starving, and boosting morale.

After Soviet forces reached Poland as the war in Europe neared its conclusion, Guide Cecylia Skrzypczak helped a British prisoner of war to hide from them, rather than hand him over. "When the Russians arrived they looked like machines, they had no expressions. The German prisoners of war were led somewhere; they were so thin they could hardly walk. I felt sorry for them. There was a lot of rape by the Soviet soldiers, one just didn't go out." First she hid the prisoner in the veterinary lab where she worked, and then in an attic. "He was called Mr Bowen but he was known in Poland as Captain Smiley." The pair married in March 1945, and five months later they flew out on the first plane to England, the first stage of their journey to Mr Bowen's home town of Hull. "We were settled in the bombed-out part, it was a horrible, two up, two down house. Air-raid shelters smelling, fish smelling everywhere, the house was broken. I put cotton wool in the cracks. It wasn't what I expected."

In 1947 some of the new German Guides trained by the Guide International Service came to Britain. Their report of the visit shows just how bad conditions in Germany were at the time: "England is a country that the war has scarcely touched. There were the undestroyed towns, quick and warm and comfortable trains, a great traffic on all the roads, full shops, healthy children, well-looking men, quiet, friendly, helpful people everywhere, and a normal life. Disciplined people in the queues — because they knew they would not wait in vain. And you felt you were in an honest country. It felt strange that the question of food, clothing, accommodations and petrol was worrying the people so much, as all that seemed to us so plenty." The German Guides met no hatred, only fear, "the same feeling towards us that we have towards Russia. The influence of the concentration camp films must be responsible for this feeling of fright. They have no idea of the difficulties facing Germany. Perhaps if you have not seen the suffering it is difficult to understand it — as we did not really realise the difficulties of refugees before we were refugees ourselves."

As rationing of clothes, furniture and food continued in Britain for ten years after the end of the war, the dressmaking, carpentry and cooking skills Guides had acquired remained imperative. Even when the school leaving age was raised in 1947 to fifteen, Guides continued to be important both socially and education-ally for many young women. What happened to some of the less famous Guides?

After returning to Britain from China, Margaret Vindon trained as a teacher. She returned to the Far East, and worked for twenty-five years in the Philippines with her missionary husband. "I can't throw things away: everything has to be passed on, but I don't think any of this did me any harm." She and her husband now support students at the University of Reading in the Chinese Christian Fellowship. Arthur Hummel, one of the escapees from Weihsien, would return to China as the US Ambassador. After rejoining her parents and returning to the USA, Mary Taylor became an English teacher, director of a County Youth Center, and won a seat as a Democrat in the state's Assembly. In 1997 she tracked down six members of the rescue mission, "to say thank you for fifty-two years of freedom". The movie star John Wayne bought the film rights to the story of the Weihsien rescue, but was forced to abandon the project when he learned that it had been organised by the forerunner of the CIA, and so, even in 1958, it was still classified.

In 1984, eighteen old Chefoo students visited the site of the Weihsien camp. The Chinese had constructed a black marble memorial with all their names inscribed on it, and had put up a stone on Eric Liddell's grave. In 2005, on the sixtieth anniversary of VJ-Day, a group of former Chefoo students returned to their old school for the first time.

Olga Małkowska ran a Polish children's home in Devon until she moved back to Poland in 1961. She died in 1979, aged ninety-one, and was buried with her husband in Zakopane. After the war, the Polish Scouting and Guiding Association was one of the few organisations that retained some independence from the Communist Party and in the 1980s many Scouting officials were arrested for their involvement in the Solidarity trade union movement.

At the age of twenty-six, Brown Owl Mary Oakley, who had taken the 1st Eynsham Brownies camping in 1939, became one of the youngest ever headmistresses in New Zealand. She taught there for fifteen years, and was a Provincial Commissioner for Girl Guides in Canterbury. She then became head of the American International School in Switzerland, followed by twenty years as head of St Felix School, Southwold. She was also only the second female lay reader in Britain.

Verily Anderson, sub-editor of *The Guide* and holder of the Authoress Badge, went on to write over thirty books, including several about Brownies. She was still writing in her ninety-sixth year.

When Josephine Klein from Holland reached her sixteenth year, she became a Sea Ranger. She left school, and her head teacher found her a job with a corn merchant where she learned shorthand and typing. "But after all that trauma, I couldn't remember the names of seeds. I was depressed and I'd run out of puff." She was determined to go to university, and her former teacher helped her to learn enough Latin to pass the entrance exam. Still only seventeen years old, she read first French and then Sociology at the University of London. She eventually became a psychotherapist, writing highly regarded books such as *Our Need for Others and its Roots in Infancy* and *Doubts and Certainties in the Practice of Psychotherapy*.

Many of the Kindertransport Guides stayed in Britain, while others emigrated to America, Canada, Australia or the newly formed state of Israel. Most of them had been orphaned since leaving their homes, losing their families in the ghettos or camps.

* ★ ★ ★

The end of the war brought new countries into the Guiding movement, including El Salvador, Austria and Haiti. In Eastern Europe, however, in countries such as Estonia, Lithuania and Yugoslavia, Scouts and Guides were replaced by Communist youth organisations.

Five years after the war's end, in 1950, the Girl Guides celebrated the fortieth anniversary of their founding. In July that year, the Thirteenth World Conference was held in Oxford. To mark the occasion, Poet Laureate John Masefield wrote "A World of Hope".

Though threat of ruin fills the world with fear,
A light of beauty shines in Oxford here.
A hope for happy life is not yet cold
In this grey City built by faith of old.
For here, amid new war's beginning scathe,
New pilgrims travel, bringing living faith,
Bringing, in glee, from our remotest isle,
A word of light to cheer man's little while.
A word of hope that, by an act of will,
Life may be surely bettered, even still:
The City rings with sound long out of use,
The footsteps of the bringers of good news.

Messages of friendship were brought from all over the world by various means, including an elephant that marched along Woodstock Road. Over 10,000 Guides from twenty-seven countries attended the campfire in Headington Park, which was broadcast around the world on the BBC World Service.

By 1947, former Guide Princess Elizabeth was Chief Ranger of the British Empire. Five years later she became Queen of the United Kingdom of Great Britain, head of the Church of England and the Commonwealth. The royal family kept up its ties with the Guide movement: two of Princess Elizabeth's bridesmaids were former Guides, and for her coronation in 1953 every Guide, Brownie and Ranger was encouraged to do something which was "useful, beautiful and gay". The 1st Buckingham Palace Brownie Pack, and then the Guide company, were re-formed for Princess Anne. Princess Margaret's daughter Lady Sarah Armstrong-Jones joined the 7th Kensington Brownie Pack, and in 1965 Princess Margaret took over from her aunt, the Princess Royal, as President of the Guides. In 2003 Prince Edward's wife, HRH Sophie, Countess of Wessex, became President of Girlguiding UK, as the Girl Guide Association had become the previous year. "I have fond memories of my years as a Sea Ranger," the Queen wrote in 2009, "and of becoming Chief Ranger of the British Empire, and then Patron of the Guiding Association. While the core values remain constant, I have been delighted to watch it evolve, led by the ambitions and needs of the girls of today." Could she have done so much, so well, without having made that Guide Promise, kept the Guide Law and passed all those badges?

Olave Baden-Powell continued her work promoting Guides. She had them to tea in her Hampton Court Palace apartment, and travelled round the world five times. In 1960 she flew to the independence celebrations for Nigeria, and attended a Guide rally inside the Emir's mud-walled palace, where she met the Emir's chief wife in her Guide uniform. The same year, the Guides of India and Pakistan began a literacy project with the slogan "Each one teach one", encouraging members to help their illiterate grandmothers and aunts. Olave refused to accept the reality of India and Pakistan's post-war partition, and arranged for Guides from both countries to meet at the border. "They clasped each other affectionately and wept at the reunion," she observed, "and the armed guards looked the other way." On Thinking Day in Pachmarchi, a hill station in central India, she was delighted to hear prayers said by Parsee, Muslim, Hindi and Christian Guides and Scouts. Olave died in 1977, aged eighty-eight, having outlived her husband by over thirty-five years. Her ashes were buried in his grave in Kenya.

As the Austerity Fifties became the Swinging Sixties, the Guides, with their uniforms and laws, came to seem very old-fashioned. More and more girls had to be persuaded to go to meetings by their parents. The journalist Janet Street-Porter didn't last long as a Guide: "I found sharing a tent with three other girls in Epping Forest a damp and depressing experience. Queuing up for the toilet block, washing with little metal bowls of lukewarm water, eating overcooked sausages and baked beans were all experiences I vowed never to repeat."

"We assembled in a large, draughty crypt in Eaton Square," remembered GP Susie Graham-Jones. "Blue uniforms, senior Guides with crimped hair and no imagination, and poorly-understood rituals. I was bemused by the rural attributions and frequent references to skills that seemed completely alien to Belgravia schoolgirl life. Knots for sailors, lighting a campfire with three matches, and orienteering. I escaped by getting a poodle."

Historian Juliet Gardiner did no better. "At Brownies we had an old papier mâché toadstool, and there seemed no way to repair it. It got tackier and tackier. I was a Pixie and we were, were we not, supposed to 'Help those in Fixes'. But I was never quite sure what a fix was. Maybe mending a collapsing toadstool would have qualified? It was all so uncool."

"My granny went on about the great adventures of Brownies," remembered artist Eloise O'Hare from Dublin. "So I joined the Irish Brownies, but they wore blue uniform, which did not make sense. They told me that I should get the silver polish out and polish my mother's pennies. Why? At Brownies we did some skipping. I wanted to go on trips away, see the world, and make a house with a Swiss army knife."

The radical American feminist Camille Paglia, author of *Sex, Art and American Culture*, found being a Girl Scout in New York in the early 1960s a metaphor for her life: "I caused a violent methane explosion by dumping too much lime into the latrine at camp in the Adirondack mountains. Toxic brown clouds churned up into the trees for half an hour. I was mortified. It symbolized everything I would do with my life and work. Excess and extravagance and explosiveness. I would look into the latrine of culture, into pornography and crime and psychopathology . . . and I would drop a bomb into it."

Despite the Baden-Powells' attempts to spread the movement to all classes and types of girl, Guides did not reach everyone. "Brownies were too posh for me," said the writer Lynne Truss. "And my parents would never have stood for getting a uniform."

But for some, the Girl Guides were an introduction to other social classes. The painter Celia Ward was born in 1960, and became a keen Guide. "We were a middle-class family, and Guides was the only place where I met the girls from the secondary modern school. It gave my twin sister and me new friends, and independence from our three brothers. The whole point of Guides was an evening out away from parents, a great excuse for giggling, something that we were absolutely forbidden to do. We adored the leaders: neither teachers nor parents, and not quite sensibly grown up, they inhabited a hinterland between ourselves and adults. It was a liberating organisation, and gave us positive values about women which we didn't get at my male-dominated home. We weren't there to look after men. You learned to do things yourself. I never wanted to give up, but I stopped at sixteen once I was allowed to go to pop concerts. Actually Guides were much better, there was more conversation."

In 1968, at a time when most teenage girls were thinking of the Beatles and Flower Power, the Girl Guide Association introduced the Three Cheers Challenge — "To Cheer a person, a place and yourself" — and a new book of rules, the first for fifty years. Mrs Troop, a Guider in Oxfordshire, offered the services of her lodger, Tony O'Gorman, to deliver it by parachute to the County Vice-President, the Honourable Vere Vivian Smith. "There weren't too many free-fall parachutists around in the UK then," he remembered. He flew up in his brother's plane from Kidlington airport with RAF parachute instructor Flight Sergeant Jake McCoughlin. "It was lovely weather and we had the Guide rule books stuffed into our jumpsuits. I climbed out onto the wheel and jumped at 6,000 feet. I pulled my ripcord and it was a joy to see that lovely green airfield below with all those little faces staring and cheering. I landed just in front of them all. Alas, McCoughlin's chute opened with a line over the top of his canopy, known as a B.P., or Blown Periphery. Unfortunately he did everything wrong. He pulled the ripcord of his reserve, which sent the 'chute straight into the flailing mess above his head. I ran to where he would hit the ground. Then, as though by the hand of God, the line fell away and McCoughlin landed safely. We lined up, McCoughlin with a cut over his eye, and presented the new Guide Rules Book to those wonderful Girl Guides." The Honourable Vere was so delighted she asked them over for a drink. "Well, that was some party, and I'm sure many of the rules in the new book were broken that night."

By the 1970s the Girl Guide Association was keen to modernise its image. The covers of *The Guider* featured Guides playing guitars and young men judging cookery competitions. Guides still knitted blankets for the poor, but they were also meeting pop singers such as the Beverley Sisters, though not The Who. When a new uniform was mooted, Mrs Pearson of Oxhey in Hertfordshire wrote to *The Guider*. "I think this style would look well in crimplene."

Things really moved when Guider Mrs King held an enrolment ceremony halfway between the Caribbean islands of Antigua and Anguilla. "A Guider and a Ranger made their promises in the army aircraft while we were in mid-air. We had the Captain of the flight holding the Union Flag and a Guider the World Flag. The army crew in the plane were almost as thrilled as we were. My next scheme is to enrol someone undersea."

By the mid-1980s it all seemed a bit outdated again. While other young women camped at Greenham Common and wrote for *Spare Rib* magazine, Girl Guides continued to work towards the Laundress Badge. The Girl Guide Association moved with the times, with Brownies working for Computer and Science Investigator Badges, and "Communicator" took over from "Telegraphist". The Hostess Badge still exists, but now a Brownie has to prepare for a sleepover, rather than a "dance social".

The Guide Law was changed in 1994 from "To do my duty to God" to "To love my God", in order to embrace all beliefs. From 1998 Guides could wear jeans, and that year over 17,000 Guides and Brownies gathered at the Millennium Dome in London, the largest ever one-day Guiding event in Britain. A year later the first "BIG GIG", a pop concert exclusively for Guides, took place at Wembley.

With the new century, the Girl Guide Association realised it was time to re-brand, and in 2002 the Girl Guide Association became "Girlguiding UK", with the motto "Surprise Yourself". Traditional uniforms gave way to sweatshirts, and Girlguiding UK joined forces with the Body Shop to develop an activity pack called "Girls Get Real", based around self-esteem and body image. When the Scout Association decide to allow girls to join Cubs and Scouts, Girlguiding UK was not worried. They knew that enough girls would always want an organisation for themselves, without competition from boys.

Baden-Powell coined the phrase, "Can we do it? Yes we can!" That can-do attitude still gives girls the self-confidence to succeed in a male-dominated world. Emma Thompson, former Girl Guide and Oscar-winning actor, worked with Guides on a project to reduce carbon emissions by switching off machines and insulating homes. In 2008, thirteen-year-old former Brownie Eleanor Simmonds won two swimming gold medals at the Beijing Paralympic Games, was voted BBC Young Sports Personality of the Year, and became the youngest ever MBE in the Queen's New Year's honours list.

Brownies have their own interactive website, and Guides from all over the world communicate on social network sites such as Facebook using language that Agnes Baden-Powell would never have understood. Gemma shared her feelings with her internet friends: "omg guides is soooo-O BAD. i have pix awesome camp. greatest times girl lol:)".

Today there are over ten million Guides in 216 countries, 145 of which are members of the World Association of Guides. Among others, Chad, Dominica and Russia joined in 2008, while the Democratic Republic of Congo (DRC), Lithuania and Syria became associates. In Britain there are approximately twelve million women who are, or once were, Guides. There are 300,000 British Scouts and Cubs, over half a million Brownies and Guides, and a waiting list of 50,000 girls without leaders.

Despite the Blitz, rationing and the national call-up of women, the 750,000 British Guides kept going during World War II because of their dogged determination and refusal to accept defeat. Their work not only made a huge difference to the lives of those around them, but also helped ensure that there would be new generations of Guides and Brownies. When they felt tired or miserable, they would sing a round together, to the tune of "John Brown's Body":

There's never any trouble if you S.M.I.L.E.
There's never any trouble if you S.M.I.L.E.
And if there's never any trouble
It will vanish like a bubble
If you'll only take the trouble to S.M.I.L.E.

Acknowledgements

The following archives and archivists have been very helpful with documents, information and photographs: Karen Stapley, Girlguiding UK Archive; Peter Elliott, Royal Air Force Museum; Bodleian Library; Cowley Library; Rosemary Dixon, Archant Library; David Hails, Old Chefusian Association; Ron Bridge, Far East Civilian Prisoners of War Society; Eileen Hawkes, Oxfordshire Girl Guide Archives; Margaret Brooks and Rod Suddaby, Documents, Film and Sound Collections, Imperial War Museum; Margaret Hawkins, Jersey Guide Association; Edith LePatrouel, Guernsey Guide Association; Kit Tranter, Norfolk Girl Guide Archive; Lynne Oppenheimer, Berkhamsted School Old Girls; Andrea Goodmaker, Kindertransport office, Association of Jewish Refugees; Ian Grant, Chefoo School Magazine; and Valerie and Joe Melnick, B'nai B'rith UK.

The chapter headings are from *Hints for Girl Guides' Badges*, published by Brown, Sons & Ferguson, and *Brownie Tests* and *Brownie Games*, published by the Girl Guide Association.

Thank you to the following for sharing their stories and for lending me their log books, diaries and letters: Verily Anderson (*née* Bruce); Carol Barker (*née* Snape); Rachel and David Bradby; Joyce Bradury (*née* Cooke); Angela Bromley-Martin; Dame France Campbell-Preston; Alma Camps; Cheryl Clark; Joyce Coterill (*née* Strank); Geraldine da Silva; Paddi Dimitropoulos; Petra Dubliski; Barbara Dykes; Kathy Evans; Martyn Farley; Barbara Fawkes (*née* Henley); Kathleen Foster (*née* Strange); Juliet Gardiner; Margaret Goldberger (*née* Gretel Heller); Elizabeth Goldsmith (*née* Hoyte) ; Iris Goodacre (*née* Calmann); Beryl Goodland (*née* Welch); Susan Graham-Jones; Rachel Hamdi; Moira B.K. Hendry (*née* Findlay); Evelyn Heubener (*née* Davey); Eric and Christine Hinkley; Monica Hobongwana; Margaret Holder (*née* Vinden); Marian Holmes (*née* Kitchen); Estelle Horne (*née* Cliff); John Hoyte; Rebecca Jenkins; Gemma Jones; Marjorie Keeble; Sylvia Kent; Melanie King; Josephine Klein; Marian Lauchlan (*née* Bevan); Beryl Laverick; Pamela Ruth Lawton; Mary Lea (*née* Allingham); Celia Lee (*née* Cilly-Jutta Horwitz); Helen Leonard; Cathy Longworth; Jane Longworth (*née* Roberts); Carla McKay; June MacKenzie; Kathleen Martin; Jane Maurin; Susie Medley; Eileen Mitchell; Jessie Nagel (*née* Ritchie); Audrey Nordmo Horton (*née* Bevan); Tony O'Gorman; Eloise O'Hare; Deborah Oppenheimer; Jenny Pagliano (*née* Bevan); Lucy Pendar; Mary Pick; Mary Previte (*née* Taylor); Helen Rappaport; Alison Richardson; Robin Richmond; Sir Samuel Roberts; Ruth Segal (*née* Wasserman); Emma Slack; Jen Smith; Marianne Talbot;

416

Gay Talbot Stratford; Jean Turner, Marguerite Tyson (née Kennedy); Celia Ward; Val Waters; Rozz Wing; June Wood (née Mackenzie); Marilyn Wordley; Christina Zaba.

Thank you for invaluable assistance to my agent Simon Trewin and Ariella Feiner; my editors Arabella Pike, Sophie Goulden and Robert Lacey; Lucinda Mahoney for keeping my arms moving; Hugh of Cowley Computer Assistance for keeping my computer going; Julie Summers for intelligent walks; Judith Kerr for permission to quote from her book *The Other Way Round*; Asha Beauclerk for her Polish translation; Deb Puleston for keeping the book on track; Charles Hampton for his constant emotional and nutritional support; and my grandchildren Bill, Matilda, Freya and Delilah, all born during the labour of this book, for their soothing smiles and cuddles.

Ging gang goolie goolie goolie goolie, watcha
Ging gang goo; Ging gang goo;

Ging gang goolie goolie goolie goolie, watcha
Ging gang goo; Ging, gang, goo;

Haila, oh, haila shaila, oh haila shaila, haila ho.
Haila, oh, haila shaila, oh haila shaila, haila ho.

Shally wally, shally wally, shally wally, shally wally,
Oompa, oompa, oompa, oompa . . .

Start again . . .

Also available in ISIS Large Print:

Danger UXB

James Owen

Autumn 1940: The front line is now Britain itself. Cities are blitzed night after night as the nation becomes the target of a campaign of aerial assault. And even after the bombers have turned for home, a deadly menace remains: thousands upon thousands of UXBs. Buried underground, their clocks ticking, unexploded bombs blocked supply routes, closed Spitfire factories, emptied hospitals and turned families into refugees. Dealing with this threat soon became Churchill's priority.

It was a battle of wits, German ingenuity against British resourcefulness. This desperate struggle against the ticking clock is told through the experiences of four key figures; Robert Davies, who saved St Paul's Cathedral; Stuart Archer, protector of the vital Welsh oil refineries; the extraordinary Earl of Suffolk, who inspired The English Patient and made possible the atom bomb; and John Hudson, the modest horticulturalist who mastered the V-1.

ISBN 978-0-7531-5255-3 (hb)
ISBN 978-0-7531-5256-0 (pb)

Battle of Britain

Patrick Bishop

From the bestselling author of Fighter Boys and Bomber Boys, Battle of Britain is a magisterial account of a defining episode in modern British history: the epic struggle of RAF Fighter Command with the Luftwaffe in the summer of 1940.

From the shock defeat and evacuation from Dunkirk in May/June 1940 to Fighter Command's assertion of superiority over the Luftwaffe in mid-September of that year, Patrick Bishop charts the key staging-posts of Britain's fight for national survival. The day-to-day progress of the battle — its dogfights, its heroes and victims, its impact on flyers and civilians alike (from the Luftwaffe's "Black Thursday" of 15 August, to the opening day of "the Blitz" on 7 September) — is evoked in a richly compelling and moving narrative. Eye-witness descriptions and extracts from diaries and journals evoke the often horrific reality of war in the air.

ISBN 978-0-7531-8778-4 (hb)
ISBN 978-0-7531-8779-1 (pb)

Voices Against War

Lyn Smith

On 15 February 2003, an estimated two million Britons took to the streets of London to protest against war in Iraq. Since the outbreak of that conflict, the anti-war movement has broadened and now has a global reach. Not all protesters would consider themselves pacifists — against all wars and violence — but whatever the basis of objection, their protest is part of one of the most enduring movements in history.

Based on nearly 200 personal testimonies from the Imperial War Museum Collections, this landmark book tells the stories of those who participated in anti-war protest — from the Great War through to the Second World War, the Cold War and up to the present day. This includes the Falkland Islands invasion in the early 1980s, the first Gulf War and the ongoing conflicts in Iraq and Afghanistan.

ISBN 978-0-7531-5243-0 (hb)
ISBN 978-0-7531-5244-7 (pb)

The Secrets of the Notebook

Eve Haas

Eve was just eight years old when, as a Jewish girl in a Berlin school, the rumblings of the Nazis' rise to power began to threaten everything and everyone she knew. Fortunately, her parents managed to get her family out of Germany and to London to start a new life.

The horrors of war were just a part of the past, until the day when Eve inherited a treasured family notebook that hid an amazing secret. Warned against pursuing the truth behind the notebook, Eve set out to discover who her family were, how her great-great-grandmother had married into a royal family, and why her grandmother perished at the hands of the Nazis. Eve was to risk her life to uncover the truth.

ISBN 978-0-7531-9544-4 **(hb)**
ISBN 978-0-7531-9545-1 **(pb)**